WORKPLACE POKER

WORKPLACE POKER

ARE YOU PLAYING THE GAME, OR JUST GETTING PLAYED?

DAN RUST

HARPER
BUSINESS

An Imprint of HarperCollinsPublishers

HarperCollins books may be purchased for educational, business, or sales promotional use. For information, please e-mail the Special Markets Department at SPsales@harpercollins.com.

FIRST EDITION

Designed by Renato Stanisic

Library of Congress Cataloging-in-Publication Data has been applied for.

ISBN: 978-0-06-240528-9

16 17 18 19 20   OV/RRD   10 9 8 7 6 5 4 3 2 1

For Paula

Who reads me better than anyone else. Damn it.

Contents

♠

Introduction   ix

1. **POKER ON A UNICYCLE**   1
   Learn to observe and read the people with whom you work.

2. **BALLET IN A MINEFIELD**   33
   Navigate the unique culture and political environment of your business.

3. **TAKE THE HIT**   73
   Embrace full responsibility for your own career failures and missteps.

4. **FUEL YOUR FIRE**   93
   Strengthen your career climb with physical, emotional, and mental energy.

5. VELCRO BUTTERFLIES AND TEFLON RHINOS 127

Balance emotional strength with sensitivity when responding to personal rejection.

6. ENJOY THE SHOW 157

Strategically promote your capabilities and contributions.

7. LIKABLE AND LUCKY CHARMERS 197

Influence others through personal rapport and connection.

8. BUDDHA, SPOCK, PATTON, AND SHERLOCK 227

Make effective decisions that will accelerate your long-term career trajectory.

9. LIKE A RUBBER CAT 255

Bounce back quickly from career adversity and setbacks.

Conclusion 281
Acknowledgments 285

INTRODUCTION

♠

I n hindsight it seems odd, ridiculous really, that I didn't see it coming. There were rumors floating around the company about an upcoming round of layoffs. And in the previous six years I had twice been directed to reduce the headcount of my department, but had received no such direction recently.

So on Monday morning when an appointment with HR popped up on my Outlook calendar, scheduled for Friday at 7:30 a.m. (which happened to be the end of the pay period), I thought they were probably executing the layoffs that day, and this meeting was to inform me of the specifics. As a senior director working with numerous business teams I would need to know who was no longer going to be around to interface with my department.

I had a brief moment of paranoia and wondered, could they be letting me go? Not likely, but just in case, should I copy anything I want to retain from my corporate laptop? Should I polish up my résumé and my LinkedIn profile? Naw. I was too deeply involved in so many critical projects. After eight years of solid performance and increasing responsibility, they had invested so much in my professional development, it wouldn't make business sense to let me go. Seriously. Those were my exact thoughts. Not me. No way.

Way.

At precisely 7:30 a.m. on Friday the HR person showed up at my office along with two unexpected guests: the VP of HR and Lloyd the security guard. Surprised and still a little clueless I joked, "Wow, it can't be good when HR shows up with security . . . heh, heh . . ."

Stony silence. The VP of HR had a folder of papers. The HR rep bit her lower lip and let me know that she felt my pain as she said, "We're eliminating your position." You gotta love Human Resources. They are always there for you. Until they're not. My head was spinning so I didn't hear most of what she said, but she took my corporate laptop, then watched carefully as I packed my personal belongings into a box (which they had graciously brought with them). Within twenty minutes I was headed down the elevator with Lloyd the security guard.

Like I said, in hindsight, it seems obvious. There is no question that I should have seen it coming. In fact early in my career I had worked for a company that suddenly went out of business, and I had vowed to never be surprised by a sudden job loss again, so I had always prided myself in having a degree of healthy paranoia. I was always observing how people interacted at work, watching and listening for the "game under the game" as I called it. While it was of course frustrating to be suddenly out of a job, it was even more so because clearly I had not played the game well—I had been played. Of course, even if I had been more aware, it probably wouldn't have actually changed anything, but I would at least have had more time to prepare and would have felt a little less stupid.

I sat in my car contemplating all of this for a few stunned minutes, then thought that some people with window offices might be staring down at me so I pulled out of the parking lot and drove aimlessly for over an hour, trying to figure out what to say to my wife.

The harsh reality began to sink in. I was now an unemployed senior corporate training leader, the economy was soft, and in the past three months I had talked to three acquaintances who were also corporate training leaders and had been recently laid off. I had felt very sorry for them as we talked about how businesses almost always reduce corporate training headcount when times are tough. They were all struggling to even get interviews, and I knew two of them were much more experienced than I. And now I was about to join them.

It turned out that more than fifty people were laid off that day. We all agreed to stay in touch, help each other, all the things you promise when everyone is nervous about the future. Ninety days later only seventeen of the fifty were reemployed. One senior leader complained about being interviewed by "clueless kids" half his age. It was so embarrassing for him that he had completely given up and decided to retire early even though he couldn't really afford to. We stopped getting together because it was just too depressing, but we stayed in touch by creating a LinkedIn company "alumni" group. At the end of six months over half of the fifty were reemployed, but most had to accept lower salaries or jobs they really didn't want.

A few, however, had managed to enhance their careers with increased responsibilities and higher salaries. Thankfully, I was one of those. And here is the kicker: as I kept track of who landed new jobs, I knew these people well, their capabilities, work ethic, and dependability. I knew which of them were great at their jobs and which were, uh, less than great. But actual work performance seemed to have very little connection to how quickly they found new jobs or whether or not they had to accept a lower salary in a tight job market. And as I thought about those who had not been laid off in the first place, many of them were clearly less capable than those who were shown the door. On that fateful day of layoffs, some career trajectories stalled, some flatlined, a few accelerated.

And these varying outcomes weren't correlated with skill, experience, ambition, or hard work. So what was the difference? That's what this book is about.

Workplace Poker introduces a set of skills, strategies, and insights that can help you accelerate your career beyond the limitations of talent, ambition, and hard work. Of course you have to be good at your job, there is no magic bullet to fix incompetency (except putting in the hard work to develop competency). But in the modern work world just about everyone is "good enough" in terms of work capability and motivation.

While most of our careers have had at least a few stalls from business downturns, failed projects, bad bosses, sudden unemployment, or other difficulties, the uber-successful continue their career acceleration through almost every tough situation. Others may hit speed bumps, but not them. Somehow they nimbly dodge the bullets that hit the rest of us, usually because they are better at playing the game.

If you are talented, ambitious, and hardworking but feel your career just isn't accelerating as rapidly as it should—or as fast as you would like it to—this book is for you.

If you have been frustrated to see others (less talented, who don't work as hard as you do) achieve rapid professional progress while your career stalls out—this book is for you.

If you've been annoyed by those who are successful primarily because of where they went to school, or family connections, or financial resources—this book is for you.

Please note: If you happen to be one of those with a privileged education or highbrow family connections, or a trust fund, just put this book down (It's kind of heavy anyway, with lots of those wordy paragraph things, ugh.) and back away. Nothing to see here.

Just to be clear, *Workplace Poker* is not a compilation of manipulative, conniving, or backstabbing strategies. It is not about pushing others out of the way of your career path. And it is not just a theoretical approach. *Workplace Poker* is based upon real-world observations and experiences over more than three decades of work in a broad range of businesses. I have had the unique opportunity to meet and work with thousands of people in hundreds of businesses around the world, from Saudi Arabia to Singapore, from Canada and the US to the EU and Australia.

The focus of my workshops and individual coaching has always been practical skill development to enhance one's career potential. And you will certainly see a fair amount of my workshop and career coaching content in these pages, but what I think you will find most illuminating are the stories and examples of individuals actually applying the techniques, skills and strategies. Plus, a lot of the best content in this book came from them, not me. It has been a real privilege to meet so many uber-successful men and women, and have them gladly share their own ideas and insights.

Unfortunately the really juicy stories of wickedly difficult employment (and sudden unemployment) are often a bit sensitive, and many of the contributors requested anonymity to protect relationships with bosses and coworkers. So I have placed all contributors in my author's witness protection program. They will recognize themselves, but there are enough adjustments to names, places, and other details to protect the innocent as well as the profoundly guilty.

When I meet someone who has managed to achieve an exceptionally accelerated career trajectory, I often pose this question: "Beyond talent, ambition, and hard work, what's the secret sauce of your success?"

You will find lots and lots of their "secret sauce" in this book.

You'll learn how to read people better than a world-class poker player. You'll learn how to navigate the land mines of office politics and understand the "game under the game" in most organizations. You will come to understand the way uber-successful people react to failure, but we won't deal with this in a self-helpy "just follow your dreams" way. Instead we will take a hard, deep look at exactly how to react when your career runs up against a brick wall.

You will learn how to effectively promote yourself, to highlight your contributions without seeming to be one of those boastful me-me-me people at work. (God, I hate those people.) Yet if we don't do a better job of promoting our own contributions, the sad truth is that those people will get more than their fair share of the recognition—and reward. Not anymore, not after you read this book.

This book will help you eliminate blind spots and develop the ability to see around corners. You will be able to identify when and where you have been sabotaging your own career progress. You'll develop greater emotional resilience while also enhancing your sensitivity to those around you. You'll learn to make better career-impacting decisions, how to have more energy for the career climb, and how to bounce back when bad things happen.

You'll even learn how to be more charming at work.

Really.

Throughout the book I will address some of the most common career-stagnating situations and walk you through the application of the core workplace poker skills. We will progress from building self-awareness to developing new capabilities that will help you respond quickly and react productively to difficult situations including:

- Dealing with a less-than-competent boss.
- Handling complex office politics.
- Working with a lot of ambitious people when there are limited opportunities for advancement.

- Working with a colleague who takes credit for your great work, or blames you for his own mistakes.
- Reacting when you are suddenly fired or laid off, and how to get back on track as rapidly as possible.
- Making the best career-accelerating decisions.
- Recovering from a bad career decision.
- Recognizing when your career is off track or stagnating, and deciding what to do about it.

This is all very serious stuff, but I have a hard time staying too serious for long periods, so please know in advance that along with the practical skills and informative stories, you're going to get more than a small helping of snark, cynicism, and borderline inappropriate humor.

I also hate long introductions—so start reading chapter 1—now.

1

Poker on a Unicycle

◆

The most profound business lesson of my life occurred more than twenty years ago, mid-afternoon in a bar near the horse racetrack just north of San Diego. The sun was shining brightly outside but the bar was dimly lit and I was sitting in the darkest corner at a table with six men and two women. Even in the low light I could see the anxiety on their faces.

The company we all worked for had abruptly gone out of business that morning. We showed up for work and the doors were locked. A note taped inside the glass of the front door said the business was shut down. Permanently. This was just before payday, so many of us spent the morning making phone calls, trying to get answers and some assurance that we would receive our final paychecks. Although our frantic calls to the home office went unanswered, a few of us did reach people at some of the other regional offices. But nobody seemed to have the full picture of what was happening. We eventually figured out that about half of the regional offices had been shut down. And the other half had been instructed to operate "business as usual" and minimize contact with anyone from the closed regions.

So no one wanted to talk to us. And even if they did, no one knew what was going on. After a tense morning, the bar seemed to be a natural choice for a few of us to gather and try to sort things out.

Final paychecks never arrived. Later we discovered that a year earlier the company had spun off half of their regional offices as a separate business with different owners. These were the offices that had just been abruptly shut down. Some spent years trying to chase down the owners and get the back pay to which they were entitled. As far as I know, none of us ever got a dime.

So our small group sat in the bar for most of the afternoon working through the stages of grief and loss. First denial, with imported beer on tap. "This has got to be a mistake. I can see why they would shut down Austin and Oklahoma City, but San Diego? No way!"

Then anger, with shots of tequila. The agave good stuff. "Those damn kiss asses at corporate are all idiots and the little guys always get screwed!"

Then there was bargaining, with a chaotic mix of gin, whiskey, vodka, and one white wine spritzer. (It was the late eighties, so don't judge.) "Maybe if we reduce our operating expenses and cut back on overtime we could show them how profitable the business here could be!"

We never really got to the acceptance stage, but I did buy a round of brandy for everyone. That was about the point when Tony walked through the door and up to our table. Someone looked up at him and slurred, " 'Bout time . . . you gotta casshh up."

"Sorry, I can't," Tony said. "I've got a couple of job interviews this afternoon."

He stood before us, smiling and upbeat and wearing a nice interview suit. We all stared at him silently, the way you look at a strange animal at the zoo—a striped tapir with one red eye, or an ocelot with five legs. Any decent group of human beings would have felt good for him and given him encouragement. All he got from us was "What the hell?"

Tony had been a telemarketer, relatively low on the corporate totem pole, spending most of his working days in a cubicle talking to prospective customers on the telephone. We didn't interact with him much at work, but we all liked him. He kept his head down, did his job well, and always seemed to be in a good mood.

He sat down with us and asked the waitress for a glass of ice water. He was annoyingly peppy and pleasant, sipping at his stupid cold water and trying to cheer us up. When someone asked him how he got a job interview so quickly he said, "It wasn't quick really, these interviews have been in the works for a while."

"*These* interviews? Meaning more than one?" I asked.

"Yeah, I've got a few solid opportunities in the works. And the one this afternoon is my third at the company, I think they're going to make me an offer today."

We all watched as the ocelot grew another leg. "What the hell?" someone said again. It might have been me.

"Come on, you guys," Tony said. "This couldn't have been a big surprise to you. The only shocker is that it took this long for them to shut down the business." He went on to describe things he had seen and heard over the past year that led him to the conclusion our office was doomed along with seven other regional locations. So of course he had started interviewing for a new job many months ago.

Tony seemed to know things he just couldn't (or shouldn't) know. Somehow he knew how each of the regional offices ranked in terms of profitability, although this information was tightly protected by the corporate home office. He knew that our region and seven others were actually owned by a separate corporate entity. He knew some of our competitors had heard rumors about how the business might be consolidated and high-value real estate might be sold off because the founder was "cashing out" in advance of an ugly divorce. Tony didn't have the time to explain how he acquired all of this information because he had to leave for his job interview.

We wished him good luck as he headed off, then proceeded to snidely rip him apart once he was gone. "Who do you suppose he's screwing at the home office?" someone asked. We continued drinking until happy hour ended and the prices tripled (and there were no more free drinks for the ladies). By then we all agreed that Tony must have done something illegal or unethical to get so much inside information, and while we certainly would have liked to be interviewing for new jobs just as quickly, it was better to have higher standards. Or something stupidly self-righteous like that.

A few weeks later I had lunch with Tony. By then the alcohol had worn off, Tony was happily at work in his new role as a telemarketing manager, and I was sending out tons of résumés to prospective employers. My head was clear—the panic of joblessness will do that for you—and I really wanted to know more about how Tony had seen the troubles coming long before they actually arrived.

We had a lengthy and illuminating conversation, but I'll give you the short version. Tony wasn't sleeping with anyone at the home office. He didn't have unique access to information that any one of us could not also have acquired. But he did pay attention in a way the rest of us didn't. He noticed things and looked for things the rest of us ignored.

Tony talked to me about his perception of many of those we worked with. He noted their individual communication styles, what seemed to motivate them and how they made decisions.

"Do you ever notice how the district director really chooses his words carefully, while the vice president is more open and willing to just talk with us casually, like a real person?" he asked. I nodded. I really liked the VP's personality and communication style. "Well, I think it's because the director really isn't comfortable giving us false information, so he carefully chooses his words. But the vice president, he's totally comfortable with just saying whatever he needs to, with a big smile, whether it's true or not."

I was surprised that Tony's take on the two men was so different, and obviously more accurate, than my own. I wondered why a guy who did most of his work in a cubicle, with minimal interaction, had even bothered to think about these things. And beyond the thinking, the fact that he was so discerning, that he was able to see so deeply into the personalities and characteristics of these people, it frankly floored me.

In addition, Tony had carefully observed how our key leaders communicated and interacted with employees, so when they sent out memos, gave speeches, or visited the office to check in on the staff, Tony was reading between the lines, discerning the reality behind the corporate-speak. He wasn't judgmental or critical as he described this to me. If anything he was flat and unemotional—like a psychologist with a patient on the couch—he just observed carefully and noted their behaviors.

At our last company holiday party Tony noticed that the founder's wife was absent, while in the past she had been heavily involved in every aspect of planning and was always a significant presence at these events. We were told that she wasn't feeling well. Tony didn't buy it, especially after he met the founder's new lovely young "assistant."

When a few of our key employees left the company to work for a competitor, Tony maintained friendships with them and was able to stay current with what our competitors were learning and saying about our business. Sometimes competitors know what's happening within a company long before the employees do.

When our paychecks were suddenly issued by a new bank and the corporate name on the checks was slightly different, the rest of us just shrugged it off as a minor curiosity. Tony, on the other hand, did the research to find out what was behind the change. This led him to understand that the business had been split into two separate corporate entities. Operationally almost nothing had changed, so the rest of us didn't really notice. But in the end, when we were trying to get our final paychecks, it was a big deal.

The point of sharing these details with you is not to revisit painful events that occurred over twenty years ago. I have a therapist for that. The point is to highlight the huge lesson I received from Tony. His deeper understanding of our work environment allowed him to be better prepared, to plan for and not be ambushed by a sudden turn of events. While most of the rest of us spent many months looking for new jobs (often settling for less than what we really wanted), Tony was able to be proactive and drive his job search from a position of strength. From that day forward I saw the value of Tony's insight and I began to pay closer attention to the people I worked with.

Over the years I've met many more "Tonys" who strive for a deeper understanding of the people with whom they work. They are able to deal more productively with a broad range of individuals, they are able to navigate office politics more effectively, and all of this helps them gain a more accurate and thoughtful perception of the particular corporate culture within which they work. I have come to view this ability—really a set of skills and capabilities—as the single most reliable predictor of one's career success.

It's tempting to oversimplify what it takes to read people well. Humans are complex creatures and to truly discern an individual's motivations, fears, wants, needs, perceptions, habits, and attitudes can seem overwhelming and inherently imperfect. This is why so many people just overlook what's happening beneath the surface of human actions. It's easier to just put your head down and focus on doing good work, hoping that will be enough. Often it isn't.

But the complexity presents an opportunity. This is why jury consultants are highly paid to divine a prospective juror's mind-set, why successful negotiators focus on psychology as much as deal terms, and why poker players who can read their opponents well are able to win big—sometimes millions of dollars big.

TOUGHER THAN A CARD GAME

The key to poker mastery isn't reading the cards, it's reading the people. It can take a lifetime to truly master the ability to recognize the "tells" of other players during a game. But as difficult as it is, poker is relatively easy compared to reading people in your everyday work life.

In a typical poker game everyone has the same objective (to win the most money or poker chips) and there is a specific structure to which everyone adheres. The rules of the game are clear, and as each card hand is dealt there is a common process—everyone places their bets in a predetermined order, etc. The goal in reading the facial expressions and body language of other players is generally to answer one question: To what degree are they bluffing? Cheating may occur, but when it is detected there is generally no question that the cheating was wrong and the punishment should be severe.

In the workplace there is less predictability and much more complexity because humans are intricate emotional and psychological creatures, and each of us has multiple, sometimes contradictory, motivations. In workplace poker the stakes are always high, everyone bluffs on occasion, and cheaters sometimes win. The rules of the game are seldom clear, and can change quickly. It's like playing poker while riding a unicycle and juggling kittens with one hand.

Rather than just wanting to win the most poker chips, at work a person could easily be motivated to:

- **Make more money**
- **Spend more time with family**
- **Be more popular with coworkers**
- **Gain more respect from superiors**
- **Work less**
- **Achieve more**

} **All at the same time.**

There are obvious conflicts between some of these motivations, but that is how most of us are built. We want to do and be and experience many different things, and generally our strongest motivations at any given moment focus on what we are lacking or feel unlikely to achieve. The promotion you are striving for (and unsure of) is a much more dominant motivator than the annual bonus that is almost certain to occur.

We tend to want most that which feels just slightly out of our grasp.

So when you are trying to understand a person's strongest motivations, ask yourself what it is they seem to want that is just not quite achievable right now. Often these deepest motivations are not openly shared with others. For example:

Highly ambitious people often feign a lack of interest in the career climb ("I have a passion for doing *this* job well, I'm really not focused on the next one.") while in fact they are planning their progress like a chess game, always three or four moves in advance. Their most INTENSE desire is the NEXT step up the career ladder.

Those who are paranoid about losing their job or something else of value at work such as status, bonuses, influence, etc. often overcompensate to hide their uncertainty. ("I'm not worried about it at all. Whatever happens, happens.")

Those who yearn for greater personal recognition often go out of their way to recognize the accomplishments of others. They may appear to downplay any recognition that does come their way ("It wasn't me really, this was truly a group effort. It's not about me, it's about the team.") when in fact, in terms of their deepest motivation, it's all about them.

So how do you gain awareness of the internal mind-set of others when their motivations are complex and contradictory, and they are often least likely to be open about the wants/desires/needs that are most important to them?

The first, simplest, and sometimes most difficult step is this: just take the time to pay attention. Seriously. Take—the—time . . . to pay attention.

We are all so busy busy busy with meetings and emails and projects and presentations and so many urgent tasks, who has the time to listen to a colleague and try to discern what's *not* being said, or the message *under* the message? And it's easy to convince ourselves that we shouldn't have to try so hard to understand people, they should be trying harder to be understood.

"I don't have time to 'read' people," a busy finance director once told me. "If they have an opinion, I expect them to share it. If they are too much of a pussy to tell me what they think, it can't be that important." Needless to say, he wasn't especially good at reading people.

The reality is that it doesn't actually take more time to read people, but it does take more energy (mental and emotional) and it can be frustrating because the outcome is uncertain and there is often no particular "aha!" moment where your objective is achieved. So it can be overwhelming to think that suddenly you are supposed to be a "mind reader" with everyone you meet, and you'll almost never know how well you are actually doing. But if you choose to ignore this, or adopt a just-do-the-work mentality, you are putting your career progress at risk.

....

If you don't read people well, you're climbing
up a wobbly career ladder. Blindfolded.

....

Ryan Holcombe was a marketing manager at Thane Logistics in Waltham, Massachusetts. No one questioned his work ethic or capabilities, in fact Ryan had become the "go to" person for just about any key marketing project that had to be delivered on a tight budget and short timeline. He was ambitious and assumed that his hard work would lead to a promotion, but he had been passed over twice when new opportunities had become available. In both cases Ryan was told that he was a strong candidate but they had found someone who was a "better fit" for the job requirements. Ryan had really struggled with this, not wanting to be a bad sport and trying hard to see it from their perspective. But he really thought that he was being objective when he saw himself as clearly a better choice for the new position. Both times. Trying to make sense of it was frustrating and distracting. So eventually he would just put his head down and go back to doing his work. To his credit he never let the frustration affect the quality of his work.

When a third opportunity became available Ryan was about to dutifully submit his résumé through the internal application system when a colleague noticed and said, "They're never going to let you out of this job. It would be too much of a risk."

The colleague went on to explain that the previous two people who held Ryan's current position had made serious blunders that cost the company hundreds of thousands of dollars. Ryan was the first person anyone could remember who seemed to have the ability to manage so many fragmented marketing projects at once and always deliver on time, on budget. And Ryan's current manager had almost lost her job because of the previous failures. So Ryan, because of his excellent performance, had incredible job security. But he was going nowhere at Thane Logistics.

This new information completely changed Ryan's perspective. It didn't make him any happier, but finally things made sense. He still wasn't pleased with the outcomes of the two missed promotions or the reason behind them, but at least he didn't feel crazy anymore. He could have easily made plans to eventually leave Thane Logistics, but he really liked the company, the culture, it was a convenient commute, and he wanted a long-term career there.

While Ryan had never bothered to think much about "office politics" or the underlying motivations of those he worked with, this experience was almost like flipping a light switch for him. "It was like playing a game of chess," he says, "and suddenly realizing that there is a whole different game *under* the game you're playing."

Ryan decided that he needed to figure out how to play the "game under the game," so instead of immediately applying for the third opportunity he began doing his homework on everyone who would be involved in the decision-making process. He talked to others who worked with them closely, and he observed them more carefully in every meeting and in other interactions.

Ryan engaged in a lot of conversations, asked a lot of good questions, and listened carefully for what was being said and what was *not* being said. Without going into detail regarding everything Ryan did, here is a summary of what he was eventually able to learn:

Yes, his manager was VERY paranoid about Ryan moving out of his current position, but she wasn't willing to admit it.

In addition, his manager had just had her second child, and the child had serious health issues. So naturally most of her energies were focused on her child, and this made it even more important for her to not "rock the boat" with a staffing change.

His manager was exhausted and stressed out, but working hard to keep all of this hidden. She didn't want her career at Thane to suffer because she was a "weak link."

But his manager wasn't the only roadblock. Ryan came to understand that his ability to "keep the trains running" had some business leaders thinking of him as more of a tactical executor and less of a strategic and innovative thinker.

One of the core skills that Thane business leaders were looking for in every new director-level employee was strategic and innovative thinking. This didn't appear on the formal job description but it was clearly an important area of focus for them.

So Ryan came to understand that he had two problems to solve:

1. Help his manager feel more comfortable with his transition to a new role, and
2. Help other Thane Logistics business leaders gain confidence in his strategic and innovative thinking capabilities.

And Ryan's big "aha!" moment was to realize that he needed to solve problem number two before (or at the same time as) solving problem number one. He could have easily fallen into the trap of just solving the issue with his own manager, then running up against the brick wall of problem number two.

I'll share with you how it all worked out, but the big lesson for you isn't in the outcome of this particular story. The big lesson is that without uncovering what was REALLY going on, Ryan would have driven himself crazy trying to solve a problem he didn't truly understand.

....

How many career issues have in the past driven you crazy, perhaps because you are trying to solve a problem you really don't understand?

....

Ryan worked to gain the trust of his manager enough that she could open up to him a little and share some of her work frustrations. He agreed to take on some of her workload, specifically projects that required him to use his strategic and innovative thinking abilities. He gave her assurance that he wouldn't "abandon" her, but the conversations also made it clear that she would need to work with him and help him grow, or she would eventually lose him, probably abruptly, to another company. And that would obviously be the worst possible outcome for her own career. He didn't threaten her, but definitely leveraged her paranoia to his benefit. Ryan's work on the new projects gave him more "face time" with other Thane Logistics business leaders and eventually led to a promotion. And they all lived happily ever after.

Your own situation may be less complex, or more so. It's hard to know until you start digging beneath the surface. So let's assume for a moment you are willing to invest a little more mental and emotional energy into your conversations and other interactions at work. As you begin to do this you'll want to make sure that your own mind-set is unbiased and neutral.

BE JANE GOODALL

If you are going to delve deeper into the motivations and behavioral tendencies of the people you work with, you have to minimize your own emotional reactions and set aside any and all preconceived notions, judgments, and expectations. This may be harder if you've worked with these people for some time, because you've already formed opinions about them.

The moment you decide that someone is "nice" or "a jerk" or "passive aggressive" or "fake," or make any other judgmental assessment, or have an emotional reaction, you minimize your ability to really see that person. Even positive emotions can block your clarity. This is one of the fundamental reasons why most of us don't really see other people clearly. We make quick judgments or have strong emotional reactions, then become blinded by them.

Highly confident people can be blinded by their certainty that they are impressing those around them. Timid and shy people can be blinded by their concern for what others are thinking about them. You will not be able to accurately observe and assess someone if you are:

- Impressed
- Annoyed
- Intimidated
- Judgmental
- Attracted
- Contemptuous
- Embarrassed
- Frustrated
- Uncertain
- Turned on

The list could go on, but you get the point. You have to be a dispassionate observer of workplace behavior. Think of yourself as a corporate Jane Goodall, observing the office chimpanzees in their natural habitat. Jane didn't pass judgment on their behavior, she merely observed. If one chimp constantly picked fights with the others, Jane noted this dutifully in her journals, was curious and attentive, but never with a sense of judgment. Even if a chimp abandoned its baby or killed another in a fit of rage, this was noted objectively without frustration, sorrow, or pity.

....

In order to really see people you can't pass judgment when they throw their poop.

....

Randall Whitcomb was the sales supervisor for a winery just north of Portland, Oregon. He loved his work and liked most of the people he worked with, but his relationship with the general manager, who happened to be the owner's son, could not have been more difficult. "I was frustrated with him from the beginning, when he dropped out of college and his father decided he needed a job—so he was given the GM position," Randall said. From his perspective, the owner's son didn't like to work, wasn't particularly bright, and had horrible people skills. But suddenly the son was running the whole winery, and the owner was rarely around.

Almost every evening Randall would go home and recount for his wife something annoying or stupid the owner's son had done that day. This went on for about six months, and it actually seemed that the son was getting worse at his job as the months passed.

Then the owner suddenly passed away. But Randall learned that it wasn't sudden at all. The family had known of the cancer for some time. The son had not wanted to drop out of college, but his father had asked him to, wanting to have more time with his son as well as prepare him to run the business. The son had no real interest in the business, but agreed, out of respect for his father. All of these details came out in the months following the funeral.

"Once I understood what was really going on," Randall says today, "I was a little embarrassed at my reaction. I probably would have figured it out sooner if I hadn't been so pissed off." Randall acknowledges that his initial frustration with the owner's son blinded him somewhat, and prevented him from discerning what was really going on. "You can't get inside someone else's head until you get out of your own," he says.

And he did pay the price for his lack of discernment. His relationship with the owner's son and other company leaders had become tense and abrasive, and this wasn't easily healed just because he came to a better understanding of the underlying issues. "I had a lot of fences to mend," he says. "And it probably set my career back at least a couple of years."

One of the best ways to read people and minimize your own emotional/judgmental reaction is to be a third party observer rather than engage directly. When you are personally having a conversation with someone it can be very difficult to stay fully engaged while at the same time being somewhat distant and objective. Over time, as your observation skills increase and objectivity becomes your natural state, this will become easier. But as a starting place, you'll gain much more useful information by stepping back and observing others, rather than engaging with them directly.

BEGIN WITH A BASELINE

Since you are observing people you work with on a regular basis, you should begin with awareness of their typical behaviors in a variety of settings. Your curiosity about these people should be almost obsessive (but no stalking please) as you notice how they speak, how they dress, how they act and interact with others. How they sound, and even how they smell. Over time patterns with each person will emerge and form a "baseline" for future observations. You'll stay attuned to notice deviations from the baseline, which can be highly illuminating.

One of the best ways to establish a baseline is to observe people in a variety of situations. During meetings, presentations, discussions, etc. you can observe how people communicate, how they dress, how they interact with others, and their general tone or demeanor. Workplace social events often present a fantastic opportunity to "people watch" and observe interactions when everyone is a bit more relaxed. Just noticing who attends, who doesn't, and who makes an appearance but quickly fades away—all of this can be helpful. Notice who is comfortable sitting with the "powerful," and who gravitates to the opposite end of the room. Notice who loosens up quickly (and what that behavior looks like) and who stays buttoned up, both literally and figuratively.

You can even establish a baseline for conference calls, emails, and other activities. Some people freely share their thoughts, ideas, and questions during group phone calls, while others tend to hold back unless specifically prompted to contribute. Some people respond quickly to every email while others might take days. Some send out lengthy email messages with an (unrealistic) expectation that most people will actually read their dissertation. While others send out brief one-sentence email blurbs. The point here is to pay attention and recognize the normal day-to-day style of each work colleague so that you can recognize when there is a change from their typical behavior.

As you establish a baseline for each key person you work with, you'll become more sensitive to those times when they deviate from the baseline. You'll notice the typically tardy colleague who suddenly starts showing up early for every meeting. You'll notice the "chatty" coworker who seems unusually quiet. The person whose emails suddenly become short and abrupt, who starts oversharing on conference calls, etc. These deviations from the baseline may or may not have significant meaning, but it is important to recognize them when they occur. And then explore further to ascertain the meaning (or lack thereof).

Derrick Adams was a Starbucks barista who took great pride in his observational skills, far beyond just knowing the first name and typical drink of his regular customers. He noticed how they dressed, their typical mood and personality, eye contact (or lack of it) and anything else that jumped out at him. "At first it was just a way to keep from getting bored," he says. "But eventually it became really interesting and fun to notice everyone's typical pattern of behavior, especially when that pattern changed."

Derrick noticed a pattern change with one of his regular customers who had always ordered a large cappuccino, paid with cash, and always dropped the change in the tip jar. This customer was well dressed, friendly but just a little impatient, always made direct eye contact, and said "thank you" when picking up his drink. This was the baseline behavior, and Derrick noticed a significant change when the customer had not come in for about a week, then came in one morning much later than usual. "Hey, we missed you," Derrick said cheerfully, but the customer was not amused. He ordered a small coffee and kept the change, and didn't make eye contact or say anything when picking up his drink order. There was also a definite change in demeanor. "I could tell there was something serious and somber going on with the guy," Derrick says.

This pattern change continued for several weeks, with the customer's clothing gradually becoming more and more casual. You have to be careful with assumptions, maybe there was another reason he was ordering smaller drinks and keeping the change, but Derrick had the impression that the guy had lost his job and money was a little tight.

One morning when the customer picked up his drink, Derrick handed him his usual large cappuccino rather than the small coffee he had paid for. Before the customer could react Derrick just smiled and said, "Some mornings a little extra caffeine is a good thing."

The customer made eye contact (for the first time in weeks), smiled a little, and said "thank you." In that brief moment there was recognition, appreciation, and a mutual understanding, without having to say anything more. Derrick continued to give this customer the "extra caffeine" every morning, until about a month later when he started ordering his regular large cappuccino again. Nothing was said, but it was clear to Derrick that the employment situation had now changed for the better.

Derrick told me this story several years ago, and today he's the marketing manager for a large office equipment company. The observational skills he honed as a Starbucks barista have continued to serve him well. "People wonder how I'm able to get stalled projects unstuck, how I avoid a lot of the political land mines in our business, and why I'm leading the department after being here just three years, even though others have a lot more industry experience," he says.

Ultimately Derrick attributes much of his success to his willingness to . . . wait for it . . . take the time . . . to pay attention . . . to the people around him. "It's second nature to me now, doesn't take any real effort, but I know it makes all the difference."

When you first begin focusing on this effort to become more deeply attuned to the people you work with and establish a baseline for each of them, you will probably find that it is easy the first few days, but it's hard to keep up the level of attention. Many of us are so used to being on "autopilot" in the workplace, not really tuning in to our coworkers, that it is easy to quickly fall back into the old pattern of behavior. Especially when you are overwhelmed with the daily onslaught of work pressures. But if you keep up the effort and push through the initial difficulty it will eventually become one of your natural habits. Remember, you aren't putting on a mind reading sideshow, so you don't need to make a snap judgment. All of your observations, over time, will help you establish the baseline.

LOOK FOR EXTREMES

When you are observing people it is often the extremes in their behavior that are the most telling. Look for extremes in clothing, hairstyle, grooming, and the way they dress. Look for extremes in mannerisms, habits, and vocal qualities. If the extremes are clearly intentional (clothing, tattoos, wild hair, choice of car, watch, jewelry, etc.) then this tells you something about the image they wish to project outwardly to the world. A Fortune 500 CEO who intentionally wears a cheap watch is trying to project something to the world, just as much as the down-on-his-luck salesperson who wears a fake Rolex. The person who regularly sends out voluminous emails filled with impenetrable data is projecting something, as is the person who signs off every email with a :)!

But not all behavior extremes are intentional. If someone is highly verbal, or exceptionally quiet, or intensely focused on data rather than people, or in any other way UNINTENTIONALLY extreme, this can also tell you a lot about them, but be careful about making quick assumptions. Every quiet person isn't shy, every verbal person isn't outgoing. Everything you observe should be thought of within the context of all the other things you observe before you come to any conclusions.

THE FACE WHISPERS

Our facial expressions, especially our eyes, can communicate—or mask—a great deal of information. Reading the facial expressions of children is easy because their emotions come quickly to the surface as they smile when they're happy, frown when they're sad, etc. But by the time we are adults, most of us have acquired the ability and habit (consciously or not) of often masking our true feelings, at least in terms of our overt facial expressions.

Masking our emotions to get along at work, at home, and in social settings isn't necessarily a bad thing. Sometimes we pretend to be interested, or we laugh at an unfunny joke, or we hide our annoyance behind a bland smile, etc. These gentle deceptions allow us to work effectively with people we might not especially care for (and/or who might not especially care for us). Masking allows us to socialize with strangers and take the time to get to know them before deciding the degree to which we are comfortable being transparent. Masking is in many ways the "social glue" that helps diverse groups of people work together productively. But those who are most productive and effective are able to see through the masks of others.

Of course, most people are not perfect at masking their true feelings and thoughts. The subtle masks we create for one person are often perfectly obvious to others. When you observe a person interacting with someone else, sometimes you'll be able to detect the mask they're putting on for the other party. Or when you see someone sitting alone, especially in a crowd or other environment where they are not concerned about being individually observed, they will often drop the mask. Sudden stress or tension or a surprise can also cause the mask to drop away, at least briefly.

As you observe facial expressions, don't get too caught up in what it means when someone glances downward or sideways, or when their brow furrows, or when they bite their lower lip, or any other specific change—these can have many possible meanings— your purpose is best served by first noticing the facial expression within the context of everything else you are observing, then allow your mind to respond instinctively. What do you THINK is really going on in the mind of this person? Often your immediate gut instinct (if you set aside your emotional reactions and have taken the time to be a good observer) will be more insightful than anything your conscious mind could have produced.

With some focus and practice you can learn to read what are called facial micro-expressions. These are brief flashes of true emotion, when the mask drops for an instant, less than a second. These micro-expressions typically only show up when we are trying to hide a very strong feeling that is in conflict with the mask we're showing outwardly. The expression of true feelings will suddenly and briefly flash across our face, then be gone.

Larry Edwards is an executive recruiter in the health care industry who carefully observes facial micro-expressions during his initial interviews with candidates. "Executive-level people are usually great at masking their true thoughts and feelings. So I'll abruptly change the direction of the conversation with a question that I know is really difficult for the candidate, and I watch carefully for their initial reaction," he says. "It tells me a lot if I see a flash of anger, or frustration, or curiosity, or amusement."

Of course, you have to be careful not to jump to conclusions too quickly. Everything you notice should be thought of within the context of your entire observation. The vast majority of people never even take the time to notice these things, are never aware of these subtle indications of emotion, so they never see behind the mask. As you develop your own sensitivity to this, be patient, don't burden yourself with the pressure of a quick definitive interpretation.

In an actual poker game you have the pressure of time because you have to assess and read the other players quickly as the game progresses. But you don't typically have that pressure at work, so be patient, don't rush it; over time your observations will educate you regarding any deeper meaning and eventually you'll gain new insight to add to your baseline observations.

THE BODY TALKS (SOMETIMES)

While most of us are pretty good at keeping our feelings out of our facial expression when we want to, we're not as good at disguising how we feel throughout the rest of our bodies. You've no doubt heard and read about the importance of noticing body language when you observe others, but be careful about your interpretation. Much of what you may have read or heard about body language is oversimplified nonsense designed for easy television or Gawker-article consumption. The biggest misconception is that specific gestures—folding your hands, or tilting your head, for example—have precise meanings. Gestures, body movement—really all body language—is somewhat ambiguous. If you cross your arms during a conversation it can mean you are annoyed, or defensive, or hungry, or cold. Or you might have a backache. You might be self-conscious about a tattoo on your arm. Or maybe you're just more comfortable with your arms folded. You could be signaling any (or all) of these things, or nothing at all.

Many of us have been wrongly advised to overinterpret or misinterpret body language by "experts" who are under a lot of pressure to provide definitive analysis in quick sound bite format. Nobody gets on television to analyze Kim Kardashian's body language while she's deboarding a flight at LAX if their analysis is "Her shrugged shoulders could mean this . . . Or this . . . Or maybe even this . . . or it might mean nothing." So the people we hear talking about body language on television are almost forced to oversimplify their commentary.

OK fine then, what are you supposed to do? Here's the big, big secret to reading body language: take a very brief glance at someone's posture and other physical characteristics (placement of hands, tilt of head, etc.) then look away. Without looking back, ask yourself, within the context of everything else that is going on, what does their body *seem* to be saying? Just as with facial expressions, more often than not your initial reaction to that brief glance will tell you what the body is saying, if anything.

And the good news here is that you don't really need to be an expert. As humans developed on the evolutionary timescale, we were genetically programmed to read one another's emotions and intents. This was a critical factor in our ability to survive as a species. We sense strong emotions and react quickly (often unconsciously) so that we can take fast action if necessary.

For many of us this unconscious expertise has been dampened (or destroyed) by the fast-paced modern work environment. But if you take the time to . . . here it comes again . . . pay attention, then over time you will reactivate that part of your brain. This is what people mean by their "gut" or "instinct." You'll become more and more tuned in to the thoughts and emotions of those around you. Simply ask your unconscious mind "What do I think is happening here?" and wait for an answer. Just pay attention—then listen to your gut—and your conscious mind will get it too. This may be a little tough and uncertain at first, but give it time and your deeper evolutionary mind will "remember" how to do this.

IGNORING THE "GAME UNDER THE GAME"

Ten years out of college, Sheree Washington had achieved a high growth career trajectory and established herself as a force to be reckoned with at her company, a high-tech engineering firm in Silicon Valley. She had worked her way up through the ranks of IT, and as a black woman with a degree in electronic engineering, she had few peers. Sheree was a hard-driving project manager, and if you were working for her you knew that the hours would be long, the work would be intense, and there was no room for error. Sheree's projects always came in on time, under budget, and the quality always exceeded the expectations of her business leaders.

In Sheree's IT organization, meetings always started on time and ended ten minutes before the hour, to give people time to get to their next meeting. It was expected that if you received an email with an action required, your response would happen before you left the office that day. Email was not allowed to pile up in your in-box. Your role on a project would be clearly defined, and your timeline for deliverables closely monitored. It had to be this way because often the work of others would be held up if your portion of the project fell behind schedule.

Her attention to detail and ability to sit down with engineers and write code herself gave Sheree high credibility with the team. And they understood the enormous pressure she was under as they worked to execute increasingly complex software projects. Over a three-year period Sheree's team launched a series of apps compatible with iOS, Android, Windows Mobile, and (even) BlackBerry.

The pressure of this high-tech development world crushes a lot of business leaders, but not Sheree. She thrived and was looking forward to continuing her fast-track career progress. Her company identified her as a "high potential" leader and to expand her capabilities she was tasked with leading the commercial (marketing and sales) organization.

Sheree was determined to make a quick study of the commercial function within her business. In her first two weeks she read through volumes of sales data, asked for a "pipeline analysis" for each salesperson, and launched a market analysis project to determine the objective sales potential of each territory. She ordered up a forced ranking of every salesperson and wanted to see the development plan for each person on the bottom tier. She held several group meetings with the senior sales directors and while she was certainly friendly with them, they all were left with that "new sheriff in town" feeling.

It never occurred to her that she should put any particular effort into studying the new people she would be working with. Over the years Sheree had met most of the people in sales and marketing, so she knew them, at least superficially. She didn't personally meet with a single big client. She didn't meet individually with any salespeople or sales leaders. When the commercial organization offered some critical feedback regarding client reactions to one of the apps her engineering team had developed, she snapped back, "They did their job in building it, now you've got to do your job in selling it." To her credit, Sheree did identify several opportunities to improve sales efficiency and productivity, but she didn't have time to implement those ideas. Less than a year later Sheree was back leading the IT organization. And her high-trajectory career path had flatlined.

Today, almost everyone who will talk openly about Sheree's experience leading the commercial organization speaks in politically correct corporate terminology that makes it hard to discern what really happened. It was decided that she should "align her leadership track with her core competencies." Who decided this? No one will say. The sales organization struggled with Sheree's leadership toward a "culture of productivity and accountability"—according to someone *not* in the sales organization.

But in speaking with several salespeople and sales managers who interacted with Sheree at the time, it is clear that she had a blind spot. She was focused on process, procedure, data, and planning. All of these are of course good things, but taken to an extreme, or applied without taking the human dynamic into account, they can do more harm than good. She made no effort to understand any of the interpersonal dynamics within the new group, had no sense of their personalities, priorities, or concerns. If Sheree had worked harder to understand the key individuals with whom she was working, if she had involved more people in her thought process, and had made an effort to personally connect with clients and top salespeople, she probably could have accomplished everything she set out to do.

Unfortunately Sheree doesn't see it that way, and even today she feels that she was "burned" by a "good old boys club" in the sales organization. That may or may not be true to some degree, but what is definitely true is that until she sees her own role in the outcome, her career advancement won't regain its momentum.

HOW WELL DO YOU REALLY KNOW THEM?

You probably feel that you know most of the people you work with pretty well. A recent survey indicated that 83 percent of employees feel that they know their coworkers "well" or "very well." However, when those survey respondents were asked to answer the questions below about even a single colleague, most were unable to answer more than just a few of them.

We think we know our colleagues well, but that's only because we don't really understand what it means to KNOW someone. If you really know a work colleague well, you should be able to answer most of the questions in each of the four categories below.

1. Work Habits and Preferences

What are this person's typical patterns in terms of communication, timeliness, and meeting deadlines? What are you comfortable depending on from this person? What can you definitely not count on from this person? What does it typically take to persuade or change the mind-set of this person? How does this person react when they make a mistake: open disclosure or cover-up? What kind of people do they prefer to work with, and why? What kind of people do they avoid working with, and why?

2. Personality Projected at Work
What persona do they want to project to others at work? How close is this to how they are actually perceived by others? In most situations do they tend to be comfortable and at ease with others, or careful and guarded? Do they tend to take control, or expect others to be in charge/make decisions? Do they tend to align/agree with others, or to instinctively find reasons to disagree? Do they tend to confidently promote their own perspective, or seek the ideas of others and gain consensus?

3. Professional Ambitions and Limitations
What motivates and drives this person at work? Are they more driven to avoid pain/failure, or more driven toward achievement/acquisition? How would you rate their level of intensity/action-orientation? What has been their greatest work-related pain/failure? What is this person most paranoid/fearful about at work? What is their "tell" when they are not comfortable, or being less than totally truthful? Does this person know how they are truly perceived by others at work? If so, how do they feel about that perception? If not, why not?

4. Personal Activities and Goals
Outside of the work environment, what is most important to this person? How do they spend most of their nonwork hours and energies? Is their nonwork personality different? If so, why? What has been their greatest life pain/failure? How has this impacted them? What do they *not* want others to know about them at work? What

does this person worry about most? How does this person's family perceive them? Who are this person's nonwork best friends and how are they perceived by those people?

> *Author's note: OK, if your eyes started to glaze over about half-way through the list and you skipped forward, do yourself a favor and stay with me on this. I know it's a long list, but you need to read through all of these. Yes, this is a lot of information, so take a deep breath, go back, and keep reading.*

So, obviously that is a lot of information. You are of course probably unable to answer most of these questions about every person at work—and that's the point. If you can't answer most of these questions about any particular individual, then you really don't know them—yet. But if you decide that you want to know them better, if you ask more questions and . . . take—the—time—to pay attention to them, you'll have a clear path to better understand and discern the deeper motivations of these individuals.

Some people read this list of questions and feel the pressure to quickly start gathering this information about their colleagues at work. But perhaps the worst thing you can do, if you want to get to know someone at a deeper level, is to go at them directly with questions from this list. Instead of asking someone to tell you what's most important to them, watch their interactions with others within the work environment, observe how their office or cubicle is organized and decorated, listen to the things they choose to talk about, etc. Over time all of these observations can help you see your colleagues at a deeper level. And then on occasion, if and when it feels natural or normal, you might ask a few direct questions.

Rather than be overwhelmed by the ominous task of discerning the deeper motivations and uncertainties of everyone in the world, just focus on a few key people. In your work life there is probably a small group with the greatest influence on your career climb:

- Your direct boss (of course)
- Your boss's boss
- Your peers/coworkers who are most influential in the workplace
- Your subordinates or others who do work for you, those whose efforts are most critical to your career success

If you have an opportunity to meet the spouses or significant others of anyone in this core group, you may want to add them to the list. These people often have tremendous influence on how you are perceived, based on nothing more than their brief impressions of you.

This may seem like a lot of work at first, with very little immediate payoff. But over time, as you acquire the ability to read people at a deeper level and leverage your greater awareness to advance your career, it will feel less and less like extra work. Eventually it will just become part of your normal thought process. And the career payoff can be tremendous.

THINK NOW

We've covered a lot of ground very quickly in this chapter, and as much as I am anxious for you to move on to chapter 2, it would be good for you to sit a moment and contemplate a few things.

- Think about the one person at work who has the greatest influence over your career progress at this point in time—probably your direct supervisor. How well do you REALLY know this person? Briefly review the list of questions provided, then think about how you might gain a deeper insight into this person.

- Think about everyone you work with, and clues or insight you may have missed in the past, and how this may have impacted your career. The purpose isn't to beat yourself up, but to simply acknowledge that we all occasionally miss the "game under the game."

ACT SOON

You may be more aware after reading this chapter, but without quick application you won't see much tangible benefit. So within the next few days there are several actions you can take that will help to reinforce these concepts and ensure that you truly apply them.

- Identify the core group of individuals who will have the greatest impact on your career progress: superiors, peers, and subordinates.
- For the next week, take advantage of any opportunities for third-party observation of those in your core group: business meetings, conference calls, presentations, workplace social activities, etc.
- During the week, thoughtfully observe body language, facial expressions, typical conference call behaviors (if relevant), and work toward development of a baseline for those in your core group. Notice when any of them deviate from the baseline.
- Take every reasonable opportunity to ask questions that will provide you with deeper insight regarding those in your core work group.
- Select one person at work with whom you tend to have intense emotional reactions (frustration, anger, intimidation, attraction, etc.) and for one full week make an effort to observe this person while setting aside all of your judgments and assumptions. This may or may not make a difference, but the exercise will serve you well nevertheless.

- Simply remind yourself throughout the next week to—take—
the—time to observe people and their natural behaviors
throughout your day. You will be amazed at all of the little
things you've been missing as you rushed through your oh-so-
busy life.

LONG-TERM THOUGHTS AND ACTION POINTS

Be aware of your own emotional reactions and judgments toward other people, and work to set those aside during your behavioral observations. (Be Jane Goodall!)

- Pay close attention to behavioral extremes, but do not make instant assessments. Instead, develop your assessment over time, with numerous observations and interactions.

- Listen actively. Pay close attention to the words people use, the ideas they choose to promote, how they structure their arguments, and when/how they back off. Listen for what is said and what is not said.

- Take every reasonable opportunity to ask questions that will provide you with deeper insight regarding people in both your professional and personal life.

Tuning in to the people around you at a deeper level is not a onetime event or something you can complete then check off your "to do" list. If you give this the proper level of attention it will eventually become your natural way of interacting with and observing others. Just as your vocabulary increases over time, your abilities in this area can also grow throughout your life.

In this chapter we've focused on the individuals you work most closely with. In the next chapter we will expand our perspective to view the entire business culture within which you work, and the often complex interactions that occur within that environment.

2

Ballet in a Minefield

◆

'm friendly with everyone at work," Tony said to me, "but, no offense, none of you are really my friends." I was confused and put off at first, because I thought I was one of his favorite people. Later I realized how many others at work felt the same way, because Tony was friendly with virtually everyone. In the previous chapter you read about Tony from San Diego and his ability to read people and gain deeper insight into workplace situations. But Tony did more than just read people—he connected with them. I came to understand that Tony had many friendly work colleagues, not only in our office but also in the corporate home office and other regional locations. He and I had worked at the same company for about the same length of time, and I was actually in a more senior role, but in the end he was much more "connected" than I was. So Tony's comment about workplace "friendships" was really unexpected.

"The truth is that none of these people are your friends. Even the ones you go to lunch with. Even the ones you sleep with," he said. "They are not real friends. Now that you've lost your job, how many of them will be having lunch with you a year from now?"

It took some clarification from Tony before I really started to understand his mind-set about office "friendships." Positive relationships at work are obviously a good thing, but his point was that it can be a mistake to assume they run deeper than they really do. And while company loyalty is a good thing it is also a mistake to assume that loyalty runs both ways.

This became abundantly clear to me years later when I had a friend who worked for Smarter Faster Stronger, a health, fitness, and nutrition company in San Diego. My friend invited me to their annual "Smarter Faster Stronger Family Fun Day" at which the CEO celebrated the corporate culture of "family first" and almost shed a tear as he described how everyone in attendance was like family to him. I was impressed with their positive company culture and commitment to the health and wellness of every employee. They seemed incredibly connected and loyal to one another, like a real family.

Then a few months later my friend told me that eight people in her department had been laid off because the company had decided to end one of their product lines. Earlier that week her boss had paid her a visit, saying, "You've been an important part of our family here, and we really appreciate your contributions, but in your business segment we're moving in another direction, so we're going to have to let you go." Really? What kind of family does that?

When I was growing up I don't ever remember anyone in my family turning to someone else at the dinner table and saying, "We really appreciate your contributions to the family these past few years, but I think we're going to go in another direction, so we have to let you go."

As much as any business tries to instill the feeling among employees that they are the "most important asset" for the organization, the truth is that they are not important—it is their output and contributions to the goals of the business that are important. As human "resources" we all serve a purpose, and that purpose advances the goals of the business. Once we no longer serve our purpose (or can no longer do it cost effectively) then the business will cut us from the herd.

And Tony helped me to understand that there is absolutely nothing wrong with this. It is the nature of business. "You are a mercenary, like it or not, and you always will be," he said.

I realize this goes against the grain of the current "family friendly" and "employee centered" facade most human resource departments aspire to today. But let's be brutally honest: even HR exists only to serve the business goals. They are there for you, until they're not.

This doesn't mean that employees aren't important, of course they are. But no one is served well by pretending they are "family," except perhaps the business itself, which creates a sense of bonding and loyalty on the part of the employees. So the business can reduce unplanned turnover because employees are more loyal and they assume their loyalty will be returned in kind. But when a company needs to restructure or downsize, loyalty to employees is rarely a consideration. Again, this shouldn't be perceived as bad or unethical or even mildly frustrating. It is just the natural state of business culture.

So I asked Tony how he could be so cynical about businesses and the people he worked with and yet still manage to build so many positive working relationships. "I think it helps that I have real friends outside of work, and a great family, so I can keep everything in perspective," he said.

Tony's attitude about the business and the people he worked with was always positive, but realistic, and tempered by his mind-set regarding "friends" and "family" at work. My own attitude tended to swing wildly up and down, depending upon how things were going with my own workplace friends, and how the company was treating me. When I look back now it is clear that Tony's more nuanced understanding of workplace relationships was much more effective.

....

At work there are no friends or enemies, just imperfect
people trying to do their jobs well.

....

When I asked Tony how he had developed so many connections at work, well beyond the people in our regional office, at first he just shrugged his shoulders as if there really wasn't anything special about it. He told me that during one of the holiday parties at corporate he had met someone in accounting and they stayed in touch. I remembered that party. I went to the party because it would look bad not to show up, and I snuck out as soon as I was sure that my absence wouldn't be noticed. When Tony and I both attended a training workshop for all of the Southern California regional offices, he met some people from the other regions and went out with them for drinks that evening. I grumbled about the wasted time and got back to our office as soon as I could.

Yes, Tony was perhaps a more naturally outgoing "people person" than I was, but nothing would have prevented me from doing the same thing he was doing. It just never occurred to me that I should expand my work network beyond what came naturally from my day-to-day interactions. Tony, however, was always stretching his network of "friends" at work.

So Tony knew a lot of people, and not just the nice ones. I was surprised to hear that he occasionally talked on the phone with our VP of marketing, who was definitely not a warm and fuzzy guy. "What in the world did you talk to HIM about?" I asked Tony.

"Career advice mostly, plus we both like golf," he said.

"But don't you think he's an ass? Haven't you seen the way he treats his people?"

"Yeah, he can be pretty harsh. I think mostly it's because he's under a lot of pressure."

"Tell me the truth. Did he tell you we were being shut down?"

"No, but all of his career advice pointed outside of the company, so that told me a lot."

Tony seemed to find a way to deal with just about anyone in a friendly and constructive manner. He seemed genuinely interested in every one of them. Yet he also seemed to clearly see their flaws—he just didn't let the flaws get in the way.

I on the other hand was in the habit of figuring out who the "jerks" and "morons" were, avoiding them at all costs, and keeping to my small group of trusted friends at work. I hated the idea of "office politics" while Tony accepted it as a fact of work life. He didn't get involved in any of the office intrigue, but he didn't ignore it either. And he was smart enough, and aware enough, to never let the politics surprise him or hurt him.

Tony helped to change my perspective and over the years I've worked hard to model his approach because clearly it was more effective and productive for his career. But I know many people who struggle with the ebbs and flows of interpersonal dynamics at work. Many years later I met a young woman who was particularly challenged in this area.

"Why can't people just say what they mean and mean what they say?" lamented Jenny, a midlevel manager for Data Dynamics, a telecommunications company in Tampa, Florida. "If we focused all of this energy on the business we wouldn't have most of the issues that cause the gossip, paranoia, and backstabbing." She was reacting to recent comments from a "friend" in the business, confiding that some of her coworkers were "worried" because Jenny had been coming in late the past week. First of all Jenny was surprised because her cubicle was in an area where no one could see her daily comings and goings. She had been arriving about thirty minutes late in the morning because her husband's car was being repaired and he needed her to drop him off at his workplace—and staying almost an hour longer at the end of each day, but apparently no one noticed THAT.

Jenny had just become a manager for this group three months ago. She knew they were a bit frustrated with her because she was more hands-on than their previous manager, who had retired after a long career with the company. What she didn't know was the group had expected that one of them would be promoted to the manager position, so they were surprised when a young woman who had no experience in their business was hired. Jenny was bright, competent, hardworking, and truly a good manager. But the director for her division realized she had a blind spot which could derail her promising career—her response to office politics and other messy human issues related to her job was to express frustration, complain to her own boss, then decide it was time to "clean house" and start to build her own team.

"She's got the potential to be a strong leader for our business," her director said to me. "And we know she has a difficult group to manage. Most of them have been with us more than twenty years and they aren't interested in changing their ways. But their deep knowledge and expertise is critical to our business and you can't simply replace them. It takes a two-year cycle to bring someone in their position fully up to speed, but Jenny doesn't know the business well enough yet to really get that." Her director was aware of her strengths and capabilities, but said, "She doesn't get the chess game here. If you let one person go and replace them with a trainee, how does that impact all of the others? How motivated will they be to help train the new person? And how many of them will start looking for a new job? All of that has to be part of the thought process. And speaking frankly, she was quite charming when we were interviewing her, but ever since she started having problems with her team, that warm charm seems to have faded away. If we can't get *that* Jenny back, I don't think she will be here long, either by her choice or ours."

LEARN TO LOVE THE GAME

I suck at golf, and not for lack of trying. I've been coached by great golfers, and I've spent many hours trying to get good. Or at least good enough not to be embarrassed. A friend took me to an indoor golf coaching clinic where you hit the ball into a video screen while being recorded from two directions in order to analyze your swing. On my third swing the ball hit something hard on the edge of the screen, deflected up to the ceiling, hit a metal pipe, then kicked back down to hit me in the forehead. Swear to God. As they were applying a cold washcloth to the growing red lump on my forehead the owner of the golf clinic said, "Maybe you should try another sport. But not darts."

So I hate golf. Now, do I hate it because I suck at it, or vice versa? You decide. I happen to love bowling and I'm good enough not to be hit in the head.

Most people profess to hate office or corporate politics. And this is primarily because they suck at it. This is of course a natural reaction. Who wants to play a game where you don't know the rules, can't understand what is happening, and lose every time?

But whether you claim to hate it, avoid it, or actively seek to eliminate it, the human dynamic is a fact of life in every business. Whether you are at the top of the career ladder or the bottom. Whether you work in a veterinary clinic or a law firm, an advertising agency or on a road construction crew, large or small, start-up or mature business, you are dealing with people and their inherent complexities.

Humans are messy, chaotic, fickle creatures. They are also very bright and alert, which just adds intensity to the intrigue. And let's be honest, you've been playing human politics almost since you were born. When you smiled and giggled to encourage your mother to hold you, feed you, change your diaper. When you cried loudly if the giggling didn't work. When you chose your friends (or enemies) in school, gave loyalty to get loyalty, did favors to receive favors—the list goes on. When you give a generous tip to the waiter at a local restaurant because you know you'll be returning many times and you want to ensure good service in the future, you are practicing human politics.

....

Everyone plays politics at work. Some hate the game, mostly because they suck at it.

....

The human dynamic in business becomes more complex because there are both competitive and cooperative pressures. Plus these are people with whom you might not normally choose to associate. We select our personal friends instinctively, and can easily choose to "unfriend" them, but work colleagues are often foisted upon us. In this unnatural tribe of coworkers, the human dynamic allows some to gain advantage personally or for a cause they support, sometimes at the expense of others.

It may not seem fair or right. Shouldn't doing an exceptional job be enough? Unfortunately it's not. The hard truth is that you must learn to do a great job AND navigate the complex human dynamics. Like dancing a beautiful ballet in a minefield. If you ignore the land mines, or do nothing but complain about them, you're likely to lose a few toes.

If you deny (or merely express frustration at) the politics that may be going on around you, and avoid dealing with it, you may needlessly pay the price for your disengagement while others gain advantage.

If you avoid practicing politics, you miss the opportunities to properly further your own interests, and those of your team and your cause. And as you get better at this particular sport, you'll come to enjoy it. I promise. Especially if you start with things like:

- Helping others more than they expect to be helped.
- Making a little extra effort to get to know people on a personal level.
- Being a good listener and a "safe" place where individuals can express their frustrations without fear of it being shared with others.

These are all things that a good decent person would do in the workplace, with or without any sort of political intent. And there are many other things you can do (or perhaps do already) that have a political aspect to them but are in fact purely positive activities in the office environment, such as warmly greeting people as you pass them in the hall, going out of your way to have brief friendly chats in the elevator, etc.

This is not meant to in any way imply that positive politics is more important than actually doing good work. Your practical job performance is fundamental to success. One of the big reasons Tony's positive office politics were so effective was that he was also really, really good at his job.

MAKING POLITICS WORK FOR YOU

The best way to develop strategies to deal with the political behavior going on around you is to first be a good observer and then use the information you gain to develop a deeper awareness of the working network you operate within. This will also help you develop a network of positive alliances and office "friendships."

So where do you start? First, you need an understanding of the formal and informal hierarchy. The formal structure is usually easy, just take a look at the organizational chart. But then take some time to think through the informal hierarchy—within the broad organization as well as within your particular work group.

- Who has real influence to make things happen? Why?
- Who has authority but doesn't exercise it? Why are they passive? (Are they trying to foster leadership in others, or are they afraid of accountability, or is it something else?)
- Who is respected? Why? (Longevity, innovation, helping others, business results?)
- Who seems to be really good at navigating the human dynamics within the organization? (Watch and learn from these people.)

These are questions you should answer over time. Unless you have had years of experience observing this particular group, you should think through these questions and then spend time noticing the interactions of your colleagues at meetings, events, work discussions, etc. You can even ask others about their perceptions of particular people, but be sure to do so in a totally benign way—don't telegraph a positive or negative perception of your own. Too often people tend to mirror the perception you telegraph, or at least soften their own expressed opinion so as not to be in conflict with what they perceive your opinion to be. So ask neutral open-ended questions like:

- "What is it like to work with Sandra?"
- "How are things going on the new project with Bob?"
- "What's the culture like in your department?"
- "How have things changed since your new leader started?"

Of course, you have to be thoughtful about how you ask these questions and with whom you are speaking. In the workplace there seems to be a common underlying paranoia that doesn't occur in natural friendships or families. Typically, if you ask a family member to "Tell me about Uncle Bob," you won't get a paranoid reaction (unless Uncle Bob has some dark secret that no one is supposed to talk about). But in the work world even the simplest questions about other people can generate paranoia.

Over time, as you gain a better sense of where the power, influence, and natural respect of others exists within the organization, you can also start to pay attention to the social networks:

- Who gets along with whom and who clearly doesn't?
- Are there obvious groups or cliques?
- Who has the most trouble getting along with others?
- Who is a "loner" and how do others view them? (Some loners are respected, some are viewed with curiosity or suspicion, others are ostracized.)

Again, the deeply valuable answers to these questions will come over time, through patient observation and interactions with people in many different situations. As you observe and deepen your awareness, you can also begin to build your own social network within the organization. You probably already have a natural network. If you are a new employee you may have aligned with other new employees. If you are an experienced midlevel manager you probably have a natural alignment with your direct reports and others at your level. But as you think about the political landscape within the organization you may want to expand your work/social network.

Don't avoid powerful people in the organization. You may be surprised at how friendly and accessible they can be (because so few people are comfortable talking to them). Make sure your relationships cross the formal hierarchy in all directions (peers, bosses, executives) and start to build relationships with those who have the informal power.

- Build your relationships on trust and respect—avoid empty flattery.

- Be friendly with everyone—don't align yourself exclusively with one group.
- Be a part of multiple networks—this way you can keep your finger on the pulse of the organization.

When Jenny, the midlevel manager with poor (really, nonexistent) political skills, was first approached by her director to discuss the challenges she was having with her team, she was probably somewhat embarrassed because she understood the value of having deeper insight into those around her, but she wasn't used to being coached or mentored. She had always been an exceptional performer in every previous job—hence her rapid career progress—and had always exceeded the expectations of her employers. So this was a new experience for her, having someone identify a "gap" in her performance. And, not surprisingly, she was defensive and impatient and wanted to rush the process, close the gap, and never have this happen again. It took a fair amount of discussion for her to accept that there was no quick fix.

But to her credit, Jenny began to apply many of the ideas just described. She came to a much deeper understanding of the dynamics within the group she was managing, and eventually someone outside of the group helped her understand the frustration they were feeling because none of them had even been considered for the management position. Right or wrong, it was as if the entire group had been dismissed, and they naturally took this as an affront. And even though Jenny was not part of that process, she was the focus of the group's frustration. Being aware of this didn't solve the problem, but it was a big step forward.

HUG THE HATERS, BOND WITH THE BACKSTABBERS

Jenny's next step was to neutralize the negative dynamics that were occurring and begin the process of creating a more positive and productive relationship with her group of employees. It takes a mature person to smile and engage positively with an individual you know has been backstabbing you. But it takes an exceptionally mature and confident person to deal productively with a whole group of backstabbers.

The director told Jenny that he truly thought she was up to the difficult task at hand. One of her early realizations was that her choice to work in a cubicle that was distant from her work group was an error. It created both a physical separation and a social distance, and she acknowledged that perhaps her own discomfort with the group drove her decision. "I guess I could tell from the beginning that they weren't thrilled with me," she said. "So when the facilities manager gave me options, I selected a cubicle away from them, sort of to isolate myself from the negative environment. But I realize now that my job is to change that environment, not run away from it."

Some negative people can be turned. Generally speaking you can positively influence those who are difficult if the root of the problem is because they see you as a threat, misunderstand your motivations, or feel slighted by you in some way. When you engage positively with these individuals, ask good questions and actively listen to them, they will often begin to turn. If you truly engage in an effort to mend fences and genuinely want to help them with their priorities, these people can eventually become allies. Sometimes they become your strongest allies.

But there will be individuals who can never be turned, and should never be trusted. There are workplace cultures seemingly designed to breed sharks and chew up the angel fish. And the broad culture of an organization is almost always more powerful than the intent of any single individual, so it is important that you understand it.

KNOW YOUR BUSINESS

Remember this comment from Jenny's director: "It takes a two-year cycle to bring someone in their position fully up to speed, but Jenny doesn't know the business well enough yet to really get that." This observation told me a lot about the kind of work Jenny would have to do if she was going to truly master the political culture in her company, because the very best political players work to understand their businesses far beyond the specific requirements of their job. They work to deeply and broadly understand the full business model, which typically includes sales, marketing, operations, human resources, creative, legal, and (sometimes) compliance, research, and facilities.

....

Develop a deep and broad understanding of your business model.

....

The more you know about the end-to-end model of your business, the better you will be at navigating the cultural waters. Of course this takes time and a true commitment, because generally no one is going to be requiring you to learn more about the departments that are unrelated to your day-to-day responsibilities.

Understand that you are not digging for dirt, you are not looking for what's wrong or faulty with the business. You are simply trying to understand the business beyond your own tactical responsibilities, and over time this knowledge will help you more fully discern the underlying culture.

RECOGNIZE A HEALTHY WORKPLACE WHEN YOU SEE ONE

As you get to know your own business better, it also helps to have a frame of reference in terms of what an ideal or "healthy" business looks like. Sad to say, but some people have spent so many years in a less-than-optimal business that they've come to assume the world they work in is normal. Like growing up in a dysfunctional family and assuming that daily loud screaming happens in every household.

Based on my observations of hundreds of businesses, from strong to weak, and conversations with thousands of employees (from happy and productive to angry and borderline catatonic), I have identified ten characteristics that I look for when gauging the relative health of a business. Most businesses have several standout strengths from this list, and a few clear weaknesses:

- **Compelling Purpose:** Do employees feel that the business exists for important reasons beyond achievement of financial targets?
- **Authentic Leadership:** Do employees trust leaders and align with their direction for the organization?
- **Clear Objectives and Expectations:** Do employees know exactly what is expected of them, and how their efforts contribute to strategic business objectives?
- **Adequate Skills and Resources:** Do employees feel that they have the skills and resources necessary to do their jobs well and achieve required objectives?
- **Energizing Environment:** Does the working environment help employees to maintain a high level of energy and motivation throughout the workday?
- **Pervasive Productivity:** Are ALL employees highly productive so the workload is broadly and fairly shared, and no one feels they shoulder a heavier burden because of their exceptional competence or commitment?
- **Joyful Engagement:** Are employees truly engaged, happy, and excited as they work each day?
- **Cooperative Teamwork:** Do employees feel that they can count on others throughout the organization to help them when needed?
- **Rewards and Recognition:** Do employees feel that rewards and recognition are meaningful, fair, and objectively targeted?
- **Development Opportunities:** Do employees feel they have opportunities in the business to grow and develop?

To me this seems like a fundamentally fair list, but I did recently have a conversation with the CEO of a large company, which must remain nameless (but rhymes with orange), about conducting an employee survey to get feedback in each of these areas. His reaction was "Well, you can't expect every employee to feel good about every one of these areas, can you?"

I gently asked him in which of these ten areas would he feel comfortable having employees who are less than fully satisfied. He thought for a moment before responding. "Well," he said, "obviously we would want every employee to feel good about each of these areas, but I just don't think that's realistic."

See what I mean? I think he grew up in a house with a lot of screaming.

You will be much more effective at understanding your own corporate culture and its unique politics if you can objectively assess the relative health of the environment in which you work. The ten areas highlighted above can give you a good framework to think through where the culture is strong, and where there might be room for improvement. Many businesses invest a great deal of time, energy, and resources into creating a work environment that feels healthy and productive for all employees. And just like an individual person who is committed to maintaining optimal health, the best of these companies are always monitoring their "vital signs." They understand that organizational disease typically arises slowly and subtly, just like real disease in most human beings.

One thing to consider as we delve into some of the more common organizational diseases (metaphorically of course) is that an exceptionally healthy company may actually provide you with LESS opportunity to differentiate yourself. If everything is going well and everyone is positive, productive, and motivated by the company mission, this is probably a great place to work, but a tough place to really stand out. However, when a company has "issues," this gives you an opportunity to differentiate yourself based upon your approach to the challenges. Just something to think about.

CORPORATE CANCER, IMPOTENCE, AND CONSTIPATION

I like to use disease terms metaphorically when discussing organizational culture issues, because I've found that (a) the metaphors are quite apt, and (b) it helps people internalize the importance of the issue. Plus it's more fun this way.

There are three common organizational diseases that can spring up in even the healthiest company. The key to maintaining a healthy business culture is to recognize the initial warning signs of a potential malady, then take quick action for early treatment. If a business waits until there is a full outbreak, it may be too late. Here are the three most common organizational culture diseases, along with a few quick points for early treatment.

The Cancer of Employee Apathy

A cancerous cell has lost its connection with the body's internal governing mechanisms, growing on its own, ignoring what is best for the host. Employees who have lost a connection with their organization's mission and purpose have the potential to become as detached as a rogue cancer cell. One or two disengaged employees may not impact the business significantly, but if a critical mass of disconnected employees arises, this can quickly grow into a debilitating corporate tumor. Early warning signs include employees:

- Regularly making snide jokes and sarcastic comments about senior leadership.
- Proudly ignoring company directives, policies, and rules of behavior.
- Unwilling to speak up and express a strong opinion in order to avoid a problem or poor decision. They see a "train wreck" coming and let it happen.

- Complaining that there is no future working for the company, unwilling or uninterested in trying to make it better.
- Taking home office supplies or other company property for personal use, and feeling no sense of guilt or remorse (unless they get caught).

When you are working in an environment with some of these characteristics, the key to effectively navigating the political landscape is to understand that virtually every person is motivated primarily by their own self-interest, not what is ultimately best for the company. You don't have to echo the common anticompany sentiments, in fact you shouldn't, but you should be sensitive to common employee frustrations and do what you can to address them. Solve problems, don't vent your (even reasonable) frustrations.

The Impotence of Flaccid Leadership

Something about the modern work environment seems to erode the confidence and competence of some leaders. Perhaps they have difficulty asserting authority within matrixed working groups—an increasingly common structure in which numerous departments and individuals (with separate formal leadership) contribute to a project or business task. Perhaps they struggle when assigned to a team in which no one is given a clear mandate to lead. Maybe they feel constrained by the need to compete for the most talented workers. Maybe it's the Millennials, they seem to reject authoritative leadership. But whatever the root cause may be, you know your organization has an issue with flaccid leadership if:

- All decisions are driven by group consensus and there is no clear individual accountability when something goes wrong.
- Major decisions are continually adjusted whenever someone expresses a strong alternative point of view. The voting booth never closes.

- Team accomplishments are celebrated, but exceptionally strong contributors do not get the individual recognition they deserve.
- There is a general feeling that no one is really in charge.

It may be tempting in an environment like this to step in and fill the leadership void, but be careful. Unless you have been given a formal leadership role, others in this culture may react with disdain if you step up and out of "your place." Even if you have been assigned a formal leadership role and have determined that more assertiveness is necessary, go slowly. The careers of many strong assertive individuals have floundered when they have come up against the cumulative power of a large group who have become accustomed to flaccid leadership. Start slowly, assert gently, give them time to adjust to the new world you are creating for them.

The Constipation of Low Productivity

Given the pressures of modern work and the fountain of productivity-boosting books, articles, and apps, it seems shocking that there could possibly be an issue with productivity anywhere in the business world. But in fact there are many businesses where projects get stalled; workers spin their wheels waiting for information, components, or clear direction; or employees are in fact busy bees but not working on the right things. So much of our work is dependent upon the contributions of others, it doesn't take much for one person to diminish the productivity of a whole team. You know your organization is straining to be productive if:

- Employees do not all have clear goals and objectives, tied to direct business impact.
- Late projects and tasks are the norm, not a rare occurrence.
- Employees tend to wait passively if their progress has been halted by another employee's failure to meet an expected timeline.
- Responsibilities within work teams are unclear or contradictory.

- Failed projects are quickly shelved and forgotten, rather than carefully analyzed and used as learning experiences.

The good news with this type of working environment is that you have plenty of opportunity to differentiate yourself by being a great example of personal productivity. When your work is delayed because someone else has missed a deadline, you can gently nudge them, and if that doesn't work then poke a little harder. The most important thing to be careful of when you are trying to make changes within a culture like this is to not let everyone dump their responsibilities on you. They will be more than happy to help you be more productive by doing some of their work for them. Avoid this at all costs. Instead help them all to do their own work by suggesting new ideas, processes, and strategies while making a firm commitment to get your own work done on time, as promised.

In the same way that we all experience occasional sickness, every organization at times will experience one or more of these three common diseases. You may notice an outbreak in a particular department or working group, or even with just a particular individual. Remember, the key to treatment is to take early action before you have an epidemic on your hands.

EXTREME CORPORATE CULTURES

In addition to the three relatively common diseases highlighted above, there are other cultural manifestations that are more rare, extreme, and difficult to navigate. Each of these can present unique challenges and different "rules" for office politics, so you should always be on the lookout for:

- The Cult of Personality
- The Culture of Contraction

- The Coliseum Culture
- The Perma-Grin Culture
- The Inbred Culture

The Cult of Personality is an organization that seems to revolve around the ego of one key leader. North Korea under Kim Jung Un would be the most extreme example, but there are plenty in the business world including Anna Wintour, Marissa Mayer, and Donald Trump.

There is only one way to survive emotionally and psychologically in this type of culture. First recognize that everything—*everything*—is about propping up the leader. Then observe carefully what the leader expects from underlings and do your best to comply with those expectations. And accept that your efforts may never be enough. The leader may never, ever be fully satisfied. Or may never give you the satisfaction of knowing that he or she is satisfied.

You can recognize the craziness of this type of culture and still make a conscious, reasonable decision to work there, because sometimes the price you pay is worth the benefits you receive. If you are exceptionally well paid, or gain extraordinary experience and/or industry contacts that would be unavailable anywhere else, sometimes it makes perfect sense to work within a cult of personality. But—and this is a BIG but—you should always have an exit timeline and strategy. Never, never let yourself think that this is your long-term career. Many people fall into the trap of the personality cult, becoming so used to the odd requests and unreasonable demands that they forget what the real world is like and how real humans treat other real humans. Over time, a cult of personality WILL erode your own psyche, so work there if you choose to—as long as you have a plan to eventually get out.

Beth Waldrup was hired as the director of marketing for a top-tier architectural firm, working for an owner with a well-known reputation for being extremely talented, difficult, picky, and unpredictable.

"I thought I was coming in with my eyes wide open, I had heard all the stories about his quirky and demanding behavior," she says now, "but I had worked for a plain vanilla corporate architectural firm for several years and I really wanted to experience something more creative." Beth expected it to be difficult working for a demanding boss. "But I had no idea. After two months I was pretty sure that I was losing my mind."

She had been advised by others in the business to make sure the owner approved all expenses in advance, but when she met with him to get approvals he snapped at her. "What do you think I'm paying you for?" he demanded. "I don't need to be involved in every little shit decision. Now go do your job!"

So two days later she approved the budget for a photo shoot related to one of their newly completed projects. She supervised the shoot and later brought in the final photos for the owner to review. The building was amazing and the photos were great so she was shocked when the owner's response was "Who the hell approved this?!"

Things just went downhill from there. Beth thought she had found a "friend" at the office with whom she could confide her doubts and frustrations. This person eventually shared Beth's concerns with the owner's admin assistant (with whom he was having an affair) and so of course the owner eventually heard all of the details. There was a brief shining moment when the owner acknowledged the results of a marketing campaign Beth had spearheaded, but this tiny scrap of positive recognition seemed to make everyone else jealous. "I came to realize that I wasn't dealing with one crazy person," she says. "I had the whole asylum to work with."

Beth managed to work in this environment for three full years, but she was only able to do so (and stay sane in the process) by following three rules for working in a Cult of Personality:

- Know exactly why you're doing it and know your endgame (including timeline).
- Trust no one, and understand that most are playing the same game you are. The rest are TRULY nuts.
- Give the Personality all the ego stroking he or she demands, but expect nothing in return. Do not expect consistency, reliability, or integrity.

The leader in a Cult of Personality has learned over time that he or she does not have to follow the same rules as everyone else. From a career advancement standpoint my general advice would be to run like hell from any of these people—UNLESS there is a specific career-enhancing reason to stay.

The Culture of Contraction typically pervades an organization that has gone through a big layoff, or a series of layoffs, or other business downsizing. Most of the surviving employees feel paranoid and wonder if they will survive the next round of cuts. Fewer people are left to do the same or increased amounts of work. Typically in an environment like this:

- No one complains openly. Everyone complains at home.
- People are very protective of their "territory"—meaning projects, responsibilities, or any other task in which they bring value to the company.
- The best and brightest are very actively looking for another job.
- Every word of every leader related to the future of the business is overinterpreted and carefully parsed to determine the "real meaning" of their message.

The key to career advancement in a Culture of Contraction is to find as many ways as possible to create genuine value for the business, especially value that is not easily duplicated by others. Do not feel bound by the limits of your formal job description. If there are ways for you to create business value and differentiate yourself from other employees, get approval from your manager and move forward with it.

Even if you do not feel that your own job is directly threatened you should be actively looking for other job opportunities. Your résumé should be polished and ready to send out. You should try to find at least one interview-worthy opportunity every quarter, more often if possible. Even if your head is still fully engaged in the work of your current employer, you want to be fine-tuning your interviewing skills (through actual interviews) and gathering up evidence of your workplace contributions.

....

The best time to find a job is when you have a job.

....

Do not share the details of your job search strategy with anyone at work. Even people who really like you may turn on you when they feel that their own job might be threatened. It is certainly possible to advance within a company even when there is a culture of contraction, but it is very difficult. They may be pleased to have you as a contributor, and happy to have you bring even more value—but PAYING you more for the greater value may not come as easily.

So take every opportunity to document and reinforce the value you are bringing to the business and don't ever miss a single opportunity to "sell yourself" when in the presence of senior leaders.

Darin Potruff worked as a field customer relations representative for a manufacturing company based in Tennessee. Most of Darin's job was over the telephone, working from his home office in Michigan, with occasional travel to meet with local customers. But as his company went through a series of contractions Darin

knew that many of the field positions like his were being eliminated and most customer relations activity was being centralized
at the home office in Tennessee. Because he was in his late fifties,
Darin was concerned that he might be perceived as an "old dog"
who could be replaced by someone younger with more energy.
Darin knew that the only way to keep his job (his wife and two
sons had no desire to move to Tennessee) was to clearly communicate and "sell" the value he was bringing to the company and its
customers. Here are some of the strategies he used:

- Documented testimonials from every customer, having them
  highlight the value of his onsite visits, especially in terms of
  incremental sales of the company's products.
- Used his webcam during calls and remote meetings with his
  team at the home office in order to make himself more "visible"
  to the team, especially his boss.
- Worked to enhance his appearance and emphasize his energy
  and vitality. Yes, he dyed the gray out of his hair (before starting to use the webcam) and lost twenty pounds.
- Made sure that he had a very bright light, good microphone,
  and clear background whenever he used the webcam, to ensure
  the video quality was professional.

Some of this may seem a little extreme to you, but ultimately Darin
became the only field-based customer relations representative at the
company, and managed to keep the job until his retirement several years
later. To survive and advance your career in a culture of contraction,
you have to do a great job and SELL the value of your contributions.

The Coliseum Culture is an environment seemingly designed to
maximize the competition between employees, pitting them against
one another in an effort to drive maximum productivity and prof-
its. In a culture like this you will see public "scoreboards" and

notifications highlighting the contributions of individual employees. Everyone will work overtime to gain exposure because being anonymous means no one will notice if you're gone the next day.

Sometimes a Coliseum Culture is combined with a Culture of Contraction, essentially having people actively competing against one another for a bigger piece of a shrinking pie.

What is most important to survive in a Coliseum Culture isn't being the very best, it's making sure there are at least two or three people who are clearly worse than you are. Think of these people as your "canaries in the coal mine." If things go bad, you know they'll be gone before you are. If you look around you and cannot see any obvious canaries, guess what . . . you're the canary.

Vivek Wadhwa was a young stockbroker at a large brokerage firm in Manhattan. The culture was brutally Darwinian, with survival based upon the number of new accounts opened every week and the commission dollars generated. At Vivek's firm the average new broker lasted eight months before quitting or being fired, and fewer than 20 percent survived the first year.

Vivek loved being a stockbroker but he was not particularly aggressive or competitive. He was also not especially thrilled with the frat boy mentality and after hours partying. "In a lot of ways I didn't fit the culture of the firm," he says. "But I knew from the beginning that only two things really mattered, new accounts and commission volume."

So Vivek set out to make sure that he won the only game that really mattered. He noticed that the more senior brokers were often very helpful to the brand-new people for the first six months or so. But once a new broker had opened up fifteen or twenty new accounts, the help suddenly stopped, and in fact the pressure was really turned up. What Vivek realized was that once a new broker had a nice book of new accounts, if he or she left the firm then those accounts were divided among the senior brokers. So the senior brokers loved it when the newbies worked for six months or a year, then quit.

What really helped Vivek was the fact that he had recognized this, so at the six-month mark when he started getting a lot of pressure from senior reps (and his manager as well), Vivek knew this was just part of the game. When his manager teased him about not coming out with the group on party nights, Vivek mentioned that he spent those evenings at the local Indian Community Center, meeting people and signing up new clients. Which he did. And suddenly there was no more pressure to party with the boys. Vivek pushed himself through the final tough months of his first year, and eventually his manager began referring to him as a "keeper." In a Coliseum Culture it is critical to know the rules of the game and how the score is kept.

The Coliseum Culture will chew you up and spit you out if you aren't clear on the particular rules of the game you're playing, and if you aren't tough-minded and determined enough to ensure that you win. On the positive side, those who do win are often very nicely rewarded.

The Perma-Grin Culture exists within organizations where negative thoughts and commentary are simply not tolerated. Where everyone smiles and treats one another kindly, and everyone loves everyone. This may seem perfectly pleasant and positive, but taken to an extreme it can be horribly stifling. Especially if you aren't naturally the perma-grin type.

Jeff Barnes was a shift supervisor for the Namaste Coffee House in New York's Chelsea neighborhood. At twenty-three he was a senior at NYU and managing to balance a full class load with a full-time job. Jeff was extremely ambitious and had decided that he wanted to continue working for Namaste after college. The company had expanded throughout the Northeast into New Jersey, Massachusetts, and Connecticut. His goal was to become an assistant store manager in his senior year, then a full store manager after graduation. From there he could progress to district manager, then regional director.

But Jeff had applied for assistant store manager positions twice and had not been selected, which frustrated him no end. As a shift supervisor Jeff ran a tight ship and he knew that his shift's productivity metrics were the best in the store. In fact they were among the best in the region. Jeff's personality was perfect for a Coliseum Culture, because he had the drive and determination to always win. But what Jeff did not recognize was that he was working in a Perma-Grin Culture, not a Coliseum.

The first time Jeff lost out on the ASM position he assumed it was probably because he was a full-time student and they thought he couldn't handle the workload. But the second time, a year later, they hired a new ASM who was from another region, and ALSO a full-time student. Jeff was ready to quit, because clearly something underhanded was going on. So he decided to meet with the store manager and give her a piece of his mind before storming out on his last day.

He stood in her office, refusing to take a seat. "I just want you to know why I'm leaving. No one here works harder, I have the most productive shift, and I'm the most committed person in this store, but none of that seems to matter because you gave the ASM job to someone else!" he said, barely controlling his frustration.

"You do work hard. A lot harder than you need to," his manager replied.

"What does that mean?"

"How much of your time and energy is spent training new people?" she asked.

"A lot. You know how hard it is to keep the good ones. Seems like I've got someone new every couple of weeks."

"Your turnover rate is almost double that of the other shifts in this store. Why do you suppose that is?"

Jeff rolled his eyes; he knew what was coming. Yes, he admitted that he could be a bit harsh and abrasive with the others on his shift. But that's what seemed to drive real productivity. Standing around and singing "Kumbaya" wasn't going to get the job done. He had

had this discussion with her before and there seemed to be no point in repeating it. But that didn't stop him.

"In the end, it's the results that count," he said.

"I totally agree, and your results include employees who leave out of frustration with your management style. Employees who take a different shift to get away from you, but never tell you. Employees who will never walk into a Namaste Coffee House again because they think you represent how we REALLY feel about them. You know it's true because we've talked about this before."

She took a deep breath before continuing.

"It's probably good that you're quitting because I had decided to let you go. As much as I love your commitment and hard work, the WAY you're doing the job just isn't working for us," she said, trying to be kind while delivering a death blow. In a Perma-Grin Culture, when they show you the door, it is always with a kind word and a sincere smile. But they do lock the door behind you once you're out.

This is not a neatly wrapped happy story where Jeff suddenly has a moment of self-realization. Instead he walked out of Namaste Coffee House in a fit of self-righteous anger.

He struggled in two other businesses, both with cultures of "niceness" before finally doing well in a hypercompetitive office supply company. Because Jeff lacked self-awareness and flexibility, it was important for him to find a business culture that fit well with his natural style. But the most successful individuals do not look for a culture that fits THEM, instead they flex their own natural style to fit the business culture that best serves their career.

....

Don't expect the culture to accommodate you.
You should flex to align with the culture.

....

The Inbred Culture stems from an organization with (typically) a long storied history which all employees can recount with pride; firm adherence to long-standing processes, procedures, and work methods (which are often outdated); and an internal language that sounds foreign to outsiders. These organizations often take a perverse pride in their insular environment and are often populated with leaders who have spent their entire careers within the business.

General Motors, Brooks Brothers, and Dupont are just three examples of deeply inbred corporate cultures. Their internal language abounds with catchphrases and three-letter acronyms any normal person would find unintelligible.

The first key to success in a culture like this is to understand it. Study it. Learn the history and talk to senior employees about the "good old days" of the company. Fully absorb the language, habits, and thought patterns of those who have been immersed in the culture for decades.

The second key is to accept that you are not going to change the culture. The careers of many business leaders have been derailed when they thought they would be able to shift the long-standing culture of an inbred organization. While there are a few notable exceptions (Abercrombie & Fitch, Harley-Davidson) your best bet is to find ways to align with the culture rather than change it.

Generally the only way an inbred culture ever changes is when there is a dramatic turn of external events that threatens the very survival of the organization. When fundamental change is necessary for survival, then sometimes the necessary change will occur. Sometimes.

A CLASH OF CULTURES

Mariana Rosado was the new vice president of sales for a direct-sale home products company ($100+ million in annual revenue) founded in the late 1800s and based in Minnesota. She had been the sales director for the South America division (with headquarters in Mexico) before being elevated to the national sales VP position by the company's CEO and owner.

In South America Mariana had driven record sales growth for several years, and had developed a highly motivated team around her. She was an inspirational leader who was able to deliver compelling speeches and presentations to large groups of salespeople at their regional and national meetings.

The business team she had assembled around her in Mexico was top-notch. She hired every one of them directly and all were devoted to her mission of growing the business and expanding the sales force every year. Mariana's hiring process was more instinctive than systematic. Of course she had to see specific competencies, but more importantly she relied on her instincts to select people who would fit into the business culture she had created. Within the South America division there was an extreme level of loyalty to Mariana and pride in the results they had all produced together. While the US-based parent company was struggling with declining sales, in South America they were averaging 23 percent growth annually.

Mariana had driven (without necessarily intending to) a classic Cult of Personality, but the parent company was so pleased with the financial results that they left her alone to continue the growth for several years. The results she was producing definitely got noticed, and when the US-based parent company continued to struggle, the CEO/owner was thrilled to have her accept a promotion to the national sales VP role and bring her to work at the corporate headquarters in Minnesota.

Mariana had visited the US corporate offices numerous times for meetings and events, but it wasn't until she worked there on a daily basis that the true culture at the "home office" began to reveal itself to her. A classic Inbred Culture of a one-hundred-year-old proudly historic company.

On her first official day in the new role, Mariana walked into the bland beige corporate headquarters wearing a blood-red business suit. She gave a speech to the corporate office employees and was surprised that the response was so muted. "Are these people awake?" she asked one of her colleagues afterward.

Over the next several months she began to hear that "some people" (never the actual person speaking to her) weren't happy with her work style. "Some people" weren't impressed with her results in South America, and she was honestly confused by the criticism.

"Some people" called her ego-driven and spoke of the "cult of Mariana" surrounding her. Some made jokes about the fact that every time she spoke in front of a huge audience of salespeople she managed to end with a (predictably) tearful story that brought the audience to their feet. Some said she was "All sizzle, no steak," while others tittered nastily, "All flash, no fajita." Behind her back they claimed she had no discernible business competency, just the ability to verbalize a compelling (and sometimes not executable) plan and inspire (uneducated, inexperienced) salespeople to take action. Mariana tried to ignore the critics but their comments still stung, and drove her harder than ever to prove them wrong.

She brought in a few people from her Mexico team, but they all struggled to operate in a culture where decisions were made by matrixed teams (not Mariana) and driven by data (not Mariana's instinct).

Ultimately there was a huge clash of cultures, egos, and personalities. And unfortunately Mariana would not win the battle. Within two years she was "retired" from the business and went back to Mexico. As she looks back at the experience now Mariana sees that she played a role in her own demise.

"I had a big blind spot," she says. "Because my team in Mexico was so aligned and supportive of me personally, I assumed that the same culture would exist at corporate. Since the owner and CEO had personally brought me in, why wouldn't everyone be supportive?

That was my thinking, and obviously I should have been a little more discerning."

Mariana now sees that she tends to instinctively like people and assumes that people like her. She "bonds" with others quickly and assumes others do the same. This left her ill prepared for a corporate environment where many (perhaps most) were not prepared to be "instant fans." And while the South American division (perhaps rightly) celebrated her leadership, the US corporate culture expected her to earn their respect, not assume it. They expected her to align with them, not the other way around.

From a recent conversation it is clear that Mariana still has a few blind spots. Most significantly she doesn't see that when she realizes someone she is working with isn't a "fan," her quick instinctive reaction is to decide that person is an "enemy." You are either on "Team Mariana" or you're not. When she had complete control of the team she was creating (as she did in Mexico) she understandably surrounded herself with people who were loyal fans. But business leaders in this position can easily, over time, begin to assume that almost everyone is a loyal fan ("Except for those backstabbing A**HOLES!") and anyone who isn't gets banished.

Even if your company culture is much more positive and empowering than these problematic examples, it is still critical to understand the specific culture within which you are working. Even companies that appear to be quite similar from the outside can in fact have quite different cultures. And sometimes it is the differences in their business models that drives the cultural variance.

For example, Whole Foods, Trader Joe's, and Sprouts Farmers Market appear to be quite similar businesses focused on healthy, natural, and organic foods. But employees who have worked for all three will tell you that the business models and cultures are different in subtle but significant ways.

Whole Foods is driven by a mission to support healthy

living—for both customers and employees. In that spirit they try to create an internal culture in which employees can truly thrive and work happily. Employee salaries (and food prices) at Whole Foods are typically higher than those at Trader Joe's and Sprouts, both of which focus more heavily on providing low-cost healthy foods. Employees at Trader Joe's tend to be short-timers, and the business expects a fairly high turnover rate. At Sprouts there appears to be less turnover and more of a focus on retaining high-value employees by providing a long-term career path opportunity. The purpose here isn't to detail out every nuanced difference between these three businesses or to imply that one of them is a better working environment than the others. Instead the goal is to use them as an example of how different the corporate culture can be, even in relatively similar businesses.

Bobbie Hartwell was an assistant store manager at Sprouts who took a manager job at Whole Foods when a store opened in her area. She could be forgiven for assuming that the jobs would be relatively similar, but for her the differences were striking. "Whole Foods was a schizophrenic working experience for me," Bobbie says. "They are so much more focused on creating a customer experience, sustaining a lifestyle for their farmers and food producers as well as customers and employees. All of that was good. And while they are much less about low cost, that doesn't mean they aren't about growth and profit. In reality, along with the pressure to create an amazing mission-driven environment comes the pressure to drive growth and profitability. Much more pressure than I had at Sprouts."

At Sprouts, Bobbie worked in a relatively low-pressure environment with what she thought of as reasonable incentives to keep costs down and manage inventory. At Whole Foods, everything was tightly tracked and measured. She was under a lot of pressure to improve profitability, not by cutting costs but by improving store traffic and sales volume.

If you fail to understand the business culture within which you work, or within a prospective employer, this can put a brake on your career progress. In Bobbie's case she eventually went back to work at Sprouts, was much happier, but had to accept a cashier's position until an assistant manager position opened up a year later. There is no question that Bobbie's career would have been better off if she had understood the business culture differences before making her decision to leave Sprouts.

Remember that the true culture isn't necessarily what people *say* it is. The true culture reflects how people actually work with each other, not how they think they *should* act and react. And the most successful people in business find ways to align with the work culture, not by giving up who they really are, but by flexing their work style and natural habits.

THINK NOW

We've covered so much ground in this chapter, it would be best for you to pause a moment and reflect on a few things before moving on. Learning to navigate the culture and politics of your own work environment is going to require both a mind-set shift and development of new capabilities.

- What is your own attitude toward office politics? Is it an annoyance to avoid? A frustrating necessity? Or can you embrace the reality that almost every activity with other people has an element of human politics, at work and in every other area of life?
- What is your perspective on workplace friendships? Do you understand they are not actually friends, but just friendly work colleagues? Do you have strong relationships with friends and family outside of work? This can help to keep your perspective clear.

- Do you have a broad network of connections with friendly work colleagues throughout the organization, not just limited to your natural day-to-day interactions? If not, what can you do to begin expanding that network?
- How well do you really know the end-to-end business model of your company? Do you understand how all the key departments work together to achieve business objectives? What makes your products or services unique? What are the main business growth drivers and potential threats to that growth? If the answers to these questions are not clear to you, what can you do to deepen your knowledge of the business?

ACT SOON

- Become a student of your business model, work to develop a broad and deep understanding of every department, function, and process that impacts business success.
- Identify those in your business who seem to be really good at navigating the human dynamics within the organization and begin to model their behavior.
- Begin playing "positive politics" immediately by taking every opportunity to help others more than they expect to be helped. Go out of your way to (authentically) recognize the good work of others.
- Play close attention to the political dynamics within your organization and work group: Who has the formal power? The informal power? How do difficult decisions get made? Who is held accountable, and who isn't?
- Notice who seems to be unaware of the "politics" within your work group and the errors they make.
- Are there any specific individuals who are particularly challenging for you? How might you employ positive politics to develop a more productive working relationship?

LONG-TERM THOUGHTS AND ACTION POINTS

How would you describe the culture at work to someone who was a complete stranger to your business? What are some of the important factors for working effectively in this type of culture?

Rate your internal organizational culture in the following areas and think about how these relative strengths and weaknesses impact the culture:

- **COMPELLING PURPOSE**: Do employees feel that the business exists for important reasons beyond achievement of financial targets?

- **AUTHENTIC LEADERSHIP**: Do employees trust leaders and align with their direction for the organization?

- **CLEAR OBJECTIVES AND EXPECTATIONS**: Do employees know exactly what is expected of them and how their efforts contribute to strategic business objectives?

- **ADEQUATE SKILLS AND RESOURCES**: Do employees feel that they have the skills and resources necessary to do their jobs well and achieve required objectives?

- **ENERGIZING ENVIRONMENT**: Does the working environment help employees to maintain a high level of energy and motivation throughout the workday?

- **PERVASIVE PRODUCTIVITY**: Are ALL employees highly productive so the workload is broadly and fairly shared, and no one feels they shoulder a heavier burden because of their exceptional competence or commitment?

- **JOYFUL ENGAGEMENT:** Are employees truly engaged, happy, and excited as they work each day?

- **COOPERATIVE TEAMWORK:** Do employees feel they can count on others throughout the organization to help them when needed?

- **REWARDS AND RECOGNITION:** Do employees feel that rewards and recognition are meaningful, fair, and objectively targeted?

- **DEVELOPMENT OPPORTUNITIES:** Do employees feel they have opportunities in the business to grow and develop?

You can conduct a thorough assessment of your organizational culture by going to www.workplacepoker.com /culture-assessment/.

When dealing with others:

- Maintain your integrity at all times—always remain professional, and always remember the organization's interests.

- Voice critical feedback or objections from an organizational perspective, not a personal one.

- Don't rely on confidentiality. Assume all things will be disclosed and decide what you should reveal accordingly.

- Be a model of integrity.

- Always be a good listener and a "safe" place where individuals can express their frustrations without fear of it being shared with others.

- Don't repeat gossip, questionable judgments, spread rumors—when you hear something, take a day to consider how much credibility it has.

3

Take the Hit

◆

Let me tell you something you already know. The world ain't all sunshine and rainbows. It is a very mean and nasty place and it will beat you to your knees and keep you there permanently if you let it. You, me, or nobody is gonna hit as hard as life. But it ain't how hard you hit; it's about how hard you can get hit and keep moving forward. How much you can take and keep moving forward. That's how winning is done . . . But you gotta be willing to take the hit.

—ROCKY BALBOA, SPEAKING TO HIS SON IN *ROCKY BALBOA* (2006)

S omething bad has happened to you at work, either recently or in the distant past. You lost a well-deserved promotion or a co-worker lied to you or someone took credit for your good work (or shifted the blame onto you for their bad work) or you lost your job or your boss is a jerk or . . . well, there are a lot of bad things that can happen at work. Whatever bad thing has happened to you, you probably feel like you've taken a hit. But let me ask, have you spent much time thinking about just exactly why you find yourself in this situation?

Sure, a bad thing happened, but why is that? For many people the deep, authentic answer to this question is the hit they try to avoid.

Because if ultimately your current circumstances are the result of your decisions, your actions, YOUR choices—if you had the power to create other circumstances but this is the situation you created—that can be a pretty devastating hit to take.

In terms of career acceleration, there is profound value in "owning" your circumstances fully, completely—totally. Not just your fair and reasonable share of the responsibility/blame, but placing the entire load on your own shoulders. This is not about beating yourself up for past actions, bad decisions, or poor choices. This is about seeing yourself and your world clearly, without self-doubt or self-recrimination, in order to prepare for the challenge ahead.

I had a unique opportunity to see this principle in action several years ago when separately interviewing two CEOs who had recently been forced to resign from their companies. Both had reputations as competent leaders but had struggled to execute business turnarounds in (different) shrinking markets. Both had strong and sometimes abrasive personalities. And both saw their relationships with employees and their boards deteriorate as the businesses spiraled downward. But as I discussed the situation with each of them, the two conversations could not have been more different.

"They wouldn't give me enough time, and wouldn't invest in the resources we needed," said one ex-CEO as he described to me the root causes for his failure. "My biggest personal mistake was in trusting the board members. I took them at their word when they hired me, but after a couple of rough quarters everyone was running for the exits." He was very reasonable and factual, walking me through his growth plan for the business and explaining where the plan went off course—because of a lack of resources, loss of patience, or in some cases poor execution by those reporting to him. I had the strong impression that everything he was telling me was true, but as I walked away thinking about our conversation I was struck by how he had subtly separated himself from the failure. He actually felt quite good about everything he had done for the company and only regretted that others didn't have his strategic foresight. My next conversation with an ex-CEO took place a few months later and the tone was quite different.

"I'm still struggling with this, even after six months," he told me. "Like replaying a lost chess game in my head, working through all the other possible moves until I figure out what I could have done differently to win." He wasn't beating up on himself, and didn't seem depressed. If anything he seemed to be looking at himself with intense curiosity, trying to figure out exactly where he made the wrong moves. He also was trying to turn around a business in a shrinking market, and struggled with an impatient board unwilling to invest in the resources he needed. But when I asked him about his biggest personal failure in this situation he didn't hesitate to explain where he went off course.

"I underestimated our competitor's reactions to our pricing strategy, and I selected leaders in sales and marketing who had been successful, but in expanding markets, not shrinking ones. This gave them certain blind spots and they in turn put together teams with the same blind spots," he told me. "I guess the bottom line is that I jumped into solving the growth problem for this company before I really, deeply, understood all of the factors—I didn't really understand our competitor's strategies, I didn't really understand how our customers were changing, and I didn't really see the limitations of my own team, until it was too late."

Both of these CEOs were tasked with growth objectives that were perhaps, in hindsight, not achievable. But in discussing the root causes of their demise, the second CEO was clearly more willing to take the hit, more willing to personally "own" the circumstances of his failure.

Today both CEOs run thriving businesses, both are certainly perceived as successful corporate leaders and feel good about their respective career trajectories. But the first CEO runs a manufacturing company, about the same size as the company from which he was ousted. The second CEO has gone on to lead increasingly larger businesses and has developed a world-class reputation as a turn-around leader. I am convinced that one of the root causes of the second CEO's success trajectory is his willingness to "own" (and then learn from) his missteps.

There is a degree of deep confidence you see in people who are fully aware of, and comfortable with, their own faults and failings. They are "comfortable in their own skin" so to speak and we often find ourselves drawn to them, at ease around them, because there is no pretense, no bloated ego, and no self-loathing. The closer you can get to this particular mental and emotional state, the better prepared you will be to face the challenges ahead of you. Remember, this isn't just about dealing with the bad situation—it is about reacting to the bad situation in a manner that serves to enhance your career trajectory.

The problem itself may be somewhat (or completely) out of your control and you may not feel as if this situation is exactly a career booster. It may not be. But your reaction to the situation can definitely provide acceleration, and that is where you have complete control.

Instead of focusing on what happened TO you, focus on what you did (or failed to do) to create the difficult circumstances. Ask yourself:

- What did I do, or fail to do, to create or contribute to these circumstances?
- Why did I do this?
- What have I learned from this situation?
- How will my mind-set be different as I move forward?

Pay particular attention to the "why" question above. Keep the focus on you, your assumptions (Why did you make them?), your blind spots (Why didn't you see it coming?), and your lack of effort, preparation, or discernment. Often the deep answers to "why" hold the key to preventing similar difficulties in the future.

THE RISKY BUSINESS OF PERSONAL ACCOUNTABILITY

Jeremy Piche is an engineering project manager for Shaw Drilling, an energy services company in Alberta, Canada. He's a conscientious and hardworking guy, well liked by just about everyone at Shaw. And he's someone who truly "owns" his projects. If something goes wrong, he takes full responsibility no matter what the mitigating factors might be. This is an admirable trait and it makes Jeremy a great project manager. But it also caused a significant career setback.

"We had a complex development in partnership with two other companies, and I was the project manager, so ultimately I was responsible for the timeline and budget," he says. He was working with a team of people from the two other companies as well as a few Shaw employees. "I hadn't worked with the other companies before, and I made some assumptions that turned out to be wrong."

When some of the required documentation wasn't filed with the proper government agencies, and certain oversight inspections weren't documented properly, the project got significantly behind schedule and was in danger of being terminated, with over a hundred thousand dollars in sunk costs.

During an emergency project review focused on getting the project back on track, Jeremy put all of the responsibility on his own shoulders even though individuals from the two other companies were in fact responsible for the errors. "I thought the best way to get things back on track was to avoid pointing fingers and just focus on what needed to happen going forward," Jeremy says. "But that ended up biting me in the ass."

Everyone on the team was more than willing to let him shoulder the blame, and to his credit the project got back on track and was ultimately successful. But Jeremy's boss at Shaw Drilling lost confidence in him. The two partner companies indicated that any future joint projects should be managed by someone else. Jeremy didn't lose his job, but his career progress definitely stalled for a few years after that.

"In hindsight," Jeremy says today, "while I still think it was my ultimate responsibility, I shouldn't have let others off the hook so easily. Because it created a misimpression that no one else was at fault, which wasn't true."

In most business cultures there is a unique cooperative/competitive dynamic. We all have to cooperate with each other in order to achieve our business objectives, but we are also "competing" with each other to advance our own careers. In business, a rising tide does not lift all boats equally. Some get more credit for a successful project, some less. Some get larger bonuses, sometimes for reasons not connected to actual work performance. Some get promotions, some don't. And again, this isn't always driven purely by competency.

So while it is important for you to INTERNALLY accept total responsibility for difficult circumstances, be thoughtful about how you communicate this externally. This is not meant to imply that you should consciously try to shift blame to others, but be careful about letting others off the hook. You can take responsibility *and* hold others accountable for their failings.

....

Taking the hit does not mean letting others off the hook.

....

Whenever I have a bit of bad luck related to my career I usually think of my old friend Alex in order to feel a little better about my own situation. Alex has been a friend for more than twenty years, and he has had horrible luck in his career almost from the very beginning.

He was two years into a four-year mechanical engineering program at college when Alex's father called to tell him the money had run out and they could no longer afford his tuition. So Alex was forced to settle for a two-year associate's degree, then look for work. With a two-year degree the best he could do was to get a job as a draftsman with one of the few companies that were not rapidly moving toward computer-based drafting. He spent six years as a traditional manual pencil-and-paper draftsman—until the company went out of business.

So Alex was out in the job market interviewing for drafting positions, but he had no computer-based drafting experience, which had become the industry standard. Obviously he needed to get up to speed with technology, but he also needed to earn a living so he took a job as a salesperson and planned to go to school at night. It turned out he had a knack for selling and he came to realize that his outgoing and gregarious nature wasn't really compatible with sitting at a drafting desk (or computer screen) all day. He seemed to be a natural salesperson, didn't have to really work at it, and the money was good. So he had a couple of fruitful years as a real estate salesperson, got married to his high school sweetheart, bought a nice house, had two children. Life was good.

Then the economy suddenly turned south. Real estate sales dried up. We had been friends for years so Alex called me to ask if my company was hiring. Unfortunately we were reducing our sales force by about 10 percent, like many other companies during a cyclical business contraction. Alex mentioned that the few interviews he was able to line up were not going well. Since at the time I spent most of my working day developing sales training and coaching programs, we agreed to have lunch and catch up while we talked about his interviewing strategy.

"Good news!" he said as soon as we sat down for lunch. "We're going to have another baby!" Alex was genuinely happy and I didn't want to rain on his parade, but obviously the timing wasn't ideal.

He had to see the concerned look on my face, and I immediately felt guilty. Of course a new baby was good news. Over lunch I learned that Alex's family life was amazingly positive. His wife was beautiful and loving and supportive. Both of his children, two daughters, were healthy and happy. And now he was hoping that a son was on the way. But his professional and financial life was a shambles. In addition to selling real estate he had invested in a big land development project just before the economic slump. That investment was now underwater with little hope of ever getting any of his money out of it.

So Alex needed a job. A well-paying job. And yet his interviews seemed to be going nowhere. So I asked him some of the normal questions I would ask of any salesperson who was debriefing a sales call, and his answers began to give me a clearer picture of Alex's entire life.

"What kind of advance research did you do before the interview?" I asked.

"Well, the interview came up suddenly so I didn't have a lot of advance notice. Plus I know the company pretty well so I didn't need to do much research," he replied.

"How did you know what specific skills and experience they were looking for?"

"The online job description was pretty detailed."

"So which of those skills is most important to them?"

"What do you mean?"

"Well, I'm sure that everything in the job description is important, but what is MOST important to them? Which skills or capabilities are they having the hardest time finding in their candidates?"

"I have no idea."

"This would be selling in a new industry for you. Different from real estate in some fundamental ways. So what kind of research did you do on the industry?"

"Like I said, I know the company and I know their products. And selling is selling."

"OK, so . . . why do you think it didn't go well?"

"First of all I'm not sure why they even brought me in. The guy didn't seem particularly interested in me. He was a little standoffish and asked some really dumb off-the-wall questions. Like if I was an animal or a plant, what kind would I be? What kind of people frustrate me? I'm in sales so I get along with everyone, but he obviously didn't like that answer. Stupid stuff like that."

"So he was a bad interviewer," I said. Apparently my sarcasm was too subtle for him.

"Yeah, he was." Alex nodded energetically. "And what kind of company has somebody like that working for them? I probably dodged a bullet because if they have people like that, it can't be a great place to work."

"Did you bring along any evidence or samples of your previous work? Like sales reports or other tangible proof of your sales ability?"

"I don't really have anything like that. The company I worked for didn't really provide us with anything like that. Plus I left pretty abruptly so I didn't get to take much with me. But I gave him some good references."

Our conversation continued for another hour and nothing changed. It was clear that Alex wasn't preparing well enough for his interviews, but he had reasons. In every case, either the circumstances didn't allow him to prepare, or he didn't have access to information, or his previous employer didn't provide him with the data. Or he was too busy taking care of his children (because his wife had to take a part-time job) or the job description wasn't accurate or the interviewer wasn't well prepared. Or . . . you get the idea. There was always a reason, and it was never Alex's fault that he hadn't been able to prepare adequately.

I really like Alex, and I would love to be able to tell you that be-cause of his conversation with me he had an epiphany, a sudden re-alization that he himself was the source of his financial frustration. That he had always been in complete control of all the circumstances of his life. But that didn't happen. In fact, as the conversation began to move in that direction Alex became a little irritated and impatient so we finished up, shook hands, agreed to have lunch again in a few weeks. That was six months ago, and I haven't heard from him. I hope he is doing well.

What I know about Alex is that he was fully aware of how tight his father's finances were before he started college. So he shouldn't have been shocked when the money ran out, but he hadn't done anything to prepare for that likely occurrence. And Alex knew that his drafting skills were quickly becoming antiquated, but since his company wouldn't pay for computers and software, he didn't do anything about it. The failure of that company shouldn't have been a surprise to him, he knew how outdated they had become, but he hadn't done anything to prepare. Same with real estate sales, he knew well in advance that the market was tightening up. And because selling seemed to be a natural skill for him he was never motivated to work at getting better. He didn't attend sales training workshops, didn't read books, didn't learn from his fellow sales-people. He just did what came naturally, which worked really well. Until it didn't.

But when you ask Alex about all of the professional challenges he has experienced, the root causes are always . . . out there some-where. As much as Alex has suffered professionally, he has never been willing to truly take the hit—to acknowledge that he is ulti-mately the master of all his circumstances. Because taking that hit can be brutally painful. If you can't blame your boss, or the econ-omy, or the company management, or your spouse, your parents, your kids, your friends—or your bad luck—if you can't point the finger outward, then the only direction left is to point inward. Getting your head around the realization that in the end, you created the circumstances within which you live today, can be tough and uncomfortable. But on the bright side, it frees us to make much needed changes in our lives. It focuses our minds on what we can control and drives action. But that initial emotional pain can be too much for many of us to bear.

There is probably no more emotionally painful professional experience than being fired from your job because of poor performance (real or perceived, the pain is almost the same). Being laid off because of downsizing or restructuring comes a close second. The pain is financial and emotional. But most of us seek to minimize that pain by blaming others for the circumstances. Or blaming the economy. Or politicians. Or bad weather. Or just plain bad luck. If you had a dishonest boss who lied to you about the company and then lied to the company about you, who engineered your firing through deception and subterfuge in order to save his own job—could any reasonable person say that you had power over those circumstances? Well, the truth is that you chose those circumstances. And even if you were deceived, you could have been more discerning.

When it comes to employment there is no luck, good or bad. There are no accidental circumstances. There are no victims. Everything happens for a reason. And just because you are surprised, or are treated unfairly, does not mean that you can abdicate your own responsibility for the situation. You have made choices. And even when you felt that you were trapped into only one option, if you think clearly, you probably made choices that resulted in the "trap."

....

There is no career luck, good or bad. No accidental circumstances. No victims.

....

A chess player halfway through the game can't complain about the poor positioning of his pieces or the limited options available, because he created those circumstances, move by move. If you rewind the chess game of your life you will often see how earlier choices and decisions put you in a position where you feel you no longer have viable choices.

But here's the *big* lesson—you ALWAYS have choices, even today, when you may feel trapped by past choices.

This can be a hard truth to swallow because if you have gotten used to bathing yourself in the comfortable warm waters of blaming others or circumstances, then the cold brisk spray of icy personal accountability can be too much to bear.

I never set out to be a career counselor, but somewhere along the way, as I developed and delivered a variety of workshops and webinars focused on career-enhancing skills, people began to come to me for individual advice. These conversations often start with some particular career difficulty, and almost always there is a strong sense of being "wronged," either by others or just by life in general. I usually try to ask questions that help clarify their ultimate power over, and accountability for, their circumstances:

WHEN THEY SAY:	I ASK:
I work in an abusive environment.	Why do you choose to do that?
I've had a series of bad bosses.	What does that tell you about yourself?
I don't play corporate politics.	Why do you refuse to play?
This was the best job I could find in the area.	Why did you limit yourself to this area?
Everyone in this industry is struggling.	Why did you limit yourself to this industry?
I don't have the right educational background.	What have you done about that?

They almost always promote their friends and cronies over more competent people	How can you become so good that they can't ignore you?
I ticked off the wrong people.	What was the point of doing that?
The job wasn't what they told me it would be.	What independent research did you do?
I don't have much in savings so I'm going to need to take the first decent job offered to me.	What choices have you made to put yourself into this financial situation?
They lied to me.	Why weren't you more discerning?

Why is this such a big deal? Who really cares if you are blaming others for the bad circumstances in your life? I care, because this limits your ability to think clearly about your future actions and decisions.

So we started this chapter by acknowledging that something bad has happened to you at work. More likely, many bad things have happened to you. But there is probably one particular circumstance that really sticks out in your mind.

So let me ask you again, just exactly why do you think this happened? What did you do, or not do, to bring the situation upon yourself? If you can think clearly and deeply, and come up with a fully honest answer to this question, this can be a huge step forward for you.

Then of course we must ask, what are you going to do differently going forward? You know the world of work is rapidly changing, and the rate of change is accelerating. But what about you? Are you changing? Are you driving the change within yourself or are you letting others (or circumstances) drive it? How equipped are you to engage the challenges and opportunities that are ahead of you?

If there is one absolute fundamental rule for your career and your life going forward, it has to be taking complete personal responsibility for every situation and circumstance. If a volcano springs up in your backyard tomorrow and spews out lava onto your entire home, you are still responsible. Shouldn't you have been paying greater attention to the geology under your home? Accepting personal responsibility means a complete rejection of blame. It means not making excuses, citing other people, or attributing circumstances to external events, unfairness, or bad luck.

Personal responsibility means accepting that you, and only you, are in charge of your own destiny. It means acknowledging and accepting that you are responsible for the choices you make, the way you behave, the actions you take and the way you think and feel. Personal responsibility means being accountable for what you think, say, and do.

Personal responsibility is rooted in the knowledge that every act, thought, or feeling results from choice, not coercion. Only you can choose how you respond. Personal responsibility is an attitude, a philosophy, a way of being. So personal career responsibility means accepting that what you've done, where you are now, and where you want to get to is entirely in your own hands.

TAKE THE HIT AND GET ON WITH YOUR LIFE

Acknowledge Your Failings: You don't have to shout them from the rooftops, but you have to at least be honest with yourself. When you haven't lived up to your full potential, "take the hit" and admit your failing. Don't beat yourself up, just admit your error, learn from it, and make a commitment to do better as you move on. Strive for perfection, but never expect it.

Watch Your Language: Avoid phrases like "it's not fair," "I can't help it," "it's not my fault." Avoid any phrase that reinforces the victim mindset. "I am ultimately the captain of my life" should be your mantra.

Build Self-Awareness: Spend quiet time on a regular basis thinking about yourself, your thought processes, how you are developing and growing emotionally. Do you understand your strengths and weaknesses, attitudes and behavioral patterns? Have you actually defined what career success means to you personally?

Be Proactively Accountable: Identify what's not working, what's in your way, and free yourself from these obstacles. "Own" your thoughts, your attitudes, your feelings, and your actions. Accept that you have a choice in all of these. What do you tell yourself that is holding you back? What behaviors do you repeat that jeopardize your success? Seek out answers; don't wait for them to come to you.

Eliminate Excuses: Times are tough, but this has been true since the dawn of man, and no matter what the difficulties may be, we always have choices. Our circumstances today are the result of choices we have made. Choices to act or *not* to act. Choices to pay attention to or to ignore. Choices to engage or to avoid. Those who survive and succeed are those who recognize this and are prepared to fully embrace their personal responsibility.

POINTING FINGERS IS EASY, SATISFYING, AND DANGEROUS

The tendency to blame others and overlook our own contributions to our circumstances comes very naturally to most of us, so we have to work very consciously to push our brains in the other direction. One of the ways I push myself in the other direction when I start to point fingers is to remember the story of Bavesh Dhirwan.

Bavesh was a programmer for the IT department of a midsized company in Brisbane, Australia. He was a conscientious hard worker and could always be counted on to stay late, work extra hours, and do whatever else it took to get a project done on time and on budget. He wasn't too fond of his boss, who he felt took credit for the hard work of others, but he assumed that if he just did his job well everything would work out for the best in the end.

The entire IT department was under a lot of pressure to execute the installation of a new enterprise-wide system. They had increased their full-time staff by 20 percent and still had to bring on half a dozen contract workers to complete the two-year project on time. Bavesh was leading the security assurance testing team and by everyone's account he did a fine job as team leader. So once the project was officially complete and it was time to reduce staffing back to normal levels, he was truly stunned to be among those who were laid off.

Bavesh's manager offered no explanation but he did ensure that everyone who was laid off received a fair severance package. As a team leader Bavesh received an especially generous severance, but he still felt personally betrayed and was furious with his manager. So he sent an email to everyone in the IT department, copying the CEO of the company, laying out everything he knew to be wrong about the capabilities and management style of his boss. It was the email equivalent of a nuclear flamethrower, and the results were predictable: he was immediately and publicly escorted out of the building by security, his severance package was pulled, and obviously he couldn't plan on any sort of positive reference from his previous employer.

Bavesh was so angry he simply couldn't focus on finding a new job, but he desperately needed one. With no severance package the financial pressure was building quickly. And as the pressure increased his job search capability diminished. Even when he managed to land a job interview, as soon as the interviewer asked about his previous employer, Bavesh couldn't help but launch into an angry tirade. He felt fully justified, and thought it was so clear that he had been taken advantage of, that any reasonable person would have to see it. But the only thing that interviewers saw was someone with "anger issues," and although he was obviously a talented programmer, they had plenty of capable candidates to choose from.

Over the years I've seen many similar situations but this one was of course among the most extreme. It was definitely among the most pointless because ultimately Bavesh burned bridges with most of the major IT employers in his area. He was forced to move (not really forced of course, it was the result of his actions) to Sydney, where he found new job opportunities and had enough self-awareness to stop letting his anger get in the way with prospective employers.

But here is the kicker. Years later when he was back in Brisbane visiting old friends, he found out that the reason he had been laid off was that his manager thought he was ready to move up to a more senior IT management position, but that type of position would not be available at his old company for years because their IT staff was contracting, not expanding. So his manager had worked out a generous severance package to ease the transition and was prepared to offer exceptionally strong job references. Yes, it would have been nice if the manager had communicated all of this to Bavesh proactively, and that was probably his intent. But the situation blew up so rapidly (because of the nuclear email) that it never happened.

As you look at your own life and the choices you have made, hopefully you can remember these three key lessons:

- I created these circumstances, and that may be painful to acknowledge.
- I will create my new circumstances, which may be good or bad.
- I am responsible for a plan that leads me to a positive outcome no matter what the external circumstances might be.

I'll step off my accountability high horse for a moment and acknowledge that sometimes I can be a little whiney. My whiney mantra usually goes something like "I work so hard, why don't they appreciate me more?" and it is easy for me to feel a little self-righteous. Then I remember a woman I met a few years ago named Grace Summers. Her story tends to bring my world back into a healthy perspective.

Several years ago I received a call from the director of a women's shelter in Texas who told me about her program for helping abused women transition out of abusive relationships and into a productive work life. Many of the women she worked with had never held a traditional job. Many did not have even rudimentary workplace skills and the shelter director wanted to leverage some of the online learning programs published by my company Frontline Learning, but of course they had no financial resources to pay for the courses. We worked out an arrangement to offer courses at no cost to the women in her shelter program, and that is how I met Grace Summers.

Grace completed the first eight courses we made available to the shelter, then asked if there were more. We opened up twenty more courses and she began to rapidly work through those. I asked the shelter director to tell me about this person who seemed to be so intently focused on learning as much as possible, as rapidly as possible. The director told me that Grace was sexually abused by an uncle from the time she was fourteen until she ran away from home at sixteen. Unfortunately she went from an awful home environment to even more horrible circumstances.

Grace ended up being held captive as a prostitute and was pregnant at seventeen. The child was taken away from her and sold. She never saw the child again; Grace escaped when she was twenty and ended up in the shelter with no money, not even a high school GED. But she was determined to make a better life for herself.

What was remarkable to me was her positive focus and desire to move forward without dwelling on the past. Grace was committed to looking forward and taking the next step in that direction. She was determined to not start off with a low-wage fast-food job or an entry-level position that would barely pay minimum wage. She wanted something more and was determined to make it happen. She focused on building her computer skills, and taught herself simple web page design.

I spoke with her several times and was impressed with her lack of residual anger, her determination to not be a victim, and her willingness to confront the harsh reality of her employability, or lack thereof. "I have a great attitude and motivation," she said, "but I don't have the skills. So I need to fix that."

It would break my heart if there wasn't a happy ending to this story. Luckily there is. Grace was eventually hired as an entry-level web page developer, and advanced rapidly. Today she has a perfectly normal, perfectly average white-collar work life. She has a short commute to work each morning, stops for coffee at Starbucks, leads a small team of web designers, and comes home to a husband and two children at night. Her life is normal, average, ordinary. Which is wonderful and fantastic and amazing.

THINK NOW

Before moving on to the next chapter, please take a few minutes to think about the key points we've made in this chapter, and how this can impact your career going forward.

- To what degree have you fallen into the habit of blaming others for circumstances over which you actually have a significant level of influence or control?
- As you tell your career story to others, how often do "villains" appear in the story? If there are villains, there must be a victim. And you're not a victim, are you?
- Who do you know in your career who does an admirable job of accepting total responsibility for all of their career circumstances? What can you learn from them?

ACT SOON

Take some time to think deeply about your life and career, the challenges you have experienced and the choices you have made. Remember these three key lessons:

- I created these circumstances, and that may be painful to acknowledge.
- I will create my new circumstances, which may be good or bad.
- I am responsible for a plan that leads me to a positive outcome no matter what the external circumstances might be.

LONG-TERM THOUGHTS AND ACTION POINTS

In terms of career acceleration, there is profound value in "owning" your circumstances. Be honest with yourself about your own faults and failings.

When it comes to your career, there is no good luck or bad. There are no accidental circumstances, and no victims. There is only cause and effect.

As you face challenges in the future, think deeply about your answers to the following questions:

• Why am I in this tough situation?

• What have I learned so far from this experience?

• What have I learned about myself?

• What changes (within me) would serve me well?

• What is my plan to make those changes happen?

You always have choices, even when you feel trapped by past choices.

Watch your language carefully to ensure you are accepting full accountability for your life and career circumstances.

4

Fuel Your Fire

♦

A sad soul can kill you quicker than a germ.

—JOHN STEINBECK

One of my challenges in writing this book has been to share interesting and informative stories without throwing any of my business clients under the bus. It's easy to change details that prevent others from recognizing the client, but when a particular story highlights the absurd and senseless actions of those involved, you don't even want them to recognize themselves. And with this particular story that's not going to be possible. So under the bus we go.

I was asked to develop a training program for a large group of telephone customer service representatives. "They have a real attitude problem," their director told me. "We need some training to make them more polite, more sensitive, and more friendly with our customers."

OK, fair enough so far. And one of my standard practices when developing a program like this is to spend some time observing the group in their working environment. So I spent a full day on the bottom two floors of a nondescript office building in downtown

Kansas City, Missouri. Their telephone customer service team took up all of the space on these two floors. Imagine row upon row of small beige cubicles, and I mean small—enough space for a chair, a workstation, and one filing cabinet.

They had plenty of empty cubicles because they expand CSR staffing by more than 40 percent during the holiday season, then scale back down quickly in mid-January every year. This was in August, so no one minded me sitting in one of the empty micro-cubicles for a day. I listened in on actual phone calls with customers, took notes, and toward the end of the day I even handled a few calls myself. I also had a chance to have lunch with a group of the CSRs and talk to others in the break room on the lower floor. I gained a realistic perspective on their working environment and had what I needed to make a strong training recommendation to the client.

The next morning I met with the director and his team of eight managers. "I'm not so sure you have a training issue, or an attitude issue," I said. "I think you have an energy issue."

I went on to explain that often what appears to be a bad attitude or low morale with employees is in fact just a natural reflection of their low energy. And telephone-bound workers in call centers are especially susceptible to the debilitating effects of low energy.

As I spoke to the group I could see them looking a little confused as I explained that there are four sources of energy that can help employees feel more engaged, motivated, and focused at work. The four energy sources are:

- **Emotional Energy:** Feeling recognized and valued as a unique human being, able to freely express thoughts and opinions in a "safe" environment.
- **Aspirational Energy:** Having a positive sense of potential growth and continuous improvement of career circumstances.

- **Physical Energy:** Being healthy and fit while working in an environment with natural light, fresh air, water, and easy access to healthy foods.
- **Mental Energy:** Staying challenged with work that requires intellectual engagement while also allowing for regular "downtime" to recharge the mind.

I described each of these to the director and his management team, then provided my observations from the day I had just spent with their telephone customer service representatives.

"You have everyone in tiny beige cubicles with strict rules about not adding personal items that would be visible to others," I said. "Some employees commented that they feel like cattle, herded in at the beginning of a shift, expected to sit in their tiny cubicles and do their jobs efficiently, with no fun, no social chatter except during the strictly controlled break times, and no sense that they are human beings, not automatons. And some have said that they've seen others pay a price for speaking up about the working conditions. So everybody just puts their head down and does the work. Naturally, the emotional energy level is really, really low."

I was watching the facial expressions of the group as I said this, looking for some reaction, even a negative one, but I got nothing. Just dead flat stares, even from the director. So I continued on. I wondered if someone was pressing a secret red button under the table to summon security and have me escorted from the building.

"Their aspirational energy isn't any better. Nobody feels that they have any sort of career path or growth potential in the customer service job here. Essentially they work here until they find something better somewhere else," I said. "And everyone has anxiety about the January layoffs." I paused for their reaction but again, nothing but cricket sounds in the room.

"From the standpoint of physical energy, they sit for two hours in a cramped cubicle and then get a fifteen-minute break. There are no windows, and the fluorescent lighting is kind of bleak. The carpet is old and musty, the vending machines in the break room have nothing but junk, and there really is no easy access to healthy food or fresh water unless they bring their own."

"But we do have a refrigerator on each floor where they can keep their own meals cold, plus a microwave," one of the managers said.

"Have you seen the inside of those refrigerators lately?" I asked. "Or the microwave ovens? On both floors, they're pretty gross."

"Well whose fault is that? They should keep them clean," the manager shot back. Clearly they were beginning to take my comments personally, so I decided to wrap up quickly.

"And finally, in terms of mental energy, you've got them all following strict scripts, so there really is not much thinking required. Hour after hour they listen to customer questions and complaints, quickly refer to the correct script, and then just say the words in front of them. I don't think even Meryl Streep could act enthusiastic reading those scripts over and over again."

I smiled at my own little joke. They didn't.

"That's the point," one of them said. "We don't want them having to think of the right answer, we have to know that they are delivering correct information with every call."

Their reaction made it pretty clear that they weren't buying what I was selling. I tried hard not to sound preachy or judgmental. I didn't mention that none of them worked in a tiny cubicle on the bottom two floors. They all had windowed offices on an upper floor. I had visited that floor and took a look at their break room. Clean refrigerator, clean microwave oven, fresh water. There was even a small exercise room with three ellipticals and two treadmills. Hmm . . . but I didn't mention any of that.

"I would love to deliver a customer service training program to your folks, because they seem like good workers who really want to do a great job," I said to the managers. "But to be honest, right now I think the money would be better spent making adjustments to their working environment."

"This is interesting," the director said. "But we don't have the budget or resources to make a bunch of changes like this." He explained that with their high turnover rate, they couldn't afford to invest too much on each individual CSR, because most of them would be gone within a year. I countered that I thought they could reduce turnover with a more energized work environment.

Crickets.

I was heading out of the building twenty minutes later, but at least I didn't have a security escort. Now, any reasonable person would have just taken the hint and moved on because clearly any further effort with them would be a waste of time.

I'm not known as a typically reasonable person, so I followed up with an email that included a list of budget-conscious steps many call centers make to create a more energized work environment for their CSRs. Simple things like:

- Encouraging CSRs to decorate their cubicles and give their work space a "personality."
- Celebrating individual birthdays, recognizing individual accomplishments, and doing other things to help workers feel valued as individuals.

They may not call it "emotional energy," but this is exactly what they are trying to foster. Plus the best of them ensure that the physical working environment is clean, well-lighted, with easy access to fresh food and water. Some even have exercise facilities or outdoor walking paths so that people can get some physical activity during their breaks (fifteen minutes every sixty to ninety minutes is ideal). And an increasing number of forward-thinking companies are offering standing desks and/or ergonomic chairs to enhance physical energy.

In my follow-up email I included a link to research supporting the positive impact on productivity in a broad range of businesses when investments are made to enhance the physical, emotional, mental, and aspirational energy of employees.

....

You can view some of this research at
www.workplacepoker.com/energy/.

....

There was no response to my email for two weeks, and then what I received was a request for my pricing to deliver a customer service workshop. No mention of my crazy energy ideas. I did end up facilitating a series of workshops for them that year, and the feedback was positive. But there were no changes to the working environment—although I heard that they did create a rotating assignment sheet to clean the break room refrigerators and microwaves.

A year later they asked me back again, and not surprisingly most of the workshop attendees were new to the company. And last year I facilitated a third series of workshops for them, same content, totally new participants. I'm not sure how I feel about all of it, but I do think the workshops help a little. This must be how country music singers feel when they go to a prison and give a free show for the inmates. It doesn't really change anything, but it helps a little.

I'm thinking once they read this book I may not have to wrestle with the moral dilemma any longer.

I share this story with you primarily because I know that high-growth career trajectories are fueled by the kind of energy I've just described—emotional, mental, physical, and aspirational. And the most successful career climbers have developed habits and lifestyles to continuously enhance these energies. You may sometimes find yourself thinking, "Well of course she's energized at work, because things are going so well for her." And while that may be true, anyone can be energized when things are going really well. The most successful career climbers understand they are building energy reserves for when things aren't going very well.

And let's be honest—no matter how much you may like your job and the people you work with, sometimes the daily grind can wear you down. You don't have to be sitting in a tiny beige cubicle in a basement in downtown Kansas City to have your internal fire dampened by the pace and pressure and vagaries of modern work life.

STARTING STRONG, BUT RUNNING OUT OF FUEL

Angela Brandt was a talented and hardworking marketing manager for Dynetron, an energy company based in Houston. She had developed her strong work ethic growing up as the only child of a cattle rancher and was the first in her family to go to college, graduating from the University of Texas at Austin. "I was used to pushing myself hard, getting to work early, staying late, doing whatever it takes without complaining," she says. And her strong work ethic served her well at Dynetron, where she quickly established a reputation as someone who could be counted on to go the extra mile and get things done. She was promoted within her first two years, becoming the youngest (and only female) marketing manager at Dynetron. She seemed to be on course for a high-trajectory career eventually leading to a VP position in a high-growth company and a dynamic, expanding market.

But six years later not much had changed and she began to feel that her career progress had stalled out. "I was getting modest pay raises and nice bonuses each year, but was passed over for two promotions," she told me in a telephone conversation.

When the current marketing director retired Angela felt she was surely a strong candidate for the position, and actually expected to be asked to apply. But no one approached her, so she applied through the standard internal system at Dynetron. And no one ever followed up with her. She made a call to the HR recruiter just to be sure her application had been received and got nothing more than a polite assurance that yes, her application had been received and there would be follow up if she was considered to be a viable candidate for the position. There was no follow up. She was frustrated and confounded, but didn't have anyone she felt comfortable turning to for answers.

Feeling that her career at Dynetron was at a dead end, Angela began to look for opportunities elsewhere, applying for marketing director jobs in Austin, Houston, and Dallas. As she prepared for her first job interview she couldn't help thinking about how sorry they would be once she left Dynetron. Maybe after she was on to bigger and better things they would finally know what they had missed out on. So there was more than a small "I'll show them" chip on her shoulder and she was excited about moving on to something new. But the first interview didn't produce a job offer. And while she continued to apply and interview for other jobs, that first failed interview had crushed her spirit more than she had expected. "I had gotten myself so worked up because it really seemed like a great fit. So when they didn't even call me back, I felt defeated. I even tried to follow up with them but they didn't return my calls. It felt like being jilted by someone after the first date. I hated it."

So hardworking, talented, and energized Angela had gone from a high-trajectory career path to feeling flatlined in six years. What had changed? And was there anything she could do to get back on track? "I just lost my fire," she says today. "It wasn't any one thing, it was a whole combination of things that gradually built up."

As her early career had progressed, Angela's aspirational and emotional energy had been exceptionally high. In fact they were so high that it masked a decline in her physical and mental energy. After her first promotion she was energized by the new work, but after a couple of years in the same role, the work was no longer new and challenging for her. So her work began to require less mental energy, and changes in her lifestyle had definitely diminished her physical energy.

Many of us start our careers with the natural energy of youthful vitality, boundless ambition, and the optimism of inexperience. We look out on the horizon and see nothing but potential. We look good, feel good, and are ready to take on the world. But it is very easy to acquire habits of living, working, and thinking that begin to erode this natural vitality. And over the span of years, in a tough and demanding career, this erosion can begin to take a heavy toll.

Angela is a classic case in point. "Growing up I was basically an extra ranch hand for my father," she says. "I could eat just about anything and stay rail thin. Plus I loved being outside, the sunshine, the fresh air, the physical nature of the work. At the end of each day you could look back and see the results of your labor. It was a great way to grow up."

In college that began to change for Angela. She spent more time sitting than walking and moving. Her diet shifted to college-convenient fast foods. She put on some weight and lost some of her physical "fire," but her aspirational and mental energy kept her going.

When she entered the corporate world her living habits shifted again, just naturally aligning with the habits of those around her. Most of her days were spent sitting at her desk or in meetings. She was a busy career-oriented single woman, so she ate out a lot. She discovered that pizza really did taste better with a cold beer. Restaurant dinners were more enjoyable with a glass or two of wine. And as she gained a few more pounds, year after year, her dress size increased and her physical energy decreased. But again, her aspirational and mental energy were high—she was energized by her career

advancement and the new work kept her mind actively engaged—
but this also tended to mask the decline of her physical energy.

HOW MODERN WORK DAMPENS OUR "FIRE"

Have you ever wondered why companies spend so much time and so
many resources trying to get their employees motivated and engaged?
Why is so much effort spent on boosting productivity? Most of us are
naturally built to be engaged and productive, so what is happening to
us that we need all of this additional "support" and encouragement?

Human beings are naturally energetic problem solvers. How do
you think we survived in prehistoric times without claws, horns,
fur, fangs, venom, or brute strength? Because we were nimble, mentally alert, fast-acting problem-solvers. Our bodies and minds are
designed to be on the move, scanning an ever-changing landscape
and staying alert for danger. In our natural state there are no fat (or
even pudgy) humans because they get caught and eaten by predators.
There are no unmotivated or disengaged natural humans because,
again, they get caught and eaten by predators. And there are no
dumb natural humans because, well, ditto.

Fast forward to the modern work environment. Sitting at a
desk for hours. Sitting in meetings for hours. Staring at a computer
screen, or a beige cubicle wall, most of the day. No sunshine. No
fresh air. Rather than chasing and killing our food, we take the elevator down to the cafeteria and feast on a modern blend of refined flour and sugar, processed meat, mass-produced vegetables,
preservative chemicals, and hydrogenated fats. And in terms of our
physical energy or "fire," we've been doing this so long now that it
actually feels normal.

Beyond the lack of physical activity and the abundance of crappy
food, the nature of modern white-collar work itself can be a fire
killer. It is understandable that most businesses would seek to create
workflow that does not depend too much on the individual creativity

or unique talents of specific individuals. If your business is too dependent upon unique contributions available only from certain individuals, your success is always at risk. However, if you can structure your workflow so that if someone leaves you can easily replace them within a few weeks, this gives your business the stability it needs. So systems and processes become standardized, all of which is logical and good for business.

But this means that many of us are doing essentially the same work every day, which has been streamlined and structured to *not* depend upon any particular individual talent. So we struggle in jobs where we try to highlight our unique individual contributions, while at the same time knowing we could easily be replaced within a few weeks. And both our mental and emotional fires take a hit.

So our natural human drive to be unique works against the business imperative that we be easily replaceable. Of course there are still jobs that require creativity, innovation, and unique contributions, but those positions are increasingly rare.

So much of corporate success truly depends upon well-functioning teams working collaboratively within an informal structure that, again, your value as a unique individual contributor is dampened. Not eliminated of course, because strong individual contributors are needed to make things happen. But it is very easy to do fantastic work and have it absorbed into the overall team-based environment, never gaining significant recognition for your truly distinct, exceptional contribution. And over time this can erode your confidence, your passion for the work, your emotional "fire." Because we all want to be known and recognized as uniquely valuable individuals, not simply valued cogs in the corporate machine.

Another splash of wet water is the sometimes arbitrary and unpredictable nature of the corporate game. Not every promotion is based upon competence. Not every decision is based upon a firm understanding of the facts. Not everyone can be trusted. And sometimes things happen that don't make sense—and you'll never know why. So think about the impact that has on the aspirational fire of some employees, especially the ones who are smart, talented, and hardworking, and expected business to be a fair and open meritocracy.

Imagine being a talented player on a soccer team where the rules sometimes change without notice. Scoring a goal might earn a point, or a penalty. Teammates might help, or sometimes not. Some teammates might actually trip you up, but then get rewarded with recognition for a scored goal that should have been yours. The "most valuable player" award sometimes goes to great players, sometimes not. How would you feel as one of the talented members of this team? Over time what would happen to your natural instinct to win?

The point of all this isn't to lament about the awful state of the modern work environment (well, maybe a little) but to acknowledge that this environment can wear you down. In fact, it does wear most people down. And while that may not be a conscious objective for most businesses, in some ways the wearing down serves them. They want you to be motivated and ambitious—within certain limits. If you are too uppity or aggressive or "needy" in terms of your own ambitions, your aspirational fire, this can make the business uncomfortable. So they work to keep your ambitions in check.

Pay grades and salary ranges are structured to dampen any desire you might have to negotiate for higher compensation. Internal job promotion processes and limitations (must be in your current role for X years, must have approval from your direct supervisor, etc.) are designed to inhibit any aggressive career climbing tendencies. Modest career expectations are set, patience is rewarded (sometimes, sometimes not), and everyone is expected to get in the career line, like obedient steers in an office cattle chute. So if you are one of those people who want to do more and be more—a lot more—the corporate grind can wear you down. Think for a moment about how your own energy is impacted by your work environment.

- **Your Emotional Energy:** Is it hard to be recognized and valued as a unique contributor? Are you able to express your opinions openly in a "safe" environment? Can you truly be yourself, or do you need to put on a "work face" in order to get along?
- **Your Aspirational Energy:** Do you feel stalled or flatlined in your career ambitions? Are your ambitions kept in check by business policies and procedures? Is career progress unpredictable or irrational?
- **Your Physical Energy:** Does work diminish your health and fitness? Are you sedentary, sitting for hours at a time? Are you indoors with little or no sunlight? Do you have easy access to fresh food and water? Do you eat for health and energy, or to reduce stress?
- **Your Mental Energy:** Is your work mentally stimulating, or can you do most of it on autopilot? Are most work requirements systemized and predictable, the same day after day, not requiring you to use your full mental capacity?

If you find yourself at a place where you clearly see that your career "fire" isn't what it used to be, you probably want to make a change, but it can be hard to know where to start. When in doubt, start with physical energy—this is the foundational energy upon which all of the others depend. Just to be clear, we are not necessarily talking about weight loss—we are focused here on physical energy, and there are many examples of relatively portly men and women with great physical energy. But it is also true that when you adopt more healthy habits at work you will tend to lose some weight.

When Angela found herself at the low point in her career she had all the classic burnout symptoms: twenty pounds overweight (on a good day), tired most of the time, unmotivated, unable to focus, bitchy.

She went back to her family ranch one weekend and decided to help her father with chores. She was looking forward to the fresh air and some stress-free physical exertion, but it didn't work out that way. She had visited the ranch many times but hadn't actually worked there for many years. After lifting her third bale of hay, she had to take a break. Her father patted her gently on the shoulder saying, "It's OK, you're a big-city girl now."

"What the hell does that mean?" she snapped. "I'm not that big, am I?"

"Wait, no, I meant that you're a girl, from the big city," her father said. "Not a big girl from the city. I mean, you're bigger than you used to be, but . . ."

She gave him a cold icy stare.

"I'm just digging the hole deeper, aren't I?"

Angela nodded, but she also knew that he was just acknowledging reality. And it sparked a bit of an epiphany for her. Or maybe it just pissed her off.

For the next six months Angela began spending every weekend working cattle at the ranch. It gave her something new to focus on, even the aching muscles seemed to make her work at Dynetron more tolerable. Her career ambitions didn't go away, but her most intense focus was on regaining her "ranch girl" energy and fitness. The food she ate on the ranch was simple, unprocessed, basic: fresh vegetables, water, meat. Back in Houston she tried to keep it simple as well, which meant more home cooking, fewer restaurants, almost nothing out of a box, and absolutely no fast food, sodas, energy drinks, beer, or wine.

"For the first month I felt a little worse each day," she says. "Headaches, muscle pains, night sweats, sugar cravings—I had it all." But eventually the tide turned and she began to feel a little better each day. The short version of this story is that Angela eventually got back to her "ranch girl" body, and more importantly she regained her energy, motivation, and focus. It is amazing sometimes how much the body leads the mind.

Today she is the director of marketing for another energy company in Dallas, happy and healthy and fully engaged in her career climb.

But most of us don't have a family ranch we can go to every weekend. So what can you do if you recognize that perhaps your "fire" has diminished somewhat? If you've put on a few extra pounds since college, if you're tired and irritable, or if you just can't seem to muster up the mental, emotional, or aspirational energy you need to really fight for your career progress, physical energy is a great place to start.

Boost Your Physical Energy

I joined a gym and got three free personal training sessions. I don't do well with personal trainers because (a) I don't like taking orders from people, (b) I don't like being pinched by those body-fat caliper things, and (c) if I'm going to strain and grunt I'd prefer to have a little privacy.

But I do like free stuff, so I did the three sessions and have to admit that the guy said something really smart about physical energy. "Your body is smart and efficient. It evolves into what you need it to be," he said. "Your physical energy will adjust, upward or downward, to what your body and mind requires. So if you sit on your ass all day, your body will adjust to produce the amount of energy you need for that. Anything more would be a waste of energy."

I thought this was borderline profound. Then I asked him, "If my body evolves in response to my needs, when will I be growing a third arm to hold my coffee cup?"

He was not amused.

But I did understand the point he was making. In order to generate more physical energy and vitality, our body has to NEED that energy. And the only way for our body to need that energy is to get it moving and pushing and straining and flexing. If you happen to be young and blessed with a naturally high metabolism, it may not take much to keep your physical energy level high, but now is the time to deeply ingrain good physical habits because eventually your metabolism begins to slow and poor habits begin to take their toll.

If you are beginning to see the early signs of vitality decline—modest weight gain, consuming energy drinks, tired in the morning, bored or sleepy at work in the afternoon—now is the time to take this seriously and make quick adjustments in your lifestyle.

And if, unfortunately, you are deep into a vitality decline, the path ahead will not be easy. But it is certainly possible to regain your vitality, your physical "fire," your motivation and energy to drive a high-trajectory career.

It is definitely not easy to create a work life that fuels your fire because, as mentioned previously, the typical work environment actually dampens the flame. And there is no single right path or program—you will need to be the expert on you and your situation, and you will need to develop a plan of action to move in a new direction.

There is no one-size-fits-all answer to physical energy, but there are a number of core elements that should always be included in whatever plan you develop for yourself. These elements should be structured and cemented into your lifestyle rather than treated as extra items you are adding on. This IS your life, not something "extra" that you have to do. Elements of your physical energy plan should include:

- Cardiovascular and strength training. At least forty-five minutes a day, at least five days a week.
- Restful sleep for a minimum of seven hours each night.
- Brief but regular "movement" breaks at specific intervals throughout the workday. Always leave your desk for these

breaks. And don't just go sit somewhere else, you should be in motion during these breaks.

Because these tend to diminish physical energy rather than boost it, you should eliminate or dramatically reduce from your diet: refined sugars, refined grains (flour, cornstarch, etc.), processed meats, alcohol, and artificial sweeteners.

OK, yeah yeah yeah—nothing new here, it's true. And I'm not interested in nagging you about this because you're either going to do it or not. You decide. But what I can tell you, without hesitation, is that if you are not committing to a regular physical energy routine, it is having an impact on your career progress. No question about it.

So your decision to NOT have a regular physical energy routine is in fact a decision to slow your career progress. But, again, it's your choice.

I guess that does sound a little like nagging. Sorry.

YOUR MENTAL ENERGY—THE PRODUCTIVITY PARADOX

Ask a typical super-busy, hyper-ambitious colleague about his tasks and projects, and he may proudly walk you through everything he has accomplished recently and all of the other important things that need to get done before the week is finished. He probably plans to work part of the weekend because there is no way he is going to feel caught up by the end of the day on Friday. And he'll let you know about his need to work over the weekend with a tone of proud martyrdom in his voice. "Gonna have to come in early on Saturday to finish up the Grainger files," he'll tell you before asking, "So, what do you have going on?"

You'll feel compelled to be equally overwhelmed. "Yeah, there just aren't enough hours in the day." Both of you are convinced the other is working harder, longer hours so you push yourself to do more, more, more.

But this blind obsession with hyperproductivity may actually be hurting your career by diminishing your mental energy. Those who just power themselves through the workday, without making a conscious effort to rest/renew in a planned manner, will subconsciously "pace" their energy throughout the day just to be able to make it to the end. They will often overcompensate with coffee or other stimulants, which only delays the inevitable "crash." This can be profoundly harmful to your actual productivity because:

- You stop discerning between low-value and high-value tasks, instead just powering through to get your task list completed.
- Sometimes you take comfort in doing mundane, relatively easy tasks, just to get the positive feeling of marking them off your list (even as more important tasks remain uncompleted).
- You instinctively distribute your energy and efforts at a moderate level spanning your whole workday, rather than pushing to your peak output at those moments when you need mental energy the most.
- You may create the illusion of productivity based upon output quantity, when in reality you are suboptimizing tasks that require creativity, innovation, or deeper thought.

The result is that you aren't able to do your best work and you aren't getting the rest you need to rejuvenate yourself either. Research and common sense have shown that the most authentically productive individuals give themselves brief moments for rest and mental restoration at regular intervals throughout the day. This allows them to operate at their "peak" energy level when it is needed most, knowing they will soon have an opportunity to rest and recover.

It is important to always have enough energy in reserve to be able to quickly dial up to your peak level during those unpredictable moments when you need to solve a sudden critical problem or address an unexpected important issue.

ALIGN WITH YOUR NATURAL MENTAL ENERGY CYCLE

You have a natural mental energy level that cycles throughout a typical workday. If you are paying attention moment by moment you can sense the degree to which you feel productive, alert, and engaged—or tired, blasé, and unfocused. But most of us either don't notice or try to ignore this natural cycle, or we try to overcome it with coffee and other stimulants.

For most people, the natural daily mental energy cycle lasts ninety to one hundred twenty minutes. Every ninety minutes to two hours our energy baseline hits a peak or trough. And most of us experience deep sleepiness troughs at around 4:30 p.m. and 11:30 p.m. each day. Many creative thinkers report having more "deep-thinking energy" in the mornings than in the afternoons. And those who align their workday with their natural energy rhythm tend to perform better. This probably makes intuitive sense to you, but if you need proof, here are two relevant case studies:

A jewelry manufacturer made an adjustment to their factory assembly line that required workers to attach small semiprecious stones to a variety of objects. The assembly line was stopped every ninety minutes for a mandatory fifteen-minute break period. Within two days, the error rate had decreased by more than 50 percent and overall worker productivity increased by 22 percent.

A study of team innovation found that daylong "brainstorming" sessions were dramatically more productive when breaks were taken every two hours. Both in terms of the quantity and quality of ideas/innovations generated during the events, regular (but brief, no more than twenty minutes maximum) breaks were clearly more productive.

To truly fuel your mental fire, it is critical that you acknowledge your body's natural energy rhythms and align your alternating periods of activity and relaxation to work in a sustainably productive way. While it may be necessary to occasionally push past or through a natural energy trough, this should never be a common practice. If you regularly push yourself to continue working through natural periods of low energy, you risk chronic tiredness and suboptimal mental performance. Here are the three most important concepts to take away from this:

- Work in ninety- to one-hundred-twenty-minute time blocks: You can schedule these time blocks within your daily calendar or set up alarms on your smartphone to remind you when a time block is coming to an end.
- After each work session, take fifteen-minute breaks: If the break is short, you will find it easy to pick up where you left off. But if the break goes on for more than twenty minutes you may have some difficulty in mental reengagement with whatever you were working on.
- Take a late-afternoon nap. Sometime between three p.m. and four p.m., take a twenty-minute nap. Use your smartphone alarm to ensure that the nap does not go longer. Research shows that a brief nap at this time of day will reenergize you, but a longer nap may make you drowsy for the rest of the day.

Intermittent breaks for mental renewal are so important that you should formally schedule them in your computer calendar system, or set up reminders on your smartphone. The length of renewal is less important than the quality. Even just a few minutes of truly "disconnecting" can generate a physical energy recovery. Take a quick walk, talk to a colleague (about something other than work), listen to music, or do anything else that feels comfortable and changes your "mental channel" for a few minutes.

GIVE YOUR BORED BRAIN SOME FOOD FOR (DEEP) THOUGHT

One of the things you may notice as you begin to manage the daily rhythm of work tasks and align them with your natural mental energy cycle is that mundane, repetitive, or "mind numbingly boring" tasks no longer provide any satisfaction at all. In fact they begin to have a clear negative impact on your mental energy.

Those who are still caught up in the hectic hyperproductive do-more-than-anyone-else mind-set generally appreciate having some repetitive or mundane tasks. These can serve as a stress reliever for them and they love the feeling of checking a few easy things off their (real or mental) to-do list. But the people who have learned to optimize their mental energy throughout the workday no longer get the same sort of boost—because they are not overwhelmed, they don't need a stress reliever, and their mind reverts to its most natural state: wanting to solve interesting and challenging problems.

So what do you do if in fact your job consists of mostly simple, repetitive, boring tasks? First recognize the problem, then put that powerful and creative brain of yours to work figuring out clever ways to automate the mundane tasks, and at the same time put some of your creative energy into thinking of new, more engaging tasks you can complete that will bring equal or greater value to the business. This is rarely an easy thought process, which makes it a great way to get your brain fully engaged.

You can also find other interesting things to think about, preferably things that will have a positive impact on your career. If you put into practice many of the tactics and strategies we discussed in chapters 1 and 2, you will be giving your brain plenty of challenging and thought-provoking assignments. In fact one of the great things about focusing on reading people and understanding workplace culture is that it is a never-ending process. People are complex, plus there are always new people coming into the business, so you have plenty to keep your brain occupied and should never have another boring day at work again after you've decided to become a better people reader.

MENTAL ENERGY—QUICK TIPS

Leverage your natural "up time" for your most important and difficult projects. For most people this is in the morning, but whatever your personal energy rhythm may be, don't waste your natural energy peak on simple or mundane tasks.

When you have a task that requires intense concentration, try leaving your office (where everyone knows how to find you) and finding an isolated space to complete the work.

When working on an important task or engaged in an important conversation, set your phone to go directly to voice mail so you can focus completely on the important task.

Rather than constantly hearing the "ping" of incoming email, check it just twice a day at regularly scheduled intervals. Schedule your email review time, focus fully on this task, and clear your inbox. Then don't think about email until the next scheduled review period. Inform your coworkers of your new email response pattern. Let them know that if they need an instant response, they should call you.

Intentionally schedule time—set up a meeting with yourself—for more challenging work that requires deeper thinking.

Rather than start each day by reading emails, invest your first hour in whatever issue or project is most critical to your business (I'm betting it isn't email response times).

YOUR EMOTIONAL ENERGY—FEELING KNOWN, VALUED, AND "SAFE"

It is hopefully obvious to you that you tend to perform best when you're feeling emotionally positive and optimistic. What may not be obvious is the degree to which a lack of positive emotional energy can negatively impact your ability to perform well. You may be able to go through the motions, thinking that your inner turmoil is invisible to those around you, but the reality is that most people see it—and the quality of your work definitely suffers.

A person with strong emotional energy at work has confidence that:

- They know me.
- They value me.
- It's safe to express myself authentically.

While most of us wear a "mask" at work to some degree, the more authentic we can be with our colleagues, the greater our emotional connection and energy in the workplace will be. We all instinctively yearn to be known as unique individuals, not merely a member of the tribe. In addition to being known, we want to be valued. Not just for the tasks we complete or the results we produce. We want to be inherently valued simply for who we are.

A workplace that does not allow for authentic self-expression, that forces individuals to check a part of themselves at the door, that does not highlight individual accomplishments and value people as people, not just completers of tasks—a business like this will never maximize the productivity of employees.

Each of us is able to tap into the energy of our unique human spirit when our everyday work and life activities are in alignment with what we value most and with what gives us a sense of meaning and purpose. If the work we are doing really matters to us, we have more natural energy, greater focus, and engagement.

But no matter what type of business environment you work within, even if it is tightly controlled and not especially employee-friendly or energizing, you can find ways to enhance your emotional energy.

- Find subtle ways to express your individuality without breaking any corporate rules.
- Ask questions of others to learn more about who they really are, then find ways to celebrate their individuality. Over time they will tend to do the same for you.
- Express appreciation of others. This practice benefits you as much as the other person. Verbal appreciation seems to have

the greatest emotional impact (for both of you) but sending a handwritten note works also. Even a pleasant email can give someone a boost, especially if you copy others so they can see how much you appreciate the other person.

ASPIRATIONAL ENERGY—KEEPING YOUR LIFE (AND MIND) IN MOTION

Neither your body nor your mind is designed to sit still for long periods of time. Even when you are deeply sleeping, your body is at work repairing muscle tissue while your mind is processing the activity of the day.

This is why a stagnated career is so frustrating for most people. It isn't just because we want to make more money or achieve more prestige—we instinctively want to keep moving, advancing, and growing.

- What is your compelling career vision for the next five years, the next twenty years?
- What impact do you want to have on the lives of others?
- What do you want to be known for?
- What do you want to be remembered for?

This is going to mean something different to virtually every person reading these words, but if you understand the core meaning, you can then decide what it specifically means for you. Sometimes it can help to hear the stories of others who have found a way to create new aspirational energy in their careers.

William Chenowith felt trapped. At the age of fifty-three he began to experience intense headaches and occasional chest pains. His doctor assured him that he wasn't having heart attacks, although he was about forty pounds overweight and couldn't remember the last time he saw a health club. The pain seemed to be stress-induced, and he had plenty of that, with a heavy travel schedule and the financial burden of two kids in college, along with a wife who had just gone back to school to "find herself." He wasn't sure what that meant, but he did know what it cost.

Two years later he had figured out how to medicate the pain away, but nothing else had changed. He hated his work, was annoyed with his kids, confused by his wife, and it seemed that there was nothing he could do about it. This was not the age to rethink one's life, he told himself. He had never really enjoyed his work in commercial finance, but it had paid the bills. He figured if he could just coast these last few years, he would make it to retirement and be relatively comfortable. He wasn't sure what he wanted to do in retirement, or who he wanted to do it with, but it had to be better than the corporate grind.

Another year later, nothing much had changed. Still trapped. Still coasting. Until the VP of Human Resources stopped in his office one morning with a grim expression on her face. "As you know, we have been restructuring the business," she said. "And I need to talk to you about your severance package."

A month later he was out of a job, with a severance package that would give him a safety net for a few months, but there was no way he could afford to retire at just the age of fifty-six. The job market was tight, and it seemed that he was going to have to accept at least a 30 percent pay cut, which he couldn't afford with two kids and a wife still in college.

"I was trapped and broken down, physically, mentally, in every way," Bill told me recently. "I hate to admit it but I even thought seriously about just ending it all. I had enough life insurance to make sure my family would be taken care of."

Although he didn't use these specific words, Bill had clearly lost his emotional, aspirational, and physical energy both at work and at home. He had little or no emotional connection with his family, no discernible positive vision for his future, either professionally or personally, and a body that was quickly breaking down. In terms of mental energy, he felt too burned out to do much about any of it.

Although Bill was pretty sure he was keeping it all bottled up inside, his family could see how difficult the situation was for him, and he was surprised by their reaction. Shocked, really. Both of his kids took part-time jobs to pay for a portion of their college expenses. His wife put her education on hold and found a job to bring in additional money. And they found other creative ways to reduce expenses, which significantly reduced the short-term financial pressure Bill was feeling.

The pressure was still there of course, but his family's willingness to step forward and proactively help was unexpected and deeply appreciated. They were willing to make adjustments, not begrudgingly, but gratefully after all the support he had given them over the years, and this energized him profoundly.

If this was a movie I would cue the soaring orchestra music and cut to a shot of Bill and his family walking on a beach at sunset. But since this is a book I'll just give you a list of the most critical events that occurred:

- With the short-term financial pressure eased, Bill decided to rethink his plans for the final decade of his career. The freedom to do this had a huge impact on his personal motivation and aspirational energy level.
- Bill and his wife together embarked on a nutrition and fitness journey that ultimately resulted in a forty-pound weight loss for him, a twenty-pound loss for her, more muscle aches than either had experienced in many years, and more fun than they had experienced together in decades.
- Bill came to a realization that he didn't hate commercial

finance, in fact he loved working with small business owners, optimizing their capital structure. What he had hated was the corporate grind he felt trapped in—so he decided to start his own commercial finance company targeting only small-business owners.

- Bill's company was modestly successful—but Bill himself was incredibly thrilled with the results, and with the extra time he was now able to spend with his wife.
- Bill's daughter is now working for the company. "I would never have considered working for the old version of my dad," she says now. "But this new guy, he's great to work for."

Bill's story is compelling, and scary at the same time. The corporate world had ground him down so far that he was actually contemplating suicide. Your own corporate grind is most likely not as dramatic, but you have to ask yourself, what are you doing to ensure that you achieve and keep the energy you need to get what you want out of life, both personally and professionally?

THE BEST CHANGES ARE USUALLY THE HARD ONES

Reese Riley was a thirty-eight-year-old operations manager for a fleet of corporate vehicles, married with two young children. Both she and her husband typically worked long hours, had no time during the week for exercise, but were both committed weekend triathletes. Both had been college athletes and knew how important exercise was to their overall physical and mental health. But for Reese it was becoming increasingly difficult to maintain her commitment.

"After our second child, it seemed like I was always exhausted," she says. She used to love her work, but it began to feel boring and overwhelming at the same time. She knew that she was not fully engaged with her family in the evenings, which of course made her feel guilty and dissatisfied. She slept poorly, began finding reasons to not exercise on weekends, and seldom ate healthy meals, instead grabbing a bite to eat on the run or while working at her desk. What made it worse was that her husband seemed to be just fine. He was as fit and trim as he had been in college, while she hadn't lost the baby weight. He loved his job and was eager to go to work every day, but he was also very engaged at home, helping with the kids and actually doing more than his share of the household chores. Which also made her feel guilty—and annoyed.

The breaking point came at work. In the past, her annual performance reviews had always been stellar, so she was stunned when her manager rated her as "needs improvement" in several areas including "dependability" and "engagement."

At home that evening she was preparing to tell her husband about the unfairly harsh review when he mentioned that his company had just renovated their office exercise facility and he was now going to be able to work out for forty-five minutes every weekday, during his lunch break. This pushed her over the edge. Her life was spiraling downward while his seemed to be getting better every day.

They went through six very difficult months trying to solve what seemed to be an impossible problem. She wanted to quit working, but they couldn't afford it. Their marriage was in jeopardy and the stress was impacting their children. "I realized at a certain point that part of what was driving me crazy was that I was trying to solve the whole big mess all at once," she says. "What finally saved me, and us, was just picking one thing, making one change, then building on that over time."

The changes Reese and her husband made may not be right or relevant for you, but the step-by-step process they used could apply to almost any complex life problem you're trying to solve. First, they set an earlier bedtime, turned off the television at nine p.m. and agreed that there would be no discussion of work, problems, or "issues" after that time as well. This was a very, very difficult change at first, but they started recording their favorite evening shows to watch on weekends, and their evenings became much more relaxing. Reese found herself waking up more rested and motivated—this was a gradual change, but at some point she remembers waking up in a good mood, looking forward to getting the kids off to school and driving to work. That was a big moment for her, and there were a number of other changes that helped to get her there.

Reese began to find opportunities for "micro-workouts" as she calls them. She began parking about a mile away from her office and briskly walking that distance each morning. This may sound crazy to you, but it worked for her. "The only downside is I forgot some important files in the car one morning," she says. "So I had to hike all the way back to the car, then back to the office again, which gave me an extra two miles of walking that day." Every progressive step forward helped her take the next step, make the next change.

The walking seemed to help with her stress, which in turn seemed to help her with food choices. She had always known what she should be doing in terms of diet and nutrition, but had just stopped making those choices. With her eating and exercise pattern trending in the right direction, Reese made a number of other changes over several months:

- She acquired a standing desk at work so that she would spend less time in a crouched, sitting posture.
- She eliminated diet sodas and "energy" drinks, replacing them with that magical elixir—water.
- She changed her eating habits from two big meals a day to smaller meals and light snacks every three hours.
- She took up yoga and found a studio within a fifteen-minute walk of her office. Her daily routine now includes a thirty-minute yoga session.

Reese still works long hours, but in less than three months she lost fifteen pounds, and over the next four months she lost all of her baby weight and then some. She and her husband have established certain "rituals" that help them both maintain their progress. Family dinnertime is now a must, helping them stay connected with their children. They insist on time with each other, and time with mutual friends, all of which helps to strengthen their connection and overall life satisfaction.

Today Reese will tell you that the hardest part for them was that first step, enforcing the "no TV, no work, no problem solving after nine p.m." rule. Again this may or may not be relevant to you and your life situation, but the process they went through is something we can all learn from.

Like Reese, we all know what to do. We all know that nutrition, exercise, and restful sleep are critical to maintain our basic energy level as well as our ability to focus attention and manage our emotions. But many of us also allow the modern work environment to slowly erode our habits in these areas. This makes it more important that we develop formal rituals to help keep us on track.

WHERE TO START?

You could make the case that aspirational energy is the most fundamental and important of the four energy sources we have covered here (Physical, Emotional, Mental, Aspirational), but it is addressed last for a specific reason. I've found that for most people, developing solid habits for the first three is an important prerequisite before addressing the aspirational energy source.

Of course you can certainly begin thinking about your aspirational energy right away, but before you dig too deep, get your other energy habits in order. Once you have experienced the positive impact of the habits you've established in other areas, you will begin to more clearly see that being attentive to your aspirational needs can profoundly impact your productivity and satisfaction at work.

> *Author's note: While I use the term "workplace poker" as a meta-phor, I had a conversation about these energy concepts recently with a world-class poker player and he nodded his head vigorously, telling me that this was one of the secrets to his success. "These games go on for hours, sometimes days, so I make sure I'm in tip-top physical shape before a tournament." He also mentioned that whenever there is a break he walks briskly up to his hotel room, takes a quick cold shower, then continues walking and moving until the game resumes. "I stay off my ass until the last possible moment," he says. He feels that his personal energy management practices are just as important as his actual poker skill in terms of winning the toughest, longest (and most lucrative) poker tournaments.*

THINK NOW

How would you instinctively rate your energy level in the four areas discussed here?

Non-existent									Exceptional
Physical Energy 1	2	3	4	5	6	7	8	9	10
Mental Energy 1	2	3	4	5	6	7	8	9	10
Emotional Energy 1	2	3	4	5	6	7	8	9	10
Aspirational Energy 1	2	3	4	5	6	7	8	9	10

Are there specific energy-enhancing habits you know should be immediately adopted, or energy-diminishing habits you know should be immediately stopped? If so, no need to make a commitment immediately, but please write down those specific habits in this book now. Use the space provided.

Being fully honest and authentic with yourself, what has held you back from starting or stopping these habits? Again no need for commitment right now, but please write your answer in the space below.

ACT SOON

Go to www.workplacepoker.com/energy/ and complete the personal energy assessment. This will give you an objective view of your current state along with customized recommendations based upon your assessment results.

When you have time and privacy for deep reflection, ask yourself the following questions (and for extra credit, write down your answers).

- "At my funeral, what do I want to be remembered for?"
- "If I could reach back in time and whisper into the ear of the younger me, what advice would I give to myself?"
- "Who am I today, who do I want to become, and how big is the gap?"

- "What do I truly enjoy at work? Where do I create the most value for the business? And what am I truly great at?"
- "Does this feel like the work I was meant to do? Why, or why not?"
- "Throughout my life, are my commitments of time and energy aligned with what is truly most important to me?"

Before you answer these last two questions, understand that if the solution was easy or obvious you would probably have already implemented it. So most likely this will not be easy or obvious, but if you are committed enough and creative enough, there is always a way.

- "Where is my life most *out* of alignment with my true value and priorities?"
- "What will I do about it?"

LONG-TERM THOUGHTS AND ACTION POINTS

Over time, the modern work environment can easily dampen one's personal energy, vitality, and motivation.

- It is important to objectively assess your current level of physical vitality, and to take quick action if your "fire" has diminished over time.

- Making many modest changes can ultimately have the same positive health impact as making a single large, dramatic change.

- Physical energy habits can help to ensure that you are taking care of your body even in the face of a stressful work environment and schedules.

- Emotional energy habits can keep you emotionally positive and optimistic even in the face of career difficulties.

- Mental energy habits can help ensure that you are leveraging your natural "up time" in terms of thought, clarity, and creativity.

- Aspirational energy habits can keep you focused, motivated, and energized for the long haul of a tough career climb because you have a long-term vision aligned with your deepest values.

5

Velcro Butterflies and Teflon Rhinos

◆

*Let's not forget that the little emotions are the great captains of
our lives and we obey them without realizing it.*

—Vincent Van Gogh

Y ou're stupid and nobody likes you."

This was the Facebook message received by fourteen-year-old Ben Dierdon. The sender was "BlastCap29" but there was
no information on the actual identity of this person, so Ben was
confused and distraught. He showed the message to his parents,
who immediately contacted Ben's school to lodge a complaint because they were sure one of his classmates was the source of the
cruel message. The officials at Kennedy High School were determined to uncover the source, but the process wasn't quick or easy.
Ben felt paranoid for weeks, his self-esteem (which wasn't great to
begin with) took a hit, and eventually his parents scheduled time
with a therapist to deal with the issue.

"You're stupid and nobody likes you."

Jessica Hershbaum, one of Ben's classmates, received the same

Facebook message at about the same time. She just thought it was dumb and deleted it. Kyle Vinson received the message as well. He laughed and replied to the message with "You smell like pig farts."

It turns out virtually every student at Kennedy High School who had a Facebook account received the same message, but it took weeks for officials to determine this and they never were able to ascertain the actual source. BlastCap29's account was eventually deleted by Facebook.

It appears the original message wasn't intended for any particular individual, it was just a distasteful prank aimed at the whole class. But some of the recipients clearly took the message very personally and experienced great anxiety. While some barely gave it a glancing thought, and others were amused.

And perhaps there is a lesson here for us all.

Because our adult lives are filled with opportunities to perceive rejection, from mild aversion to outright disdain. Some of the rejection is very real—there are in fact people who don't like us or don't care for our ideas. Some of the rejection is clearly a misunderstanding, just like the misperception of some of the students at Kennedy High. And most of the rejection falls somewhere in-between.

Some people are very sensitive to even the slightest perceived negative comment or judgment from others. We call them "Velcro Butterflies" because they are easily buffeted by gusts of strong emotional wind, and rejection seems to stick to them. Every insensitive or derisive comment seems to adhere permanently to the psyche of the Velcro Butterfly. Every harsh judgment (real or perceived) sticks to them like permanent glue. Over time their emotional Velcro is covered with layers upon layers of perceived rejections and judgments that they can often recall on a moment's notice.

There is a very different type of person for whom rejection, even strong intentional rejection, just doesn't seem to stick at all. Sometimes these individuals don't even perceive rejection that would seem blindingly obvious to others. We call these people "Teflon Rhinos" because nothing sticks and nothing penetrates their thick skin.

Most of us fall somewhere on the continuum between extreme "butterfly" and total "rhino," and it is important that you are aware of your own typical reaction to the rejection or judgment of others (again, real or perceived). Because whether the rejection itself is real, imagined, or somewhere in-between, your typical response will have a huge impact on your career trajectory. Ultimately your rhino/butterfly perceptions and reactions will determine your willingness to:

- Share your own (potentially unpopular) ideas.
- Seek out "stretch" jobs and projects.
- Advocate for out-of-the-box solutions.
- Learn by doing (and sometimes failing).
- Work with talented (but abrasive) people.

In short, if you do not handle real and perceived rejection effectively, your comfort zone becomes constricted and some of your most critical career-building habits are never developed.

Imagine for a moment you are in a weekly business meeting with perhaps a dozen colleagues and a senior executive in charge of the group. This is your regular weekly meeting so you know these people well. Someone shares an opinion and the executive briefly responds with "Very good. Let's keep that in mind as we move forward," and the meeting continues. Then a few minutes later another colleague shares a thought and the executive responds with "Great idea, I think we can implement that without negatively impacting the timeline," and once again the meeting moves on. Then perhaps ten or fifteen minutes later you have an idea that you share with the group. You notice the executive grimacing a little when you speak and when you're done he makes no eye contact with you, looks a bit impatient, and says to the group "Let's focus in on the timeline so we can be sure everything stays on track." Then the discussion moves on from there, without any reaction to your comment.

What is most likely going through your mind as the meeting progresses? Are you fully engaged in the discussion or is part of you wondering why the executive didn't make even a slight positive comment about your idea? How likely are you to share another idea during this meeting? Or in future meetings? And what, by the way, really happened?

A butterfly would probably assume the worst ("He hated my idea, or he has something against me!") whereas a rhino might not even discern the possible rejection, and probably wouldn't care if he did notice it. Neither reaction is inherently right or wrong, but which reaction would be better for your career? Most likely, neither extreme would be ideal. You want to be at least sensitive enough to notice the executive's different reaction to your idea, but then be strong enough to address it if you think it could be important. So more of a rhino, just not extreme.

This example is actually taken from my own life. And for a full week I stewed over the executive's non-response to my idea. The more I thought about it, the more frustrated I got, because the idea was a GREAT one—I love my own ideas, don't you?—and he just seemed to blow it off. I had myself worked up into an emotional churn of anger, paranoia, and indignation.

At the start of our next regular weekly meeting the executive smiled sheepishly at all of us and asked, "Could we go over again the second half of last week's meeting? I wasn't feeling well and it turns out I had a stomach flu, and all I could think about was ending the meeting and getting to the men's room." He noticed the uncomfortable expressions on our faces. "Sorry, probably too much information. But I don't think I really heard anything that any of you were saying, so could we review?"

What scares me about this story is that I'm pretty sure if he hadn't acknowledged what had happened, I probably would have kept stewing on it. If I was bothered by it I should have just talked to him and addressed my concern directly, but at the time I was too much of a butterfly to do that. Instead I would have just let the perceived rejection attach itself to my Velcro skin permanently.

Even if the executive had in fact not really liked my idea, this would have been a relatively minor workplace rejection. But most of us at work don't commonly experience dramatic moments of massive rejection. Instead we endure occasional "micro-rejections" and while these small moments may not individually be debilitating, for some people their long memory of disrespectful remarks, whispered comments, and unspoken disapproval (real or perceived) can have a cumulative negative effect.

"I've learned to avoid people and situations that don't support or encourage me," says Emily Harding, a product manager for Hall Graphics in Wisconsin. "Life is too short to deal with the haters."

Emily's perspective is perfectly reasonable, but also likely to limit her career trajectory. Because those who tend to avoid rejection and withdraw from situations in which they may feel rejection will inevitably back away from opportunities as well as difficulties. They may not seek a promotion or may not take on a challenging assignment. They may not be willing to take a risk or may avoid working with difficult (but talented) people. In contrast, most hyper-successful individuals are confronting potential rejection all the time, because they're constantly pushing themselves beyond their comfort zone.

....

You can't win at workplace poker if you only play the games that are comfortable.

....

But handling rejection can be a touchy subject to discuss, because many of us don't necessarily want to admit that we sometimes have an issue with rejection. We're supposed to be strong, hard-charging, fearless work machines with rhinoceros-thick skin. We admire the "rhinos" and disdain the "butterflies" so why would we ever want to acknowledge that on occasion we might have some butterfly-like tendencies?

No one at work would ever think of Samia Al-Falah as a "butterfly." She is a project management engineer for the Kuwait National Petroleum Company. Samia grew up in Kuwait and attended the University of Waterloo in Canada before returning to her home country, where she has worked at KNPC for more than twenty years. She worked very hard to establish a solid professional reputation and her (mostly male) colleagues have genuine respect for her depth of knowledge and engineering expertise.

They have also learned that she can be demanding, strong-willed, and abrasive. "It is not possible to have a mild disagreement with her," says one of her colleagues. "Everything is either sweet agreement or a total battle. There is no middle ground." They will also begrudgingly acknowledge that when there is disagreement with Samia (typically about engineering processes, procedures, or compliance requirements) she is almost always right.

Many of her coworkers still remember an incident several years ago when a group of engineers was determined to quickly restart an oil platform that had been idled for routine maintenance, but Samia was insistent that they follow all standard protocols. "She would not budge, not an inch, and we were furious," says one of her colleagues today. "This meant we would miss the monthly quota, and would not receive our usual bonus." But more than her actual refusal to bend the rules, it was her manner (harsh, sharp-tongued, sarcastic) that really set them off. Even today, years later, some will speak to her only when absolutely necessary.

Outwardly Samia is tough, thick-skinned, ready to fight, and not at all concerned with the negative perceptions of others. She seems to have mastered the art of handling (ignoring) rejection from her co-workers. A classic "Teflon Rhino," right? Well . . . not quite so fast.

Samia's husband will tell you that he has spent many nights consoling her at home as she cried in his arms after a particularly tough argument with someone at work. She hates feeling that others don't respect her or like her. "What I dislike most is the fact that I care what they think, I wish I could just ignore it," she says.

In fact it is precisely her difficulty with the feeling of rejection and disdain that causes her to overcompensate with her own brand of harsh judgment. I asked her what she thought her coworkers would say if they were asked about her skills and capabilities.

"They have no respect for me," she said, with an edge to her voice. "They do not see me as an engineer. They do not value my opinion. They only see me as getting in the way."

In contrast, when I asked several of her male coworkers for their opinion, they all mentioned that she was exceptionally capable, they trusted her opinions and thought process, they respected the fact that she had worked her way up through the KNPC system, so she truly understood how things needed to be done. Over and over again, the only negative feedback was regarding her harshness and abrasiveness whenever there was a disagreement. So most of them had learned to avoid situations, if possible, in which disagreement with her might occur.

So Samia was harsh and abrasive because she perceived that they didn't respect her. And the primary reason they lacked respect for her was the harsh abrasiveness. Crazy, right?

When I first met her in Kuwait, Samia had recently been passed over for a promotion and was steamed about it. And the same dynamic was in play; she was sure "they" didn't respect her, and thus she didn't get the promotion. On the other hand "they" felt that she couldn't lead a larger team because of her abrasive manner. When Samia attended a leadership-development workshop I was facilitating, we had an individual discussion about her sensitivity to rejection and judgment. The discussion was brief.

"I don't have a problem with rejection. I have a problem working with imbeciles."

Samia, like many Velcro Butterflies, finds it difficult to truly let go of perceived rejections, slights, and insults (hence the "Velcro" in the name) and over time these can build up to create intense internal pressure. Eventually the emotional volcano blows. This is why some Velcro Butterflies suddenly lash out fiercely—I call them Velcro Butterflies with fangs.

Her unwillingness to be introspective and consider her own role in being passed over for the promotion means that for the most part Samia's career path has flatlined. She will probably become more frustrated and abrasive, with self-righteous certainty that she has been wronged.

In contrast, Charlie Malrose is an example of a "butterfly" willing to take a deep, difficult look at himself and make the change necessary to get his career back on track. Charlie was a midlevel manager at Community Commercial Bank in Minnesota. No one ever had anything bad to say about Charlie because he was dependable, hardworking, and conscientious. A classic "nice guy" and "Boy Scout," Charlie's personality seemed to be a perfect fit for the banking industry because he was friendly, responsive, definitely not a risk taker or someone who would push the ethical envelope.

But his cautious demeanor also led him to avoid "stretch" projects and other assignments with uncertain outcomes. At one point he was offered the opportunity to lead a new initiative to introduce retail "micro-banking" kiosks at shopping malls. Charlie thought that instead of kiosks, automated teller machines would be more cost effective, so the project would most likely fail. He declined to lead the project team, and ultimately he was right. The kiosks didn't generate enough new business to make them cost effective so they were replaced by ATM machines. "I felt good that I had dodged a bullet and hadn't wasted my energy on that project," he said.

When the kiosk project leader had to deliver a postmortem review for senior leadership of the bank, Charlie sat in the back of the room grateful that it wasn't him up there. Who wants to stand up and walk everyone through all of the details of how and why your project failed? Certainly not Charlie.

He had been regularly promoted during his first seven years at CCB. But after that, the progress slowed, then stopped. Charlie was surprised when he was overlooked for several promotions even though his annual performance reviews were perfectly fine. But Charlie didn't complain or make waves. That wasn't his style.

But then he missed out on another promotion, and the person who got the job was the project manager for the failed kiosk initiative. And this person had led several other projects that had not been especially successful. Charlie was confused, and finally frustrated enough to ask why he was being overlooked. The answer surprised him.

"I'm not sure you can handle the stress of uncertainty," his regional vice president told him. "And at this level, we just don't have the same predictability as we do in our day-to-day banking operations." The regional VP went on to explain that Charlie was perceived as a dependable and careful tactician, but not a strong leader.

He sought out additional feedback from other key leaders within CCB and heard similar comments. "We need leaders who can manage appropriate risk, not eliminate risk altogether," one leader told him. Another said, "To keep growing we need innovative ideas, and leaders who will take risks to champion out-of-the-box thinking."

It wasn't easy for Charlie to hear these comments, but he knew himself well enough to know they were mostly correct. He wasn't a risk taker, didn't feel comfortable advocating potentially unpopular ideas, and he tended to avoid conflict. For him it wasn't so much about the possibility of failure as it was about the judgment of others—he didn't want to be thought of as a failure. Our goal here isn't to psychoanalyze Charlie, but the truth is he had a difficult childhood, was abused at home and teased at school, and stuttered severely until he was fifteen.

Charlie was ambitious and understood that some aspects of his cautious personality were now holding him back. And to his credit, he was willing to do the hardest thing possible. He spent a lot of time thinking deeply about himself, his personality style, the reasons for his caution, and the degree to which he could realistically change. He didn't think it was likely that he could ever be a total hard-driving "rhino," but he was determined to at least move in that direction.

Ultimately he came to realize what his fear (of failure, embarrassment, judgment) was costing him. So the next time he had an opportunity, he took on a business project that wasn't a sure bet—a new initiative to expand CCB beyond the Upper Midwest, into a territory dominated by one of their strongest competitors. They opened five new branches outside of their traditional market area. "The best thing that ever happened to me," Charlie says now, "was this project failing after my team and I worked so hard, determined to make it a success against all odds. Because after all of the panic and anxiety I was experiencing, once the dust settled, I was all right, everyone else was all right, and we all moved on." Charlie even had to deliver a postmortem review presentation to senior leadership. It was awkward and uncomfortable for him, but it didn't kill him.

Charlie attended a workshop on public speaking and joined a local Toastmasters group. His goal was to become less sensitive to the perceived judgment of others, and since public speaking was definitely outside of his comfort zone this seemed to be a good way to stretch himself. About a year later he decided to stretch even farther—Charlie took a kickboxing class at a local gym. "This was totally out of character for me, and my friends and family were shocked," he says. "But I think I needed it. Something about the brutal intensity has really helped me to be less concerned about the perceptions of others, less sensitive. It also helps that if I wanted to, now I could kick the ass of most of the guys in my office."

Charlie's personality didn't change. He is still inherently conscientious, risk-averse, and dependable. But the self-doubt that was underpinning these qualities began to fade away and not surprisingly his career path eventually accelerated. Today Charlie is a regional vice president for CCB Bank in Wisconsin. "Yes, I'm still a nice guy," he said to me in a recent telephone conversation. "But it's different because I think I used to be nice hoping that others would be nice to me, but now I'm nice, and it doesn't really matter what others think."

So should you take up kickboxing? Not necessarily, but the point of sharing Charlie's story with you is that he was (a) willing to look at himself deeply and objectively, and (b) willing to take action to make a change.

Experiencing rejection or the negative judgment of others is a part of almost every successful career. In fact, the more successful you want to be, the more challenging situations you will have to face. Most exceptionally successful people are confronting fear and hesitation all the time, because they're constantly pushing themselves beyond their comfort zone.

So is the key to success having a rhinoceros-thick skin, emotionally speaking? Well, there are a lot of benefits. You don't let rejection slow you down. It's easier for you to talk to influential, powerful people without being intimidated. You're more likely to ignore the lame criticisms of others. You persevere through obstacles. Accept no excuses. Drive yourself hard—and drive others even harder. You achieve your career goals, and in the end, that's all that really counts, right?

Not quite so fast. Because having a thick skin is a double-edged sword with a potentially significant downside. The emotional wall or barrier can work both ways: preventing negative emotions from getting through to you, but also blocking the positive emotions that spring from genuine connections with people.

You've probably met at least a few extreme Teflon Rhinos who never genuinely connect with others emotionally. They are so driven and so focused that others feel railroaded by their intensity. These extreme Rhinos sometimes create barriers to their own success without ever realizing it because others aren't comfortable with them, or feel intimidated by them. So jobs aren't offered to them, people choose not to work with them, not to help them, not to contribute to their projects—and the Rhino can't figure out why it is so hard to get things done, so, of course, he just pushes harder.

Teflon Rhinos sometimes create their own barriers to exceptional career success.

So having, or developing, a thick skin may not be the ultimate key to career success. Especially since most truly successful career professionals are very emotionally connected and in tune with their colleagues and customers. They typically have very strong interpersonal skills—they're usually sociable, interactive, outgoing, fun, intuitive, people-oriented—and they genuinely like and care about the people with whom they work. These are not characteristics we usually associate with extreme rhino-thick skin.

But wait a minute. Being a "Butterfly" means you are too sensitive and concerned about rejection or the negative opinions of others, and being a "Rhino" means you're a bully who can't motivate people to proactively work with you. So how do we square this contradiction?

On the continuum from extreme Butterfly to extreme Rhino, generally the most successful people are typically more of a Rhino, without going to the extreme. Somewhere in the zone indicated here:

Velcro Butterfly ———————————————— **Teflon Rhino**

So how do these successful individuals handle the fear and rejection? First, they don't pretend to feel nothing. Instead they acknowledge their negative feelings when they fail or when they're rejected, when they lose out on a big promotion, when an important project they were leading doesn't go as planned. When they lose a sale, or lose the support of colleagues. They're honest with themselves that sometimes the fear of potential judgment or rejection holds them back.

What about you? What's your level of self-awareness regarding fear of failure or potential judgment, or having a negative reaction to circumstances where you are in fact rejected? How do you know if fear of potential rejection is holding you back, to any degree?

You can be very successful building a career because of your work ethic, your people skills, your knowledge and capabilities—and yet still dread going to work every day. You can meet your goals and financial objectives, but never reach your full potential. You can be doing quite well, but completely avoid a certain path or direction that could bring you extraordinary rewards, because fear of judgment or rejection stopped you. That doesn't sound like real success, no matter what the financial accomplishments are.

And if you lack self-awareness in this area, your passion and talent may still propel you forward if there are no major challenges that test your emotional resilience. You may still be able to succeed and progress and advance your career.

Until you can't.

When Eric Urtiaga started his new job as a product manager for a nutritional products company in San Diego, he was looking forward to having an impact on a market that he cared a lot about. Eric was passionate about maintaining a healthy mind, body, and spirit at work and in the rest of his life. His previous employer was a small nutrition and fitness company with an energetic, positive culture. Eric had been told by colleagues there that his attitude and energy were some of the reasons they looked forward to coming to work each day. He was considered a rising star at the previous company, and loved working there, but the opportunity to step up into a bigger role with a much larger company was too good to pass up. If his star was rising, he wanted it to rise as far and as fast as possible.

So after less than two weeks at the new company, it came as a shock to Eric when he heard that someone was talking about him behind his back, and not in a good way.

"He doesn't have the educational or research credentials we need to advance our products," sniffed Marlene, the corporate communications manager. She seemed to take every opportunity to second-guess his ideas for new product introductions and current product promotions. And when he went overbudget on a trade show booth, she mentioned "our budget problem" at several meetings, just to be sure Eric's boss was aware of it.

At first Eric tried to take the high road. The criticism really stung, but he wasn't comfortable addressing it directly. As a positive, optimistic "butterfly" he just kept his head down and focused on doing a good job. But Marlene was a longtime employee with many friends and acquaintances in virtually every department. Over time her behind-the-scenes whispering campaign began to take its toll. Eric could tell that he was losing the confidence of some people, so he tried to address the issues directly with Marlene. And in typical butterfly fashion, he tried to be overly nice and gracious.

"I think somehow we got off on the wrong foot, and I'd like to start over," he said to her in a private conversation.

Marlene looked stunned. "I have no idea what you are talking about." Eric began to give her a few examples but she cut him off. "I thought you wanted open communication. That's what you said, right? I've been clear with you about my concerns, and when it seems appropriate I've shared those concerns with others. Our culture here is an open give-and-take environment where people are free to express their opinions."

Eric was getting nowhere with her, so he ended the meeting and thought perhaps she might at least think twice before talking about him behind his back again. Instead, Marlene went immediately to the HR manager and filed a complaint. She mischaracterized the nature of the conversation and told HR that she "felt threatened" by Eric's anger at her criticisms.

When Eric was called to the HR director's office and given an opportunity to respond, he was shocked and embarrassed and (unfortunately) angry. Marlene had so clearly lied, and the surprise of it all caused him to lash out. The Velcro Butterfly grew fangs as the intense pressure from all of the judgments and rejections he had held on to for months came bursting forth. "I'm telling you! She is a conniving, lying bitch! That is *not* what happened! I don't know what it is, but she has had it in for me since day one!"

His intense overreaction did not serve him well. The HR director was left with the impression that, yes, in fact, Eric probably did make Marlene feel threatened.

It would be great if this story had a happy ending. If somehow Eric and Marlene eventually developed a productive working relationship. That would be nice. But Eric's "butterfly" tendencies caused him to avoid difficult situations and people. He tried to just focus on doing his job well, but even that was difficult because he felt so depressed and angry coming in to work every day.

For the next six months Eric's career at the nutritional products company spiraled slowly downward. More controls were put in place over his budget. His boss began to second-guess many of his ideas and encouraged him to "Just keep the trains running. No need for new ideas right now." Eric could see the writing on the wall. And his emotions spiraled downward as the work environment became more and more difficult.

Eric lacked the emotional resilience to deal with these issues productively. But he had never in his working life had to deal with a situation like this, so it was totally new terrain for him. Rather than stay and try to grow from the experience, Eric started interviewing at other companies and was able to land a new position before the old one was taken away from him. It was a big step down, from a career perspective, but he was happy to get away from what he called a "toxic environment."

But in the end, Eric didn't really learn anything about how to handle the tough situation more effectively. He felt wronged and it is a story he now loves to tell anytime someone mentions the old company. I've heard the story several times over the past few years and each time "Marlene" gets nastier, more clever, and more powerful.

So is there anything that Eric could have learned? Anything he could have done to make things better at the old company? Could he have beaten Marlene at her own game? Well, Rhinos do tend to have a unique way of dealing with difficult people at work.

TEFLON RHINOS KEEP THEIR ENEMIES CLOSE

While the "butterfly" instinct is to avoid difficult people at all cost, this only gives them more room to maneuver against you. So a Rhino will sit *near* them at meetings, not at the other side of the table. A Rhino will give them compliments in an open forum so that others hear them saying *nice* things about the other person. The Rhino won't lie, but may say things like:

"You've got an experienced perspective on this."

"I appreciate how much you care about this."

You get the idea. Without going overboard, these compliments are intended to let others know you have an appreciation for this person. It will make their behind-your-back negative comments seem small and spiteful.

Should this person offer any criticism publicly, be sure to thank them and let them (others really) know how much you appreciate the candid feedback. But try not to argue the point in public. Instead try something like "You've made an interesting point and I really appreciate the candid feedback. I want to think about it, to make sure I give this the level of thought it deserves, then we can talk further."

A Teflon Rhino deals with difficult colleagues publicly by expressing kindness, appreciation, and professionalism. Even in private the Teflon Rhino understands that in the mind of an extremely difficult person, this is all a human chess game. So be careful about every move you make.

Eric's biggest mistake was in assuming that there could be a win/win outcome, because that was his personality type. And inherently positive people often get steamrolled by backstabbers in the workplace because they don't understand the win/LOSE mind-set. But you have to assume that some people will always take every opportunity to defeat you, step by step.

So get close. And never let them know that you are aware of their behind-the-scenes activity against you.

TEFLON RHINOS RECRUIT ALLIES—CAREFULLY

Rhinos tend to avoid letting others at work know their inner frustrations because they can never be sure which side other people are really on. And they know that in this particularly ugly part of the workplace poker game, loyalties can easily shift. Most people want to be on the side of the "winner," so if it appears that the difficult colleague is getting the upper hand, this is the direction most will gravitate to. Don't let this frustrate or depress you, it is simply human nature. We are all drawn to perceived strength.

At the same time, even if you can't express your own frustrations, you can see the signs of frustration in others. Look for a subtle roll of the eyes when the backstabber takes credit for a project she only briefly worked on. Or indications that others are getting impatient with the backstabber. You can get closer to, and align with, these people. And if they begin to openly express their frustration you should listen attentively, but don't join in. This is still a chess game.

Don't vent, just bite your tongue and take a deep breath. The same goes for sharing your feelings with your boss; when it comes down to it, to your supervisor (and to companies in general) it only matters that employees are performing. Any personality clashes you're having with a colleague tend to be low on their priority list. What they appreciate is the person who can work productively with difficult people, not the person who whines and complains about backstabbers.

TEFLON RHINOS USE THEIR HUMOR AND GOOD NATURE

Bullies feed on the fear and frustration of others, so give them NOTHING to feed on. Never let a colleague's comments ruin your day. Don't let the bastards beat you down. In fact, you should take pride in the fact that they are unable to intimidate you or throw you off your game. Instead you should focus on elevating others to show the dramatic contrast between your style and that of the difficult person.

If someone comes to you and tells you about a colleague's negative comments about you, shrug it off with a laugh and say, "I'm going to have to spend more time with her so she gets comfortable sharing these things with me directly. That way we can have a productive conversation."

If they criticize you publicly, at a meeting for example, you can laugh and say with gentle sarcasm, "Don't hold back, tell us how you REALLY feel."

RATIONAL VS IRRATIONAL DISCOMFORT

When your fear, discomfort, or uncertainty is based on an objective understanding of a situation, the discomfort is rational. If you don't have experience giving speeches to large groups, you'll probably be uncomfortable at least the first few times. If you continually propose creative ideas to your boss and they are always dismissed, you're going to anticipate and fear this response every time you have a new idea. This is rational.

If you've never had a conversation with an upper-level executive and you are suddenly sitting next to one on an airplane, you're going to naturally feel a little uncertain.

These types of rational discomfort have one root cause: a lack of knowledge, experience, or preparation. In fact, in these situations, something would be wrong if you didn't have some discomfort or fear of potential rejection. You're inexperienced and/or unprepared and you don't know what to do or expect.

Rational discomfort or fear often serves us well. Have you ever known someone who was so overwhelmingly confident in their ability to do something that they didn't feel a need to prepare or practice? Most of us have encountered at least a few of these people who don't experience even rational fear of rejection or failure—often these are classic extreme Teflon Rhino types. And while they may manage to do quite well most of the time, eventually the overconfidence catches up with them and they end up bombing miserably, often with spectacularly bad results.

The overconfidence of extreme Teflon Rhinos may cause them to underprepare.

So rational discomfort, uncertainty, or fear of potential rejection is a very good thing, because it can serve as a wake-up call—a flashing warning beacon—indicating you need more information, more preparation, more experience. Once you have those, the rational fear should fade away.

But fear of potential rejection isn't always rational—sometimes it isn't based on an objective understanding of the situation—and this means that increasing your knowledge, experience, or skill level won't make it go away. Irrational discomfort can take many forms. Some salespeople spend countless hours practicing their answers to objections yet still can't shake the feeling that a customer or a prospect is going to come up with an objection they can't answer adequately. Some people work hard to "connect" with others at work, to establish rapport with colleagues, and in fact often do develop strong bonds with people, yet they still can't shake the feeling that others secretly think poorly of them.

At its most basic level, this is an irrational fear of not being liked. There's nothing wrong with wanting to be liked, but taken to an extreme, a compulsive need to be liked can inhibit your abilities at work. You may come across as a bit too friendly, a little too accommodating. While your coworkers will like you, they're less likely to respect you.

But it doesn't always have to be that direct or dramatic. Irrational fear of potential rejection can manifest itself as occasional procrastination or indecisiveness. Even laziness, boredom, and negative thinking can all be signs that a person may be holding back due to irrational fear of potential rejection or judgment.

Over time, if it's not dealt with, this irrational fear can blossom into desperation, overreacting to failure, sabotaging yourself and others, not keeping commitments, going overboard on people pleasing, trying to be someone you're not.

Almost all people have to deal with both rational and irrational fears during the course of their career. With irrational fear, often the only effective answer is to push through the fear. If you recognize how much the hesitation is costing you in terms of career progress, this can help push you forward. And the more often you push yourself through the irrational fear, the easier it becomes to push through other irrational fears as your career progresses.

A good example is Debra Adamo, who is the creative director for Red Leather, a creative design agency with offices in New York, San Francisco, and Atlanta. Her career progress has been unusual to say the least, and she could easily have ended up as an art teacher in suburban Chicago had she not addressed her rational and irrational fears effectively.

As Debra describes the path her career has taken, it's clear that her ability to handle disappointment, uncertainty, and rejection—or lack thereof—has been a decisive factor. "I wanted to be an artist, a painter, and everyone in high school and college reinforced how talented I was. I loved art school, it was the best time of my life," she says. "What I wasn't prepared for was my first big gallery showing, when most of my works went unsold. It was emotionally crushing and started a downward spiral for me."

After college Debra spent two years trying to make a living as a painter. Those years were certainly difficult financially, but the lack of money wasn't the real challenge for her. "It was the visceral sense of personal rejection whenever a painting didn't sell," she says. Debra eventually decided that if she was going to be relatively poor, she might as well be poor doing something that made her feel good every day. So she became an art teacher at a local college. She planned to continue her own art "on the side" but her motivation eventually faded. "It just became harder and harder to feel good about putting myself out there, to take a chance that someone wouldn't like my work," she says.

After five years as an art teacher, now in her early thirties, Debra grew less satisfied with her life, and especially her financial situation.

She wasn't poor by any means, but she found herself wanting a life with more options, more opportunities, more freedom, and more money as the way to achieve all of those things. "When my art students would talk about their goals and dreams, I found myself responding negatively and cynically. As if I needed to crush their spirits the way mine had been crushed." Once Debra realized that her own unhappiness was having an effect on her students, she knew that she had to do something different. "But financially speaking, every reasonable career option that felt comfortable for me was just another average job," she says. "And every job that had real financial potential felt uncomfortable and scary."

Debra spent almost a full year being stuck at this crossroad. The comfortable path really wasn't all that comfortable, and the uncertain, scary path seemed to have the potential she was really looking for.

"I think eventually the pain of doing nothing became greater than the fear and uncertainty that was holding me back," she says. "Mostly it was my fear of what others would think of me. And I can't honestly say that I've gotten rid of that fear even today, but I guess I learned to face it, step by step."

Debra applied for a job as an ad agency sales rep. The interview was painful, she was clearly unprepared, and the interviewer commented that it wasn't really clear that Debra wanted the job. So she didn't get it.

But Debra interviewed for another ad agency sales position, and another, and each interview got better. Eventually she was hired. "And then the fear kicked in all over again," she says. Her first six months in the sales position were incredibly uncomfortable. They wanted her to make prospecting phone calls, so she was experiencing rejection every day. Every hour really. "God, I hated that," she says. "It was like calling a stranger and asking for a date, and being shot down most of the time." And when she did manage to get an appointment scheduled, the face-to-face meetings weren't that much more comfortable.

And then one day, she landed a new account. "The cloudy skies parted, a ray of sunshine came down on me and life was good," she says. "But the cold calling still sucked." After two years in new account acquisition, Debra wanted to move into an account management position. But these positions were rarely available and when one did open up, the selection process was very competitive. She could have applied for account management positions at other agencies, but didn't feel confident enough to do so.

When a position opened up at her company, she dropped some hints and hoped that her manager would recommend her for the job. But she never actually applied, and apparently her manager didn't get the hint. So a year later, when another account manager position became available, Debra applied. And got the promotion. "I probably could have accelerated things by at least a year or two if I had been braver," she says.

She was thrilled with her new job as an account manager, and especially pleased with the fact that she would not have to do any more cold calling. But she soon realized that there was just as much opportunity for disappointment and rejection, in fact even more so, because when a current client decided to give a project to a different agency, everyone knew about it. "Getting shut down on an initial phone call, or not landing a new client was always a downer," she says. "But it was nothing compared to being told by a current client that they were going with another firm for a big project." There was much more pressure than she had expected, but Debra managed to do well and learned to set aside the sometimes rough treatment from existing clients.

A few years later Debra realized that what she really wanted to do was to move into a creative position for the agency. She had learned a lot about the business and felt that her innate creativity would make her a good fit. She also thought (wrongly, it turns out) that this would be a lower-pressure position because she wouldn't have the day-to-day pressure of keeping clients happy. She would be part of the team generating new ideas and pitching them to clients. It sounded like a perfect fit for her, fun and creative, and the money was really good. But the opportunities in the Creative Department at her company were even more scarce than account manager positions. So rather than wait a year or longer for something to open up Debra began applying at other agencies.

"That was a brutal process," she says. "I had no idea how tough those interviews would be. They were looking for people with amazing ideas who could execute those ideas and really sell them to clients." Luckily for Debra she had a series of interviews with other companies before she interviewed at Red Leather. "I had a chance to polish my pitch, get more comfortable with the idea of not just presenting my ideas, but advocating for them."

Red Leather hired her to be part of their creative team, and for the first time in her adult life she felt as if she was doing what she had been born to do. Eight years later, when the company was planning an expansion into the Atlanta market, she was surprised to be asked to interview for the director position. "I initially said no, because it just didn't feel right to me," she says. "But eventually I realized that what was holding me back was fear. Fear that the expansion wouldn't be successful, fear that it would be my fault, fear that people who now respected me would then see me as a failure." Debra once again decided to step forward into the discomfort. The first few years in the Atlanta market were tough and there were plenty of failures and difficult situations. But eventually Red Leather gained a foothold in that market and they are now contemplating another expansion, this time to Toronto.

As Debra looks back at her career, one big lesson occurs to her over and over again. "I'm grateful that at each critical point in my career I eventually stepped into my 'discomfort zone,' but I wish I had done it sooner."

So how can any of us determine whether or not we are experiencing rational or irrational fear, and what can we do about it? Debra provides a great example because she recognized the fear she was experiencing and thought about it deeply enough to understand the root causes.

When you are experiencing discomfort or something about a work opportunity just doesn't "feel right," try to identify the true root cause of your discomfort: What is it that is making you uncomfortable? Fear of losing control? Fear of looking incompetent? Fear of being laughed at? Fear of the unknown? Fear of looking like a fool? Fear of not being accepted? Fear of not being liked? Fear that, as it turns out, you're really JUST an average person after all? What's the REAL, underlying source of the fear?

When Debra felt stuck, she found a compelling positive motivator to help move her forward: What goal or objective would truly motivate you to break through the fear? Specific financial goals? Personal growth and development? The joy of living and working without emotional limitations? The desire to see what you're really capable of achieving? You've got to come up with powerful reasons or goals that compel you to break through the irrational fear and move forward.

And in addition to positive motivators, Debra also used compelling negative motivators. She focused on the pain of NOT changing and what that would ultimately mean for her life. In fact it was probably the negative motivation that had the greatest impact for Debra, and this is true for many of us. As much as we want the positive outcome, often we are more willing to take action to avoid the negative outcome.

SOMETIMES THEY REALLY DON'T LIKE YOU

Whether you are anticipating rejection or not, it is occasionally going to happen. There will be people who don't like your ideas, don't like your appearance, don't appreciate your contribution, or just don't like you. No one can promise that life is fair. Or that a career will be fair. In fact, the opposite is probably more true—sometimes bad things happen to good people, and good things happen to bad people. So when rejection occurs, remember:

- Teflon Rhinos don't get angry or frustrated.
- Teflon Rhinos don't dwell on it.
- Teflon Rhinos laugh it off. (Seriously, they do. I've seen this in the wild.)
- Teflon Rhinos LEARN from it.

You can learn a lot from people like Debra because they do not allow the circumstances of life to determine their career success. They push through and CREATE success by first taking control of their emotional reactions to life's circumstances.

There is a lot to think about in this chapter, so before moving on please take a few minutes to contemplate the questions below.

THINK NOW

Where would you place yourself on the continuum below:

Velcro Butterfly   ⟵————————————⟶   **Teflon Rhino**

- Is this the ideal for you in terms of your career progress?
- In what ways have your tendencies, either way, helped or hindered your career?
- Is there any adjustment that you should make in one direction or the other?

ACT SOON

If you find yourself to be an extreme Teflon Rhino or Velcro Butterfly and think that your career would benefit from making a change, follow the process outlined below. Forewarning: a lot of this may at first feel VERY uncomfortable for you because making real change in the fundamental nature of your psyche will not be easy.

Make a list of what you have lost and/or not gained because of your extreme tendencies. This is important because most of us are exceptionally results-oriented in our careers, and we need practical reasons to make significant changes. So make a list of at least three things you have lost and/or not gained, five or more would be better.

Think about the root causes of your extreme tendencies. Were there experiences in your early life that contributed to the development of your extreme traits? You may not have thought about this much in the past, but often our more extreme behavioral tendencies are a result of extreme early life experiences—they are a coping/survival mechanism that served us at the time, but may now be holding us back.

Be self-aware as you work with others, reflect on the way you react to other people: to who they are; to how they act; to the things they say; to the values and beliefs they express; and especially to anything about them that tends to spark your extreme tendency. For Rhinos, who causes you to instinctively shut down or thicken your skin? For Butterflies, who causes you anxiety or anger? What specifically do they do and what are the typical circumstances? Be thoughtful and honest with yourself: What does your annoyance at them say about YOU?

If you are serious about making a change, keep a journal of your most intense reactions to others. Spend some time quietly writing and thinking about the thoughts and feelings that these people spark in you. This isn't about judging yourself, but about recording your observations for self-reflection.

When you have internal conversations with yourself, what do you hear? What do you think of yourself? Are you supportive or critical? Can you identify an inner critic and/or an inner victim? Record these reflections in your journal as well. No judgment, no drama, you are just exploring your own typical thought process.

Over time, as you pay closer attention to your emotional responses to the actions of others, as well as your internal thought process, often a natural shift will occur where you will begin to be less reactive and more responsive.

For Rhinos, reactive responses are often instinctively shutting down or protecting your rhino-thick skin.

For Butterflies, reactive responses are often instinctively lashing out (internally, not directly) with anger, frustration, or anxiety.

Being responsive rather than reactive means having thoughtful and considered responses that previously would have sparked a more instinctive reaction.

As you progress with this process, whether a Rhino or a Butterfly, you may come to realize that your extreme tendencies were putting up unneeded barriers between yourself and others. If you are an extreme Rhino you will likely never become a total "butterfly," but you could evolve into a Teflon Rhino with wings. Or a horned Butterfly.

After you have spent some time reflecting on your own behavioral tendencies, select one person at work with whom you tend to have extreme reactions. Over time, work to adjust your instinctive reaction to this person. Observe them more carefully, listen to them more actively, ask better questions and show a genuine interest in them, as fellow human beings, not just work colleagues. This may be very uncomfortable and counterintuitive for you, so focus on just one person at first because trying to do this with many people at once might be overwhelming.

LONG-TERM THOUGHTS AND ACTION POINTS

- Accept that some level of rejection is inevitable in any career.

- As your career progresses, the opportunities for rejection will most likely increase.

- You will need to be highly active and engaged, and push beyond your comfort zone in order to be successful.

- The more active and engaged you are, the more you push beyond your comfort zone, the more rejection, uncertainty, and fear you will experience.

- Pay attention to your emotional reactions and acknowledge the extreme feelings when you experience them.

- If you experience rational fear of rejection, the key is knowledge and preparation. And sometimes you will simply have to go through the experience to gain the knowledge.

- Some of your discomfort may be irrational, and you may have to just force yourself into and through these uncomfortable situations.

6

Enjoy the Show

◆

All the world is a stage, and all business has an element of theater.
—WILLIAM SHAKESPEARE *(SORT OF)*

Without promotion something terrible happens. . . . Nothing!
—P. T. BARNUM

L ani Matheson is one of the most talented people I have ever
worked with. Many years ago she was my technical systems an-
alyst, and I eventually promoted her to a technical project manager position before I left the company. We didn't stay in touch but I
fully expected that her career would progress nicely because she was
so bright, hardworking, and capable.

Last year I reached out to her because the company I now worked
for was looking for a director of technical systems, someone to lead
a team of analysts and project managers, and I thought she would be
a great fit for the position. It had been almost a decade since we had
last spoken and I expected that she would have risen to some type

of senior technical leadership role, but in fact she hadn't progressed much beyond where she was when we last met. My good luck, I thought, because it meant that the position my company needed to fill would be a big step up for her. I wasn't the only decision maker, but I had a strong influence over the final hiring decision.

So I called first to gauge her interest, and she was definitely enthusiastic about the chance to make an upward career move. She even commented on how "stagnant" she had felt the past few years. So I forwarded her résumé to our HR department and asked them to schedule interviews with each of the decision makers. About two weeks later I met with her in my office first, and it was great to get reacquainted before she went on to the other interviews. She was clearly still the incredibly capable person I had known many years earlier. At the end of the day all of the interviewers met to debrief their conversations with Lani and the other three candidates.

I felt that I was being very objective, and Lani was clearly more competent and a better fit than the other candidates. But it turned out that none of the other interviewers agreed with me. They were all in favor of another candidate who was certainly impressive, but I knew for a fact that Lani was smarter, more competent, and would be a better fit for our particular needs. I found myself getting frustrated as I listened to their observations and the deficiencies they perceived.

"I asked for examples of her work and she really didn't have much," one of them said.

"Well, I can give you a couple of great examples," I replied.

"She was OK, but the other candidate's answers were crisp and detailed, and he had done a lot of homework on our company. I think she just kind of showed up . . ."

"Well, maybe that's my fault," I said. "I asked her to come in, so maybe she didn't think she needed to do any research."

"The other candidate asked great questions, took notes, and he was dressed pretty sharp. I got the impression she just drove over on her lunch break and was impatient to get back to her office. And her manner and attire were . . . pretty casual."

"Well, she's a workhorse, not a show horse," I replied. "I've worked with her and I know how good she is . . ."

"She certainly has the technical knowledge we need, but I'm just not sure she's the best personality fit for us."

"Believe me, once you actually see her in action—"

Suddenly I stopped myself. I realized that I was trying to sell them on her, and the bottom line was that she had done a poor job of selling herself. I had known this about her, and in fact when we worked together I appreciated the fact that she rarely tooted her own horn. She kept her head down and just focused on doing a good job, which was great for me and my needs. But I could see now that it wasn't great for her.

And as I thought about it, I began to understand why her career had not progressed as far or as rapidly as I had assumed it would. Not many people would pay close enough attention and take the time to get to know her well enough to understand her amazing capabilities. Even I wouldn't normally have done so, but the first project we worked on together many years ago helped me understand her expertise. Unfortunately her almost complete lack of self-promotion capability (and interest) meant that most people just didn't see how good she was. It probably isn't fair, but it's how the world works.

You probably do great work in your particular field of endeavor. If not, fix that problem first. But let's assume that you are exceptionally competent and doing a great job. That's great, but a lot of other people are doing great work too. You work hard and go the extra mile. So do a lot of other people. You make important contributions to the business. Other people, ditto. So how do you make sure that your achievements and contributions are recognized by the right people in order to maximize your potential for career progress? Because if you don't find a way to toot your own horn, your strong performance can get lost in the orchestra of other horns blaring loudly.

In today's hypercompetitive world, where no one wants to get caught up in the next round of layoffs, and everyone is competing for the fewer promotion opportunities available, it is not enough to just do good work. You have to go out of your way to make sure the right people KNOW your good work and your exceptional capabilities.

If you aren't finding ways to promote yourself and your work, you are essentially demoting yourself, while other people are *proactively* promoting themselves. Business schools offer courses in "career advocacy" and "marketing yourself." Business books advise professional women to "lean in" and advocate for themselves. Everyone is swimming upstream against a current of other people promoting their own capabilities, building their "personal brands" and highlighting themselves as "thought leaders." So if you aren't swimming, the current will eventually take you downstream.

"Every day each of us puts on a show, whether we know it or not, whether we like it or not," the director of a large Chicago advertising agency once told me. "There is no point in being annoyed or frustrated by it, because it is just human nature, so to do well in business you have to learn to ENJOY the show. And the best way to enjoy it is to put on a GREAT show."

The idea of business having an element of theater and showmanship is off-putting for many people because we are inherently uncomfortable with the idea of self-promotion. Blatant self-promotion feels unnatural. And bragging is considered poor form in virtually every culture on the planet. Most of us would prefer that the quality of our work speak for itself.

We get annoyed by those who are obviously promoting themselves and their work to the people who have the most influence over career progress. It is even more frustrating when they (successfully) take credit for the work of others. But the show at work is playing every day, whether we like it or not.

Don't you hate it when someone in a meeting answers emails on her iPad the whole time, not contributing in any way, but when a senior leader walks into the room she suddenly has lots of ideas and opinions? And when the senior leader is clearly impressed with one of her thoughts, doesn't that just burn you up inside?

OK, sure, but what did you do about it? Did you step up and share your own ideas? Did you find a way to highlight yourself (without being so obvious about it of, course) or did you sit silently stewing over the unfairness of it all?

Proudly refusing to "play the game" or "put on a show" may help you feel good and self-righteous. Or maybe it just masks the fact that you're uncomfortable, unsure of the quality of your work, or just doubt that you can in fact put on a good show. And maybe that's just because up until now no one has ever shown you how to do it graciously and professionally. We're going to take care of that in this chapter.

YOUR DAILY BILLBOARD

"I don't hire ugly people," said the owner of a high-end jewelry store chain based in Vancouver, British Columbia. We were discussing a customer service training program for his staff and I had just commented on the stunning architecture of his store, the beautiful furnishings, and how his staff was impeccably dressed. All of it created a unique and compelling experience for his customers. I thought he might respond with "thank you" or "It's kind of you to notice," but, no, instead he smiled proudly and said, "I don't hire ugly people."

He must have seen a reaction on my face because he went on to explain himself, and while I was a bit taken aback that he would actually *say* these things, in hindsight I do see his point. These may be hard truths that people in polite company never verbalize, but if you are going to effectively promote yourself at work you have to deal in reality. Here are a few highlights from the jewelry store owner's comments:

- "Every now and then, we all undress each other with our eyes."
- "Everyone is more easily persuaded by someone they find physically attractive."
- "We all suspect that fat people lack self-discipline or intelligence."
- "It isn't pretty when we undress fat people with our eyes. But we still do it anyway."

OK, don't shoot the messenger. I know his comments are a little harsh, but of course it's better to be pretty or handsome. If you (like me) are among the legions of average-looking people, and you had a choice to be exceptionally handsome or beautiful, everything else being equal, would you turn it down? Of course not. Because being physically attractive comes with many benefits, and one of those benefits is that people are more willing to listen to you, more inclined to believe you, and more likely to trust you.

This is more than just a personal perception. The issue has been recognized and studied for decades. So I'm not going to bore you with more research—I'm just going to cut right to what you can do about it. Ultimately you have to do the best you can with what God has given you and what time has allowed you to keep.

Billboards are designed to grab attention and deliver a quick message before each car speeds past them. Think of physical attributes as your "daily billboard" that advertises to everyone who comes into your presence or quickly passes by. Here are a few quick tips.

Dress a Step Up: Always dress just a little better than your peers. Look to the people one or two steps above you and emulate their attire, as long as the difference isn't too dramatic. When it comes to work clothing, quality counts, people do notice. Even a construction foreman who wants to be a site manager should make sure he is dressed for the job he wants, not the one he already has.

Reject Business Casual: Even if you have to dress "casually" in order to fit into your environment, take care to select quality apparel, subtle colors, and patterns that reflect professional taste, and never forget that people ARE noticing what you wear every day, and judging you.

Bright Eyes and Brighter Smile: You know this, but many of us still don't make enough eye contact. No need to stare at someone like a stalker, but when you are addressing people during a meeting or hallway conversation, make direct eye contact. If your teeth are a bit dull and dingy, do something about it. When our teeth are white and healthy, we instinctively smile more. And smiling more with bright, attractive teeth is like shining a light on your personal billboard.

Manage the Gray: Don't be afraid to color it away. This goes for men as well. Yes, for men, a little gray can SOMETIMES look distinguished—here's the rule: If you are clearly fit, trim, healthy, and have an air of youthful vitality, then gray hair is OK, even distinguishing. If you are average (or below) in terms of your outward vitality, then gray hair just emphasizes that you are getting older. And a pudgy gray-haired person walking slowly down an office hallway—not a career enhancer.

Pay Attention to the Details: The people we work with every day take notice of even the most minor details. They will almost never say anything, but people do notice the smell of your breath, your body odor, your fingernails, your shoes, etc. Even younger generations notice details and make judgments; Apple or Android phone, jeans or chinos, smartwatch or sportwatch or (probably fake) Rolex or no watch at all, easy listening music or Scandinavian techno punk. Everything gets noticed.

DETAILS FOR MEN:	**DETAILS FOR WOMEN:**
Trim away nose and ear hair, eyebrows. Closely clip nails.	Keep your posture straight, bushy women have a tendency to slump forward.
Men tend not to notice the severity of their bad breath or body odor.	Hair and makeup attractive, but not overly glamorous or sexy. Subtle perfume. Manicured nails.
A white T-shirt underneath makes your dress shirt "pop" a little more.	Professional clothing, tasteful and well-fitting, few accessories, carefully chosen. Stylish shoes, but not extreme.
Nicely tailored suit, well-fitting slacks and shirts. No jingling coins or keys in your pants pockets.	Confident speaking voice, your lowest natural pitch, calm and steady.
Don't buy shoes just for comfort. Buy professional shoes that are also comfortable, and keep them polished.	Confident strides while walking, not too fast, not shuffling.

Obviously the standards and norms for every business environment are unique, but the most important point to be remembered here is that your physical appearance is part of the show, and every aspect of you is going to be noticed. This doesn't mean that we are all shallow or judgmental or licentious, it just means that we all notice these things. Your goal is to stand out, ever so slightly, because of the quality of your physical appearance.

But you don't want to stand out so much that it appears obvious or extreme. Individuality is good, as long as it is within the professional bounds of your particular work environment.

We have an intern who comes to work every day wearing a tie, his shirt and pants crisply pressed, shoes polished, etc. I hate to say it, but we used to rib him good-naturedly about it, because we work in a business casual environment. He is also hardworking, dependable, and clearly focused on doing a great job. We've already started talking about finding him a permanent position here once the internship ends. Is it about the tie? Not really, but in a way it is, because the tie is a reflection of all the other good things we know about him.

We had a much more casual intern last year, both in the way she dressed and the way she approached her work. She's not here anymore, but we still sometimes joke about her ankle tattoos.

DOES THIS JOB MAKE ME LOOK FAT?

Here's another hard truth for some people. The world notices when we are fat, or even just a little pudgy. They may not say anything to us about it, but people respond to us differently when we are overweight. Even just a few extra pounds can make a significant difference in the way people perceive us and react to us. Ask Paul Morse, a fifty-something sales and marketing director for SamCo. Paul travels throughout the US meeting fast-food franchise owners, selling his company's marketing software system.

Because he is often meeting the owners in their fast-food stores, he eats much more than his share of unhealthy food. "Unfortunately I'm a classic yoyo dieter and exerciser, I have a forty-pound weight gain/loss range and typically I'll spend a year or more at the high end, then get motivated and lose forty pounds in six months. I may keep it off for a year or two, but eventually it creeps back, and the cycle starts all over again."

Paul kept meticulous records of his monthly sales results for years, and he has also tracked his weight carefully, but it had never occurred to him that there might be a correlation until a few years ago when he was transferring sales data to his phone app, and then a few hours later he was entering his weight into another app. "At first it was just curiosity, since I was looking at two different graphs that looked similar, but inversed," he says. "So I decided to go back through my records and enter data from the last couple of years." After he entered over two years of historical data into both the sales-tracking app and the weight-tracking app, he was stunned to see the correlation. "It was shocking really, the two graphs were almost exact opposites. When my weight was up, my sales were down, and vice versa."

Having gone through this cycle numerous times, Paul started noticing the difference in the way people reacted to him depending upon his weight. "I do think people laugh a little more at 'Big Paul's' jokes for some reason," he says, speaking of himself in the third person. "But that's about the only positive reaction." When "Big Paul" travels to meet with a prospective client, his presentations are interrupted more often, he isn't introduced to others in the business who weren't part of the planned meeting, and he doesn't get invited out for evening social activity nearly as often as "Thin Paul" does. This had apparently been happening for many years but he only became sensitive to it after he had compared the two graphs.

Big or thin or somewhere in between, Paul manages to sell his marketing systems effectively. But the weight definitely creates an interpersonal barrier. And you have to wonder what other impediments are being created that Paul isn't aware of. What relationships aren't developed, what referrals aren't given, what opportunities are missed?

I know this is a sensitive issue for him because even with this awareness Paul hasn't changed his cyclical pattern, and at this writing he is currently in his "Big Paul" phase. Men are just as insecure about their physical appearance as women, they just tend to do a better job of keeping that insecurity under wraps. Paul is one of the most confident men I've ever met, but I absolutely know that "Big Paul" suffers from a crisis of confidence, and it seems to get worse with each loss/gain cycle.

Weight gain and lack of vitality hurts us in three ways:

- We have less energy and mental clarity.
- Others react to us with less natural acceptance.
- Our confidence and self-esteem take a hit.

It's not fair, but women pay a higher price for their weight gain than men do. A man can be ten or twenty pounds overweight and cover it up with a well-tailored suit. (But just to be clear to all of the slightly overweight men reading this: we STILL notice, and it DOES impact the way we perceive you.) For women, even a modest weight gain will change the way they are perceived by others, and the way others treat them.

"I never lost the baby weight after having two children, and after five years I had sort of gotten used to it. I just assumed that this was the 'new me' and I never noticed that people were treating me differently," says Barbara Kern, marketing director for SunSoft Systems, Inc. "But after I got serious about diet and exercise, and got back to my prebaby weight, I could definitely tell there was a difference in how people reacted to me. It was strange, really. They liked my ideas better. Interrupted me less. Laughed more at my jokes. Acted more quickly on my requests."

This is not a book about weight loss. Or diet. Or exercise. This is a book about hard truths related to our career progress and here it is: If you are overweight, it is costing you. Probably a lot more than you think it is.

....

If you think you need to make a serious effort to lose weight, whether just a few pounds or much more, go to: workplacepoker.com/weight-loss/.

....

SOCIAL MEDIA: SCRUB UP, THEN SCALE UP

Your online social profile is an increasingly important self-promotion resource that many business professionals underutilize. LinkedIn is the most used social media site for professionals. Many employers review a candidate's LinkedIn profile as a screening process to learn about their education and work history, skills, endorsements, recommendations, professional affiliations, and more. Your LinkedIn profile can be a powerful personal branding tool that conveys the same information as a résumé, but it can also showcase a much bigger picture of who you are as a professional. While LinkedIn is mostly for business connections, Facebook is used largely for social reasons, but it can also help people to connect with others and increase their professional network.

Yes, it can be annoying to see people you know puff up their LinkedIn profiles, or have people you barely know overshare on their Facebook pages, but this is the world we live in. Personal blogs, Twitter feeds, Tumblr profiles—it is easy to throw up your hands and say "not for me!" It is also easy to hurt your career ambitions by not carefully thinking about your online social media activity.

Barry Postrum was a thirty-something health club manager in Manhattan, with a nice professional LinkedIn profile that highlighted his formal education and passion for health, nutrition, and fitness. He posted regular updates and articles to his profile sharing tips and advice for weight loss and general wellness. Barry encouraged his health club members to connect with him on LinkedIn, which many of them did. Barry thought of his LinkedIn page as his professional social media, and his Facebook page as personal. Of course some of his club members crossed over into both, especially those he had dated.

This wasn't really a problem until Barry found another health club he wanted to work for. The new club was in TriBeCa with a very upscale clientele, and the management position would be a big step up:

more money, greater long-term career potential. Plus the chance to meet a few celebrities and ultra-wealthy folks. His first interview with the general manager went incredibly well. In fact the GM even mentioned some of Barry's LinkedIn articles and hoped he could bring some of his writing ability to the club's e-newsletter for clients.

And then . . . nothing. The follow-up appointment was canceled because of "scheduling issues" and never rescheduled. Barry's calls the GM went unanswered. It was the strangest thing he had ever experienced. Weeks went by, then a month, and eventually Barry heard that a new manager had been hired.

Months later Barry was sharing this story with me. "Do you know the name of the guy they hired?" I asked. Barry gave me the name and we googled him. He seemed to have a solid background in health and fitness, similar to Barry's. We checked out his LinkedIn profile—ditto. His Facebook feed showed a lot of group selfies taken with smiling clients in the health club, so I decided to take a look at Barry's Facebook—and this is where it got, uh . . . interesting.

Barry had quite a few individual selfies showing him posing in the club, and in the locker room. None of the locker room photos were totally naked—I'd give them an R rating mostly. He also had some photos of clients working out, and it wasn't clear if they knew they had been photographed. Some of the commentary from his Facebook friends was definitely X-rated, and it was clear that some of the club members he had dated were no longer big fans. Here are a few examples:

- "Nice photo. Must have had your package photo shopped unless things have changed since we dated."
- "I was going to unfriend you but I get too much of a laugh from these cheesy shots."
- "I've already seen you naked, how about some shots of the other guys in the locker room."

These and other comments showed a very different side of Barry's life. And I think what struck me most was that as we sat at a Starbucks and I scrolled though his Facebook photos and comments from friends, he mostly smiled. Kind of proud, in a strange way. I asked him about the ex-girlfriends who were still posting harsh comments. Why hadn't he unfriended them, or at the very least deleted the comments?

"I don't know, I guess I'm just OK being an open book. Plus, it's really not anyone else's business."

Really? Did he just say that? Yes.

"If your prospective employer saw these photos and comments," I asked him, "what would they think?"

He shrugged his shoulders. "I don't know."

Eventually Barry acknowledged that a health club with an elite clientele would probably frown upon its employees dating the members, taking locker room photos (even individual selfies), and posting "funny" photos of some members as they exercised awkwardly. But in the end he really, really didn't get it.

"This isn't any of their business. This is just for my friends," he said.

"And bitter ex-girlfriends, apparently."

"Well, yeah."

Barry was a lost cause, so I stopped trying to convince him. But you don't have to be a lost cause. I totally understand that many of us have tended to think of Facebook as our personal space, and LinkedIn as the professional space. But if you are serious about maximizing the trajectory of your career, you just can't afford to think that way.

....

Mind-Set Shift: EVERYTHING online is part of your professional self-promotion.

....

An increasing number of employers review candidates' online profiles, so it is important for you to understand how to use social media to best demonstrate your talents, experience, knowledge, and career goals to potential employers. In addition, you should assume that your current employer and coworkers visit your online profile at least occasionally. And what they find can either help or hurt your career climb goals.

PROFESSIONAL SOCIAL MEDIA ACTION SELF-CHECK

Search your name in Google and other major search engines to see what shows up on the first three pages. If anything problematic appears delete it immediately if you have control of the content. If not, immediately ask whoever controls the content to delete it.

Protect outside access to all of your social media connections. LinkedIn and Facebook allow you to make your own contacts private so that no one else can see them. Do this now. If you plan to use Facebook for social friends and LinkedIn for professional connections (which is what many people do) then adjust all of your Facebook privacy settings to prevent nonfriends from seeing any of your content (warning: this isn't fail-safe so you still have to be cautious about what you and/or your friends post).

Within your own social media accounts, review all content from the past three years and delete anything that might be considered less than ideal by current or prospective employers. Enter your public Facebook ID or username to see what is publicly available from your Facebook profile.

Ensure that your main social profile photos are professional, and that all other photos present you in a positive light.

On LinkedIn find your workplace "competitors" and review their profiles. This means your boss, your most talented coworkers, etc. Then search for people at other companies who have jobs similar to yours and the job(s) you aspire to. Gather ideas and the best practices from all of them, then apply these to your own profile.

Ensure that your LinkedIn profile fully describes the good work you have done, particularly highlighting the positive business impact of key projects, etc.

After you feel that your LinkedIn profile is top-notch, send out connection invitations to all of your coworkers, your boss, and other key leaders in your company.

Build your network. Join relevant groups within LinkedIn, connect with key clients, reach out to colleagues inside and outside your organization to expand your circle of contacts.

If for some reason your online self-search brings up something significantly negative and you are not able to get it deleted easily, there are still actions you can take to minimize the downside impact. You should also know that even if you do get something deleted, it really hasn't gone away. There are virtual archives (caches) of everything that has ever been posted to the Internet, and while these sources typically won't come up in a casual web search it is important for you to know they are there.

For negative information you cannot get deleted (or even if you do manage to get it deleted) your best response is to add enough positive information about yourself on a variety of platforms to ensure that when someone does a web search all of the negative items are pushed down to the fourth page of links or below.

Karla Schleck went through a bitter breakup with a boyfriend she refers to as "a hybrid of Charles Manson, Saddam Hussein, and Hannibal Lecter." Charming guy, and he apparently was also quite fluent with Internet technology because after they broke up he began posting crude images of her online as well as scathing comments about everything from her lack of personal hygiene to her questionable morals. She eventually got a restraining order and he was forced to remove many of the items, but enough remained that she was aghast at the thought of anyone ever searching her name online. (Please note, at her request, I've changed her name in this story. She didn't want anyone reading this and getting the bright idea of looking for some of the bad things online.)

After doing everything she could to remove offending images and other content, she then took the additive approach. She was able to obtain the URL for her own name and set up a personal hobby blog using Wordpress. This was easy and she made sure that every blog page and posting had at least one reference to her name. She updated her LinkedIn and Facebook profiles to add several more references to her name. She created new Google+ and Twitter profiles and did the same thing. She found other areas on the Internet to add content with reference to her name and within six months a web search for her name would produce only positive (or bland) information on the first three pages of search content links. This wasn't a perfect solution, but it was the best she could do to protect her professional reputation.

BLOGGING AND TWEETING–DO YOU REALLY HAVE SOMETHING TO SAY?

As much as I am a fan of leveraging social media for professional self-promotion, let me tap the brakes a bit. When it comes to building a "personal brand" and being a "thought leader" as many career guidance consultants will advise you to do, there are a few fundamental questions you must ask and answer first.

Are you in fact a thought leader in your field? Do you have the depth of knowledge, a well-informed point of view, or at the very least a discernible expertise?

If you cannot credibly and confidently answer those questions with a resounding "yes," then perhaps you have some work to do before sharing your thought leadership with the rest of your professional world. The first step is to become a deep expert in your field.

Don't just know enough to do the job well. Know enough to help others do the job well; then let people know by blogging and tweeting and speaking on the subject.

Nothing is more hurtful to someone's professional "brand" than loudly shouting out, through blog posts and tweets, one's banal comments, mundane opinions, or copycat perspectives. But that doesn't mean you have to wait until the light of profound wisdom shines from your eyes—you can begin blogging and tweeting as a curator of others' content. If you are deeply engaged in a particular topic you probably read something every day (online or offline) in that particular arena. Over time you develop a knowledge of websites, blogs, and other resources you can depend upon for insightful education. Perhaps without even realizing it you are already a curator—you quickly discern whether a particular article or blog post has unique valuable content and if it doesn't, you move on.

If you want to blog and/or tweet regularly to build your professional brand, a good place to start is simply sharing the content of others that makes it through your personal curator filter. Over time you will develop your own deep expertise and point of view, and can begin sharing this as you find your "voice." Take it slowly though. Few of us, yours truly included, are as profound or as deeply insightful as we think we are. We fall in love with our own ideas too easily. So just be sure to consistently remind yourself that the ultimate purpose of the blogging and tweeting is to promote your professional career progress—and if it doesn't do that, don't bother.

THE DANGER OF OVERPROMOTION

Maybe you are one of those rare birds who are in fact quite comfortable promoting yourself at work. Good for you. However, you may want to think carefully about how you highlight your contributions, because if everyone at work perceives you as a "horn tooter" they will tend to discount what you say, maybe even talk about you behind your back. Most of us cringe internally when we hear someone brag about themselves in any way. From a self-promotion standpoint the worst thing that can happen is to gain a reputation for "putting lipstick on the pig" of your subpar work, or taking undeserved credit for the good work of others.

Clyde Barnes graduated from the Wharton School of Business with an MBA in marketing and was immediately hired into a Fortune 500 company as part of their leadership development program. Clyde would work in four business units over a two-year period, six months per unit, gaining experience across the entire organization before he was placed in a formal leadership role. This was a huge opportunity and Clyde was determined to make the most of it. In each of his four assignments Clyde made sure he was tasked with high-profile projects that would highlight his leadership capabilities. He had no direct reports but was expected to leverage his informal leadership skills with matrixed teams of employees from many different departments.

At the end of each assignment Clyde was expected to deliver a presentation summarizing his key project and the business impact. He worked for days on the PowerPoint slides and felt great about every one of his presentations. At the end of his final assignment Clyde firmly expected to be given an early-career leadership role within one of the business units.

However, Clyde was not offered a permanent position, and unfortunately the HR representative gave him very vague feedback. Something about the overall tough market, business contracting, budget cuts, and not finding a good fit for his competencies in any of the four business units. What Clyde did not hear was the direct feedback that had been offered by several of the people with whom he had worked closely. Some of the comments were:

"He didn't seem to understand that this wasn't about him, it was about the business."

"He was all about making sure his project was on track, not really appreciating that his team had many other responsibilities beyond his priorities."

"I don't remember him actually doing anything, just directing others to do things and then putting together really nice PowerPoint slides to take credit for the work."

"Really smart guy, but kind of annoying to work with. Loves to give orders."

Clearly this was a case of being overly focused on self-promotion. Both common experience and psychological research tells us that being perceived as competent, yet modest, is almost universally attractive to others. But Donald Trump-ish overconfidence and self-promotion is off-putting to most people, particularly when it isn't backed up by genuine competence.

......

Promote yourself without appearing to be a self-promoter.

......

So how do you confidently promote your own good work without gaining the reputation as someone who promotes his own work? That is a conundrum, and unless you develop skills and strategies to solve this problem it will have a negative impact throughout your professional life. The negative impact may be subtle, even invisible to you.

YOU'RE NOT THE ONLY SHOW IN TOWN

Megan Postram worked hard to maintain a 4.0 GPA in college while also being quite active as a community volunteer and working part-time in a shelter for abused women. After graduating with a degree in accounting she received no quick job offers, but her college roommate, with the same degree but not nearly as hardworking or dedicated, had two strong offers almost immediately. This was of course frustrating for Megan. And even though she eventually landed an accounting position she felt good about, she couldn't shake the nagging feeling that something just wasn't right or fair. Years later she had completely forgotten about it until by chance she reconnected with her college roommate. Sitting in her ex-roommate's apartment admiring the furnishings and having a few drinks, Megan once again began to have that nagging feeling of unfairness as her friend mentioned a recent promotion and other opportunities on the horizon for her. Megan's job was fine, but the career growth potential at her company wasn't exactly stellar.

When they were in college Megan had been too uncomfortable, maybe a little too jealous, to ask her roommate how she had landed the job. But years later after a few drinks, laughing about their college days, she was finally able to get it out.

"No offense but, how did you, with your grades and frankly, you spent as much time partying as you did studying, how did you land such a sweet job?" Megan asked. "Did you know someone? Or . . ."

"Or sleep with someone?" her friend finished the sentence with a smile. "No, nothing like that. Maybe I was just lucky. But they did like my portfolio. Do you want to see it?"

Her friend went to a closet and pulled out a binder she had created for the interviews. The binder contained highlights from key accomplishments and activities that had shaped her life. There was a photo of her as an eleven-year-old Girl Scout selling cookies door-to-door, along with a spreadsheet detailing her year-over-year cookie sales volume for four years. There was an award certificate from her high school swim team. A ribbon from the chess club. Exhibits from several key projects she completed in college. Her transcripts, plus testimonials and reference letters from numerous professors—Megan noticed that some of the strongest testimonials were from professors in whose classes her grades weren't especially strong. She even included the results of a career aptitude test and several psychological personality profiles.

"Wow," Megan said, thinking back to the thin folder of transcripts and reference letters she had taken to her interviews. "I would have hired you." Clearly her ex-roommate had done a much better job of selling herself to prospective employers. "This is so great, why didn't you show it to me back then?"

"Well, no offense, but I knew we were going after some of the same job opportunities. And if I'm competing against '4.0 Megan,' as we used to call you, I needed every advantage I could think of. That's why I put the whole thing together in the first place."

Megan didn't take offense, either because this had all happened so many years before, or the drinks had kicked in, but she did take away a big lesson about self-promotion. The negative effect of not promoting yourself is often invisible. If her friend hadn't shared the details of the binder, Megan would have been left with nothing but a sense that somehow, many years ago, she just had some bad luck in the post-college job search process. Megan also learned a tough lesson about the competitive nature of modern employment. We shouldn't assume that this is always a team sport because other people, even people we really like and who like us, sometimes have a competitive mind-set—especially when it comes to job opportunities, promotions, and bonuses.

....

Career climbing is not a team sport.

....

Rather than thinking that self-promotion is obnoxious, the most successful career climbers accept that it is a necessary part of managing one's livelihood. Even though success is often a team sport in the corporate world, getting the individual recognition you deserve is something you will have to drive. This means documenting or archiving samples of your work and also making sure that key leaders are aware of your individual contributions. Don't expect that the value of your work will speak for itself. And don't be afraid to "advertise" any individual recognition you receive, as long as you do it in a subtle and gracious manner.

BUILD A CAREER PERFORMANCE PORTFOLIO

Megan's story highlights the tremendous power in showing your work, not just talking about it. Creating and regularly updating a career performance portfolio should be standard practice for every career professional.

Paul Walthman is a senior executive in the automotive industry who has navigated a high-growth career through numerous ups and downs in the market. He has a four-inch "master portfolio" containing work samples, awards, reference letters, certifications, success stories (with evidence), annual performance reviews, volunteer activities, commendations, certifications, etc. From this master volume he will pull specific pages that are most relevant to his particular self-promotion objective.

"I use a few pages from this portfolio when I'm introducing myself to a new boss, which happens quite often in our business. Or when I'm interviewing, internally or externally, for a new position." First he decides on the skills and competencies he wants to highlight, then he pulls the pages from this master portfolio that provide the most compelling evidence for those skills. "I've attended numerous leadership courses over the years, and of course I include a list of those. But what really grabs their attention is my certification as an underwater search-and-rescue team leader. I include a team photo and a commendation we received from the local police chief."

Paul has each page of his master portfolio flagged with small removable notes indicating which competencies or skills the specific item relates to. For example his underwater search-and-rescue-team photo and commendation has a removable note that indicates leadership, teamwork, volunteerism, problem solving, and personal energy. This last factor—personal energy—Paul added when he turned fifty because he knew that in many situations he would be interviewing against younger men and women. And if this was the case he wanted to be able to highlight his level of fitness and stamina without talking about it overtly.

So when the time comes, he pulls the relevant pages, peels off the removable notes temporarily, and puts the pages into a folder or binder. If he's just introducing himself to a new boss he might bring a folder along with two or three pages highlighting his relevant background and accomplishments. If he's actually interviewing for a job then of course he uses more pages from his master portfolio and puts them into a leather binder.

One of the reasons that a career performance portfolio is such a powerful tool for job interviews is that employers are increasingly skeptical of the claims that job-seekers make on their résumés. Misleading information on a job-seeker's résumé ranks as one of the top recruiter pet peeves. And a career performance portfolio can address their concerns by providing evidence rather than just telling a story.

Whether you are just beginning the search for your first post-college job, or in the last decade of a long career, having a career performance portfolio should be a standard practice. Even if you don't use the portfolio for a job interview, the process of acquiring and maintaining the information can boost your career confidence. Here is a list of potential items you can include in your career performance master portfolio:

- Evidence of key/unique accomplishments/success stories/ narratives.
- Project summary reports.
- Samples of work and reports.

- Performance reviews.
- Transcripts, degrees, licenses, and certifications.
- Awards and honors, letters of recommendation, commendations, testimonials.
- Volunteering/community service.
- Professional memberships and development activities.
- Personal information and/or hobbies—LINKED TO PROFESSIONAL COMPETENCIES. (In other words, sharing a childhood photo is OK if you have a compelling story that illustrates your abilities, unique competency, etc.).

Career performance portfolios should be filled with artifacts and information that clearly show evidence of your accomplishments and career progress, and tell a story of why you are the ideal candidate for the position you are seeking. Emphasis should be on skills, abilities, accomplishments—tied directly to the stated need of the hiring company.

MASTER THE WHITEBOARD

I sat in a meeting with a group of marketing folks who were discussing the "value proposition" of this book. Because the book contains such a wide range of tips, strategies, ideas, and stories there were plenty of opinions in the room. It felt as if we had been talking in circles, everyone contributing good ideas and insight, but no one was really "nailing" the core value of the book. And then a young woman stood up and walked to the whiteboard. She was relatively new so I wasn't familiar with her. She was a marketing assistant who was there essentially to take notes for the meeting. "I'm trying to get all of this clear in my own head," she said. Then she drew this diagram, which essentially captured the thoughts of everyone in the room:

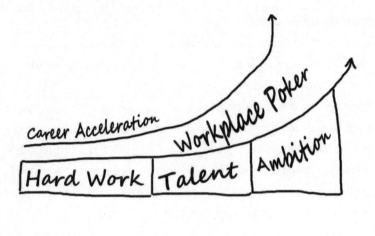

"We all want to accelerate our careers," she said. "And the foundation of our success will always be hard work, talent, and ambition. But workplace poker can help us accelerate our careers beyond that foundation, faster and higher than we would otherwise achieve."

We all sat back, pondered her drawing, looked at each other, and without a word, we all knew that she had nailed it. But what is MOST important is that in that moment, without any (apparent) effort at self-promotion, this young woman added value to the discussion and helped to move things forward in a productive manner.

If you think carefully about what she did, the self-promotion was almost invisible, yet powerful. First, just the act of standing and going to the whiteboard essentially demands the attention of everyone in the room. Then, summarizing the discussion in a visual manner lets everyone know she is actively engaged and thinking strategically, not just taking notes on all of the good ideas. We no longer saw her as "just" a marketing assistant, but as an important contributor to the discussion.

The essence of good whiteboard communication is to take a complex issue, thought process, or idea and convey the essence of your message through simple line drawings. In an age of PowerPoint and Keynote slides, YouTube videos and digital photographs, we've lost sight of the instinctual power of simple line drawings produced by hand (not animated on a screen).

But the power is there. And BECAUSE it is so rarely used, there is great potential to add this to your arsenal of self-promotion skills. Of course, like any good weapon in an arsenal, you have to be careful when you use it. If you haven't crystalized a thought in your mind, don't attempt "whiteboard brainstorming" in front of a group, unless that is their specific request.

I do a lot of random whiteboard brainstorming on my own, in private, but the process is often messy and time consuming and it would certainly not enhance my personal reputation to force others to endure this. When you are whiteboarding to enhance your professional reputation, make sure that you first have a clear message and specific visualization in your mind. Ideally you want to be talking and drawing at the same time, explaining your thought, not figuring it out while you draw. Used appropriately, whiteboarding represents a great opportunity to promote yourself, without promoting yourself.

Paul Watford was the new sales and marketing leader for a Midwest manufacturing company. At the annual all-employee meeting he was scheduled to introduce himself while also laying out his sales/marketing vision for the coming year. While he had been in the job for less than three months, his team had pulled together all of the metrics and data that were typical of these presentations in past years, along with a powerful set of PowerPoint slides to reinforce his message.

"Everything they put together was fine, exactly what you would expect," he told me a few months later. "And that was the problem. It was exactly what they expected."

So instead Paul decided that for his presentation there would be no PowerPoint slides (gasps from Marketing) and no materials for anyone to review in advance (gasps from Corporate Communications); the only thing he needed was a flip chart, several markers, and a video feed to ensure that everyone could see on the big screen what he was writing on the flipchart.

In his presentation Paul described the various business forces that were pulling the company's attention and resources in different directions. He highlighted new regulations and the systemic costs of compliance along with the need for increased investment in technology security. His ultimate point was that there would need to be a dramatic increase in new products, new markets, and enhanced sales effectiveness to overcome these increasing costs. As he spoke, Paul illustrated his presentation with this drawing:

All of the important data that his marketing team had pulled together for him made its way into the presentation, but he didn't read any of it from a slide on the screen. He knew the numbers and was able to talk about them fluently. He provided plenty of detail and metrics, writing the most important numbers on another sheet of flipchart paper. His entire presentation was low-tech, casual, almost like a conversation with a friend at the dinner table. And the feedback was interesting. Every year the company sent out a post-meeting survey, and here are some of the verbatim comments:

"Can't believe he's only been here three months. Seems to really get our business."

"First one of these presentations I actually stayed awake through."

"I've been here a long time, but he opened my eyes to some new ideas."

"Great job. He should be CEO."

Now, in terms of actual content, there was nothing dramatically new or earth shattering in Paul's presentation, but something about the way it was delivered clearly had more impact than a typical series of PowerPoint slides.

Research and common sense tell us that concepts are much more likely to be remembered if they are presented graphically (with pictures, illustrations, or drawings) rather than just verbally. This is one of the reasons why PowerPoint is so popular. But whiteboarding can have even more impact than PowerPoint.

....

When you have a key insight to communicate, whiteboard it.

....

In a recent set of experiments, Stanford University Graduate School of Business professor Zakary Tormala tested the potential effects of whiteboard visuals against more traditional PowerPoint approaches. The aim of the research was to determine whether whiteboarding can enhance presentation effectiveness.

Tormala found a statistically significant difference in favor of the whiteboard approach:

- Engagement—People pay more attention as the whiteboard drawing is created.
- Credibility—The whiteboard creator is more credited with "owning" the ideas presented.
- Recall—People are more likely to remember the content of the presentation.

This of course is not meant to imply that PowerPoint slides should never be used, just that in terms of self-promotion, whiteboarding represents a significant opportunity to differentiate yourself from your peers.

So why don't more people use whiteboarding? The act of standing up during a meeting, stepping forward, and grabbing the whiteboard marker can be pretty intimidating for some. Plus during business presentations PowerPoint is such a comfortable crutch.

We love PowerPoint because all of those bullet points keep our presentation on track. We don't have to worry about forgetting what to say next—when in doubt just click to the next slide. Even if we don't verbalize the presentation very well, we know the audience will get our point because it's all up there on the screen. But let me ask you . . . if it's all up there on the screen, what's *your* job? Are you just the slide reader?

You know how YOU react when someone delivers a presentation with a bunch of text-heavy PowerPoint slides. Part of your brain goes to sleep, you can read faster than the presenter can talk, so the presentation always seems to move too slow.

Of course whiteboarding is harder. It requires that you know your presentation end to end and that you synthesize your content into a compelling story. And that is the self-promotion opportunity. BECAUSE whiteboarding is more challenging, it will always be less common. Which makes it a big differentiator for those who do it well.

CAN'T SHAKE YOUR JONES FOR POWERPOINT?

If for some reason your business requires that you use PowerPoint during a presentation, or if you just can't break your addiction to the slides and bullet points, here are a few things you can do to make sure you don't bore your audience. You can still differentiate yourself from all of the other PowerPoint-addicted drones if you:

- Use a single high-impact image on each slide to reinforce the message you are delivering.
- Create a whiteboard-type drawing in advance and paste the image onto a slide.
- Pose a single challenging question on a slide.

If you must use text, keep it very, very short. A SYNTHESIS of your message, not the whole thing.

IF YOU WANT THEM TO KNOW—TRY TELLING THEM

While career portfolios and whiteboarding and blogging and tweeting are interesting to think about, much of the most important self-promotion activity is more basic; just telling people what you want them to know.

At the most fundamental level, we need to tell our bosses (and anyone else with influence over our career progress) what we're doing and the results we've produced. This has nothing to do with bragging or bluster. Just the facts.

A surprising percentage of supervisors (more than 60 percent according to recent surveys) really don't know the specifics of what their people are working on, and the ultimate impact of those activities. So what follows are a few specific strategies you can employ to ensure that the right people are aware of your contributions to the business.

RECOGNIZE INFORMAL SELF-PROMOTION OPPORTUNITIES

Often the most effective self-promotion opportunities are not formal presentations or meetings, but the informal day-to-day interactions. When your boss or someone else of influence asks you "What's up?" or "How are things going?" for most people the typical response is "Not much" or "Pretty good." Instead take the opportunity to say something like:

"Things are going well. We're pretty excited about the progress on

_____."

or

"Good. A lot of focus on the _____
project right now. And we're making significant progress."

or

"We're focused on _____ right now.
Do you have time for a quick question? We could use your perspective on

_____."

Use these informal moments to express your enthusiasm for the work and give a brief update regarding your latest priority or project. If it makes sense for the situation, ask the person for her perspective on some specific aspect of the project.

Don't just ask them what they think of your work. That's too obvious. Instead identify some aspect of the work that would genuinely benefit from another person's perspective. This isn't just playing the self-promotion game, this is authentically engaging with a leader to get his or her perspective knowing that this also helps to keep you on the "radar" of a busy leader.

MAXIMIZE FORMAL SELF-PROMOTION OPPORTUNITIES

Most businesses schedule regular performance reviews for each employee. Often these are annual reviews and the allocation of bonus dollars may hinge on the results. More than 70 percent of employees take a passive approach to these reviews, expecting that their manager will put most of the time and energy into preparing for the meeting. But managers may have numerous employee performance reviews to complete and often feel overwhelmed by the burden, so they put in the minimal effort necessary to complete the paperwork and move on.

Decide on your specific career advancement objective(s) prior to the meeting. Rather than just hoping the discussion goes well, you are much more likely to get the outcome you desire if you go in with something specific in mind. Perhaps you want to be included in an upcoming leadership development workshop. Or you want to achieve a specific bonus percentage. Or you want to be actively considered for an upcoming promotion opportunity. Or you want your manager to agree to assign you to "stretch" projects that will prepare you for future promotion opportunities. The bottom line is that if you don't know what your specific action objective is for the performance review, you certainly can't expect your manager to know it.

Proactive career climbers do not leave these formal performance reviews to chance or let their results depend upon the manager's capacity or commitment. At a minimum use the following checklist to prepare for any formal performance review:

- Go back to your calendar for the year and review every major event, project, task, etc. Build a list of every major task accomplished (or to which you contributed) along with a brief summary of the business impact.
- If you have been keeping up with a career performance portfolio, as advised previously, pull out any pages you created this year to highlight your most significant contributions.

- Create a brief description of your career goals with the organization, your current strengths, and also your development
  needs—those areas where you have room for improvement or
  additional learning.
- Prepare the questions you want to ask during the discussion.
  For example, even though you will share your perspective, you
  should also ask your manager for specific examples of your
  unique strengths and also your development opportunities, from
  the manager's perspective.
- Let your manager know that you take this feedback opportunity seriously and view it as an important part of your career
  progression plan. Employees who merely "check the box" and
  do the minimum required preparation tend to get the same level
  of engagement and commitment from their managers.
- If you receive an especially positive performance review, save
  the documentation and consider adding it to your career performance portfolio.

LET THEM SEE YOU SWEAT . . .

Some people make the mistake of underselling their greatest talents.
Because some unique capability comes so easily to them, they don't
understand that others (without the capability) may place an exceptional value on something they take for granted.

If you have the ability to churn out detailed financial analysis
much more quickly than others, with higher quality and deeper insight, you might naturally take a certain pride in responding with
lightning speed to every request for a financial analysis. But the un-
fortunate effect of your speed could be that those receiving your
report assume it was relatively easy for you to produce (perhaps it
was) and may tend to underappreciate the value you are contributing.

If you are an exceptionally creative marketer and a client asks you to come up with a great promotional idea for their next product, if you send them something in two hours they will inherently undervalue your work—even if your idea is amazing and hugely innovative. They will tend to think—at least subconsciously—how hard could it have been for you if you generated it in just a few hours? And if it didn't require much effort, how good could the idea really be? And even if it is really good, why should we pay you a TON of money for something that was so easy for you? Of course they will never say these things directly, but your speed may in fact create some of these perceptions.

So am I saying you should intentionally slow down when working on projects or tasks that are highly valued by your boss or client? Well . . . yes. This is a dirty little secret among some of the most talented and creative people I know in business. They have figured out that it isn't enough to have amazing ideas or produce amazing work. You have to "romance" the process and make it appear to be difficult, challenging, gut wrenching—then, when you present the client or boss or colleague with your work, it feels as if the stormy clouds have parted and a choir of angels is celebrating your awe-inspiring creation.

Of course, this has to be done within a range of reason—you have to deliver your work on time, and others should be able to depend upon you to NEVER miss a deadline. But even as the deadline approaches you can let them see you sweat.

"I will send a client an email three days before the deadline to let them know we are working furiously on their project, even if it is already completed," the owner of a creative ad agency once told me. "I want to create a vision in their mind that our whole staff is staying up late every night, determined to go the full distance for their particular project." She also says that you have to be careful about not overdoing it, because clients (and bosses) are great BS detectors.

. . . BUT DON'T LET THEM SEE YOU SWEAT

If you are in fact struggling to meet a deadline or uncertain about your ability to produce quality work, this is not the time to "romance" the process for your boss or client. This is the kind of sweating they should never see. If you are having interpersonal conflicts at work, severe enough that the boss needs to get involved, keep it calm and positive and fact-based. Again, your personal brand is not served by letting them see all of your sweaty emotions of anger and frustration.

So sometimes you make things seem more difficult and challenging than they really are, and sometimes you make them seem easier than they really are. Always with an eye to what is going to most enhance your personal brand. Yes, this is theater; yes, it is a game: yes, it probably shouldn't have to be this way—but in workplace poker, either play the game to win or don't play at all.

HELP OTHERS

If your work projects and assignments are tightly controlled by your boss, then of course your personal productivity and ability to meet/beat deadlines is important. If you are able to work more quickly than expected and have extra capacity, here is a way to ensure that you maximize the self-promotion impact of your personal productivity. You could say to your boss:

"I just wanted to let you know that I finished the ___ project ahead of schedule, so I have some extra capacity. Do you know of anyone who could use my help?"

Note that part of the key here isn't just being helpful and generous to your coworkers, but making sure that your boss knows about your extra effort, and also appreciates that the effort is focused on areas that he or she has recommended.

Even if you have a more independent work environment, before deciding to help someone on a project you should mention it to your boss. Something like:

"I'm planning to help Donna on the Mayfair project, but I wanted to run it past you first just in case there are other projects that you think should be a higher priority, or need a little extra help."

Again these should be genuine questions because you really do want the feedback, but you are also ensuring that the boss is aware of your "extra" activity. It isn't enough to just be generous with your time and energy. You have to make sure the right people know about it.

PROMOTE OTHERS

When you know that someone has done an especially good job and is perhaps uncomfortable tooting their own horn, go out of your way to toot it for them. This should be authentic and gracious, not an obvious attempt to gain recognition for yourself. But doing this can generate tremendous goodwill and also help to minimize any perception that others might have of you as a self-promoter.

If there is a project for which you have done significant work and made a genuinely positive contribution, go out of your way to mention the efforts of others on the project. Again, this needs to be in the form of genuine appreciation. But the natural impact will be to also have others highlight your own contributions.

If you go out of your way to generously highlight the good work of others, there is a natural reciprocation that often occurs. They will feel compelled to return the favor at some point.

However, occasionally you will recognize that someone in the work environment is nothing but a "recognition vampire." They suck up all possible recognition and give nothing in return. Once you recognize who these people are, never again give them even a tiny drop of your recognition blood.

It is easy to get overwhelmed by the concept of self-promotion, particularly if this is something that is not inherently comfortable for you. As you begin to put some of these ideas and thoughts into action, and as you start to see positive results, hopefully you will not only embrace the value of self-promotion but will actually come to enjoy the show. That is the most critical development—not just doing it as a necessary chore, but actually beginning to enjoy the theatrical element of your career growth. This is what will give you the maximum acceleration.

THINK NOW

- How comfortable are you with the idea that self-promotion is an important element of your career progression plan?
- How effective have you been in terms of highlighting and promoting the value of your contributions at work?
- What can you do to adjust your mind-set and "enjoy the show" by developing genuine enthusiasm for the promotional aspects of career success?
- Are there any ways in which you have suboptimized the perceived value of your ideas or other work because you have been too speedy or have appeared to produce the work too easily? What can you do about that in the future (without hurting your personal brand)?

ACT SOON

- Take every opportunity to help others at work a little more than they expect to be helped. If the opportunities don't present themselves to you, go find them.
- When you have a chance to, go out of your way to express authentic appreciation for the work of others. Make this a regular habit, not just a one-off task to be completed and forgotten.
- Ask someone you trust (spouse, partner, close friend) who has good taste and good professional judgment to give you absolutely objective feedback regarding your physical appearance (clothing, grooming, mannerisms, habits, and weight) at work. You want brutal honesty, not nicey-nice words of comfort.

- Take action on your social media presence, following the guidelines provided. This should become part of a routine for you, regularly updating and enhancing your social media presence, always with an eye to how this will impact the job you WANT, not the one you have now.
- Begin development of your career performance portfolio, and work continuously to keep it up to date.

Practice whiteboarding on your own first, then with small groups. Whenever an opportunity presents itself to summarize an idea or strategy in a visual manner, either do it on your own notepad for practice as you sit in meetings, or go ahead and step up, take the power scepter (the marker), and start drawing.

LONG-TERM THOUGHTS AND ACTION POINTS

- Many of us are uncomfortable with the idea of conscious self-promotion.

- But in today's hypercompetitive world, you have to make sure that the right people know about all of your good work.

- You can promote yourself without appearing to be a self-promoter.

- Don't assume that your career climb is a team sport. Even people who are your "friends" at work sometimes have a competitive mind-set.

- Build a career performance portfolio and keep it current as your career progresses.

- Master the whiteboard to highlight your best ideas and contributions.

- All social media is part of your professional image. Scrub up, then scale up.

- If you want people to know about your abilities and contributions, find gracious and subtle ways to tell them during informal conversations.

- Maximize the impact of your formal performance reviews by being exceptionally well prepared. Don't expect your manager to do the heavy lifting, that's part of your job.

- Help and promote the work of others.

- Never ignore the fact that your physical appearance is a BIG factor in the way people judge your competency. This may not be fair, but it is true nevertheless.

7

Likable and Lucky Charmers

♦

You know what charm is: a way of getting the answer yes without having asked any clear question.

—ALBERT CAMUS

Being likable isn't the same as wanting to be liked. Trying too hard or wanting too much to be liked can be especially unlikable. Being charming isn't the same as being witty or funny or outgoing. In fact, some of the most charming people are relatively quiet and even shy.

This is a bit of a paradox because truly charming people may care about others and have empathy for others, but they do not put a lot of energy into worrying about what others think of them. This doesn't mean they are oblivious to how others perceive them. They are very much aware of those who like them, and those who may not, but none of this causes them any angst.

Much like pornography, charm and likability may be hard to define, but most of us know it when we experience it.

"I'm likable enough," she said.

I was leading a workshop on productive coworker relationships and the group was discussing the benefits of having a pleasant personality. The topic of self-awareness had just come up and I had asked each participant to rate their own likability on this scale of 1 to 5:

5. Exceptionally likable to all humans on the planet.
4. Very likable to most people at work.
3. Likable enough to do my job effectively.
2. Not especially likable, but pets let me feed them.
1. Humans (and pets) avoid me at all cost.

In my experience most people rate themselves either a 3 or 4 on this (admittedly tongue-in-cheek) scale. When the young lady in the workshop characterized herself as "likable enough" I couldn't help but notice the smirks and rolling eyes of some of her coworkers—those who give themselves a 3 are usually closer to a 2.5, or lower.

If you are perfectly happy with your current career progress and your likely prospects for future growth, then being somewhere between "very likable" and "likable enough" is perfectly fine. Perhaps you're thinking "It depends on who I'm with. For some people I'm a 4.5, and for others, not so much." Which again is perfectly fine if you are happy with the career status quo.

But I am assuming you are reading this because you would like to accelerate your career potential, and if that's the case then I'm sorry, but a 4 just isn't enough. Being "very likable to most people at work" isn't going to drive your career beyond average growth.

Do you remember Tony from San Diego, who we introduced at the beginning of this book? One of the things I mentioned about Tony is that I always thought I was one of his favorite people in the office, but later learned that a lot of other people felt the same way. Tony wasn't just likable, he was exceptionally charming and fun and a joy to be around. And not just to a few people. Literally everyone liked Tony.

Tony didn't play office politics, at least not overtly. Sure, he knew all the workplace drama—who was mad at whom, who was sleeping with whom, who could be trusted and who couldn't, who was competent and who wasn't—but he rarely had something bad to say about anyone. He just seemed to instinctively focus on the positive. He could get angry and frustrated, but would quickly apologize if he lashed out at anyone in particular. He could be wickedly funny, but knew when to temper the humor. And of course he was great at his job, so he wasn't just an empty suit. We all knew that we could depend on him to do the work that was expected, so his upbeat spirit and humor and kindness were just a bonus.

So Tony set the "likability" bar pretty high for me personally, and I definitely saw the value of his warm attitude toward people. But for me it was never as simple as just deciding to be more pleasant at work.

....

Be somebody who makes everyone feel like somebody.

....

I'm not naturally outgoing, extraverted, or funny, especially at the office. I've been told that people used to assume I was always working on some big problem in my head because of my furrowed brow and the slightly pained expression on my face. And I can get easily bored by a conversation, letting my mind drift away to more interesting things while the other person drones on. Eventually they notice and of course this annoys them. Some have said that I'm not very approachable and not good at small talk. Plus I'm horrible at remembering names—Tony was great at remembering names and regularly used everyone's first name, like "Hey, Beth, how's your afternoon going?" or "Charlie, could you follow up on the weekly metrics report?" or "Dan, sorry we missed you last night, hope you can make it next time." You get the idea. Goddamn friendly bastard.

I saw firsthand how Tony's personal warmth and likability enhanced his career. Plus, in addition to seeing the tangible value of being more charming at work, over the years I've also noticed something strange and unexplainable—the truly charming people are not just more pleasant to work with, they actually seem to be luckier than the rest of us. I'm not kidding about this, there seems to be some sort of metaphysical relationship between personal charm and good fortune. Of course maybe when we are nicer to people they are nicer to us, and this sometimes looks like good luck.

This is not to say that abrasive people never succeed, of course they do, especially if they have uncommon talent or unique knowledge that helps the business. Steve Jobs and Anna Wintour could be jerks and still succeed because they had unique talent and insight. But the vast majority of people who think that they have some fantastically rare ability, which means they don't need to be warm and pleasant with others, are fooling themselves.

....

Start liking people, a lot. Most of them will like you right back, even more.

....

"I'm not what you would call a people person. In fact, whatever is the total opposite of a people person, I'm that, only less friendly," said Herb Luttrell, the CEO of PlayerTrak Systems, a casino industry marketing firm. He and I were having a get-acquainted lunch prior to a strategic planning session with his entire management team. I had been hired to facilitate the meeting and was hoping to get a sense of Herb's leadership style before we started. I tried to ask a few thought-provoking questions as he ate his lunch quickly, answered my questions with efficient grunts and terse comments, then stood up to leave as soon as he was finished eating.

Definitely not a people person.

What was supposed to be an afternoon of give-and-take discussion about the future of the company and changing dynamics in the casino gaming industry turned out to be a series of mini-lectures from Herb. He dominated every discussion and while everyone on his team put on a happy face, it was clear to me there wasn't much love in the room.

Herb had hired me to facilitate an engaged back-and-forth discussion among his team members, but every time I tried to draw one of them out, if they said anything that contradicted Herb's point of view a quick intense debate ensued, and Herb always won.

"He's not a genius, but he's pretty damn smart," the PlayerTrak marketing director told me days later during a private chat. "He gets away with being such an ass because he knows this business top to bottom, better than anyone else. He has more industry contacts than anyone I know, and he can read a casino metrics report and see things the rest of us just can't. And he gets results."

Sure enough, PlayerTrak had grown by more than 8 percent every quarter since Herb had been hired as the CEO two years before. When you can grow a company by more than 30 percent annually, year after year, people will forgive a little personal abrasiveness. In Herb's case, it was a LOT of abrasiveness.

Even the board members who hired him were sometimes put off by Herb's lack of civility. "When we interviewed him, it was clear that he was a master of data, and not especially personable," a board member told me. "But he was at least polite and somewhat friendly." After Herb was hired, much of his "polite and somewhat friendly" demeanor faded away.

"We lost some good people in the first six months of Herb's tenure here," another board member told me. But the board knew Herb was intensely focused on turning the company around and that might create some tension. By the time he began showing actual growth results, everyone who was still working there had become accustomed to his tough personality, and no one wanted to rock the boat.

If you are fantastically talented, and able to produce exceptional results, of course people will forgive (or at least tolerate) a lack of personal grace. But that also puts a huge amount of pressure on the graceless person to keep performing, because no one will tolerate an abrasive jerk if he or she is unproductive and ineffective.

A year later I received an email from PlayerTrak's marketing director, asking me to schedule another annual planning meeting. When I asked for an update on the business I got a terse response: "Growth stalled last two quarters. Herb's gone."

It turns out that once Herb was no longer producing stellar growth numbers, the board members weren't willing to tolerate his personality (or lack thereof). "It actually got worse as the growth slowed," a board member later told me. "Under a lot of pressure, he became more rude, even abusive. And he started making decisions without informing us, then screaming that we were getting in his way. Ultimately the board had no choice but to let him go."

Because I am intensely curious about situations like this, I followed up with Herb Luttrell a few months later and asked him to have lunch with me. I was actually surprised when he agreed. "Not much else going on," he said with a little edge in his voice. "As you obviously know."

But before I get to the details of my lunch with Herb, a few thoughts on the value, perhaps even the necessity, of personal charm in our day-to-day business lives. Some people seem to be born with the innate ability to connect with others and build strong, deep bonds very quickly. Others, like Herb, have virtually no natural capacity to muster up even the most basic level of human-to-human kindness. Most of us fall somewhere between these two extremes, but we can definitely learn new skills and techniques to improve our charm quotient.

Because true charm is becoming more rare in today's workplace, there is a greater potential to differentiate yourself based upon your exceptional people skills and habits.

WARNING—As we start to focus on specific skills and techniques, nothing is less charming than someone trying too hard to be charming. If you've ever experienced a colleague trying too hard to "work you" to gain your trust and confidence, you know how off-putting this can be. That's not to say that truly likable people aren't working at it, because many of them are. But they do so in a way that doesn't feel like they're trying. So try harder to be likable, but don't *look* like you're trying. Got that?

How do you really feel about people? This is a question you should probably ask yourself and think carefully about your answer. More specifically, how do you really feel about the people you work with? If, in general, you are annoyed or frustrated by people, or if you don't trust people, or have any other sort of negative judgment as your baseline reaction to most people, then you are going to have a tougher time beefing up your charm quotient. It can still be done, but you'll have better results if you ease up on your negative judgments of others.

> ### It is possible to clearly see the flaws in others without judging them harshly.

One of the common characteristics in exceptionally charming people is that they see the rest of us, they REALLY see us, and we often have a sense that they see our flaws as well as our good qualities. And yet they still like us, still find us interesting, still want to spend time with us. This unique perspective—seeing flaws without judging them harshly—is a fundamental element of the truly charming person.

In many ways charm is really simple. It is the art of letting people know that you feel good about them, without embarrassing them or asking anything of them in return. Whether you are a CEO of a major corporation or just starting your first job out of college, your personal warmth toward others can serve you well. It will not only enhance the likelihood of career progress, but will make the journey more pleasant for yourself and others.

Is there someone in your professional or personal life you would view as being particularly charming, not just when interacting with you but with a broad range of other people as well? Just observing these people a little more carefully can be instructive. Have you noticed how they always make direct eye contact when speaking with you? Not in a creepy stare-you-down way, but when they engage with you, they REALLY engage with you. There is no sense of distraction or thinking about something else while talking to you.

So if you are focused on enhancing your own level of personal warmth and charm as you deal with others, first see them without judgment, then engage fully, without distraction.

Full engagement means when you talk to them, let everything else go for that brief moment in time. If you are so distracted by something on your mind that you can't fully engage with the other person, then at least apologize. "I'm sorry to seem so distracted. I have a few challenges that are occupying my mind, and it's hard to let them go." Even if you continue the conversation from that point, at least you've been polite enough to acknowledge your less-than-complete engagement.

....

To accept the flaws of others, you must embrace your own.

....

Charming people typically have a degree of humility and comfort with their own flaws. Not the humility of embarrassment or shame, but instead a sort of humble confidence. If you are caught up in your own insecurities and uncertainties, you cannot possibly give someone else the honest and objective respect they deserve.

This is all easier said than done of course. We are asking you to respect others in spite of their flaws, to embrace your own flaws with humility, and to engage with others fully without distraction. If this isn't already part of your natural thought process, it's going to take some time, some deep reflection, and a serious commitment from you to make the transition. And you'll probably catch yourself occasionally drifting backward into harsh judgments of others or yourself. When you do, don't beat yourself up. Just take a deep breath, smile, let it go, and get on with your progress.

SMILE. LAUGH. GUFFAW. CHORTLE.

Charming people may not tell jokes, but they certainly make us smile and laugh. So if your goal is to become more charming you need to enhance your ability to make others laugh. This may be difficult, because you either have the natural gift of light humor, or you don't. If you have it, you almost certainly know it. And if you're wondering, "Am I naturally funny?" well then, I think you have your answer. Which doesn't mean you can't develop a greater capacity for humor, but you have to be careful. Giving comedy tips to the humor-challenged is like handing a loaded shotgun to a six-year-old. Shots may be fired, chaos may occur, and unintended damage may result.

But there is so much power in a lighthearted humorous touch that it is worth the risk to try to develop it, or to enhance the natural capacity for humor that you already possess. You already know that making people smile or laugh (or just grin a little) puts them at ease and creates an atmosphere more conducive to productive discussion and agreement. The difficulty for many humor-challenged people is that they may want to be wittier and more charming, but their social shyness and nervousness make them tend to fumble, stumble, act awkward, etc. When they try too hard to be funny, it can be kind of pathetic and cringe-inducing.

So rather than pressure yourself to try to be something you're not, just focus on being confident, relaxed, and genuinely interested in other people. Your innate charm and wit will show naturally. The three broad guidelines you should follow are:

- Poke fun at yourself, not other people.
- Keep it clean. Very, VERY clean. Squeaky. Sparkling.
- Make light of situations and circumstances, not individuals (except yourself).

When I told my wife that I was planning to include a few tips on humor in this chapter of the book, she asked me if I would be using a ghostwriter.

See what I did there? Comedy gold.

Bob Monroe is a midlevel manager for an oil field services company based in Dallas, with field operations in Texas, North Dakota, and Alberta, Canada. He is by nature a thoughtful, serious, studious man. Very task-oriented and fact-based in his decision making. In the past some of his direct reports have referred to him as "Bloodless Bob" because he seemed to be devoid of emotion, with a thick, dark beard, making it even harder to read his facial expressions. Bob was being considered for a senior leadership position in the company, and they asked him to complete an executive coaching program as part of his preparation for the role.

"Honestly, I was a little put off at first," he says. "I know how to lead people and thought it was a waste of time and money to go through this. But I figured that I had to play the game in order to be considered for senior leadership, so I played."

Before the formal coaching began, Bob was asked to complete

several psychological profile tests, and his coach also asked for telephone interviews with some of Bob's peers, some of his direct reports, and also a few personal friends and family members. Bob had no idea why the executive coach would want to interview his friends or family, but he complied and provided the contact information. By the time the actual executive coaching sessions started, Bob was getting impatient and anxious for the process to be finished.

"The people who know you personally seem to think you are fun to be with, amusing, you laugh a lot, and there is even a rumor that you play the accordion," his coach mentioned during their first session.

"Only after a few beers," Bob replied with a smile.

"Does anyone at work know you play the accordion?"

"No, why would they?"

"Well, I think the deeper question we are going to try to answer is, why *don't* they?"

Bob's executive coach met with him every two weeks for the next three months, and during every conversation they returned to the topic of Bob's two personalities. "Work Bob" was serious and flat and hard for people to read. "Family and Friend Bob" was relaxed, fun, easy to talk to. The coach was hoping to help Bob bring some of his relaxed and friendly personality into the workplace, but this turned out to be easier said than done.

"I don't want to fake it," Bob said.

"Fake what?"

"You know. I don't want to pretend to be someone I'm not at work."

"So when you are friendly and easygoing with your friends, are you faking it?"

"No, of course not."

"So if you were more friendly and easygoing at work, why would that be faking it?"

"Because that's not how I feel at work."

Ultimately they came to an understanding that Bob's emotional state at work (serious, stern, flat) was a reaction to stress and uncertainty. Bob had always been an ambitious, hardworking, and conscientious person at work, and it had never occurred to him that he might benefit from easing up a bit. Plus he didn't think people would take him seriously if he was "all jokey and casual," as Bob put it.

The executive coach encouraged Bob to bring some of his lighter, friendlier side to the office. Not by making any big dramatic change, but in baby steps. Bob tried a little harder to have light banter at the beginning of staff meetings rather than immediately plow into the agenda. He even managed a little bit of humor. "My executive coach had recommended that I show a little more emotion at work," he told his staff at the start of a meeting. "I told him that I only have two emotions, frustration and disappointment—so I'll let you guys decide which one you want me to share more of today." After a nervous moment, they got it. It turns out that Bob is actually pretty funny, with a dry sense of humor, and he's become quite comfortable poking fun at himself.

But what we are describing here in a few pages actually took many months and long conversations for Bob. He had to develop a greater awareness of what his *lack* of humor and positive emotion was costing him in the workplace. And then he had to do something about it.

"I didn't put any pressure on myself to be suddenly funny or charming or whatever," he says. "I just relaxed, reminded myself how much I really like the people I work with, and how much it helps if we can have a laugh together every now and then."

....

Lack of fundamental courtesy and respect is a charm killer.

....

Bob eventually came to realize there were numerous small ways in which he was showing disrespect to the people who worked with him and for him. It took the executive coach to help him see that some of his typical behavior patterns at work were putting up barriers between himself and others—and more importantly, the coach helped him to see how those barriers made him comfortable. If people were hesitant to talk to him, they weren't likely to share problems unless they also had a solution. If people tended to leave him alone, he had more time and energy to focus on projects and tasks. Bob came to realize that he had actually created these barriers to relieve his own stress and anxiety.

One of his behaviors included showing up to meetings exactly on time (or a little late) and immediately getting down to business without any social chitchat. And always having a full agenda so the pace of the meetings always had to be fast. When the executive coach asked him how his wife would react if this was the way things went at the dinner table—if he always showed up a few minutes late and rushed in order to eat "efficiently" at every meal—it helped Bob to see that his overfocus on meeting efficiency was actually perceived as rudeness.

Bob also worked harder at truly seeking out the opinions of others. Even when he was absolutely certain about the rightness of his own opinion, he developed the habit of first asking others for their perspective, then listening to what they had to say before expressing his own viewpoint. He stopped speaking over people, interrupting and cutting them off midsentence. "A bad habit," he admits. "I never used to be that way, but I acquired it over the years."

Bob still remembers the stunned expression on some faces the first time in a business meeting he said to someone, "I have a different perspective, but I can understand how you might have come to a different conclusion. So let's talk this through a little more." He was sure some of them were wondering if this was some sort of trap, until they got used to the new Bob.

Essentially what Bob learned (or had to relearn) was to treat *everyone* with fundamental courtesy, politeness, and kindness. There will always be some people in the workplace with whom you do not have natural rapport. There may even be people you actively dislike. Go out of your way to be especially respectful to these people. Not necessarily because they deserve it, but because others will notice your good manners. They will especially notice it when you are polite and gracious when dealing with difficult (or impossible) people.

BE COMFORTABLY CONFIDENT

This is not about being the blustery hyper-confident alpha dog in the room. In fact few things are less charming than this type of confidence. A comfortable confidence comes from someone who is simply at ease with themselves. Not intimidated by others, and not intimidating to others.

I saw a great example of this recently on a flight from Boston to Seattle. I had an aisle seat, and on the other side of the aisle sat a man with the classic CEO look: Brooks Brothers dark suit, French cuffs, polished black oxfords, close-cropped gray hair, wire-rimmed reading glasses. He was deeply engrossed, making notes on a report of some kind as he read through it, and somewhat annoyed when a young man boarded the flight and took the window seat next to him. The younger guy couldn't have looked more different: jeans, T-shirt, canvas knapsack. As the flight took off I fully expected the CEO to stay focused on the report he was reading, but I heard the young man ask him a question.

"Are you from Boston?"

"No. Seattle. On my way home," the CEO said without looking away from his report.

Now at this point most people would have decided to leave the CEO alone to let him keep reading his incredibly important report. Even I was a little intimidated by him, and I was seated across the aisle.

"I'm Peter," the young man said, smiling and extending his hand.

"Doug," said the CEO, shaking the younger man's hand, still not making eye contact.

"I promise not to bother you," Peter said, glancing at the report in Doug's lap. "You've obviously got a lot of work to do." The younger man was warm and friendly, clearly not intimidated by the CEO, but also not interested in being a pest. The CEO spent a few more minutes focused on his report, then took off his reading glasses and rubbed his eyes.

"Are you from Boston?" the CEO asked.

"Yeah, but I'm moving to Seattle for a job."

"Must be quite a job."

"Yeah, Microsoft. Programmer."

"Good for you."

There were a few more minutes of silence before Peter asked, "Doug, what do you do for a living?"

Yes, it was rude of me to eavesdrop. But there was so much magic within that one question. It was casual, conversational, and he used Doug's first name. In the conversation that followed, Peter showed genuine curiosity about Doug's work in commercial finance, asked great follow-up questions, and had no agenda other than finding out more about someone he found interesting. This young man was genuinely warm and charming, and for the next couple of hours these two, who couldn't have been more different, enjoyed a wide-ranging conversation.

As we were told to put our tray tables up and prepare to land, I heard Peter make a comment. "There's going to come a time in my life when I need to wear a suit, and when I do, I want to look just like that," he said, motioning to Doug's suit. "Where should I go?"

Doug laughed out loud and agreed to give Peter the name of his tailor. And what flashed through my mind was a vision of what would have happened if I had sat next to the CEO. I would have been a bit intimidated, wouldn't have made any effort to engage with him, and we would both be sitting in silence as the plane landed.

And I know it's not just me. How many times have you missed out on great conversations and connections because you just didn't bother to break through the initial barrier? Truly charming people seem to do this instinctively, but most of us, myself included, have to remind ourselves and work at it a little more consciously.

THE BOSS WHISPERER

Bill McElroy had a serious problem, and it could cost him serious money. He was a senior account manager for a boutique advertising agency in Manhattan, and his biggest client was unhappy. The creative work for their upcoming ad campaign had just been presented to the client and their marketing director asked Bill, "What the hell happened here?" Bill had managed this account for over two years and the client had always been very pleased with the agency's creative work, but not this time. And what made it worse was that Bill wasn't really surprised by their reaction. He had predicted it.

Sheila Kushtana, the ad agency founder and creative director, had assigned a new designer to the project over Bill's protestations. "This will be his first project for us, and I don't want to risk my best client," Bill had told her. "They like the designer they've always worked with, he really gets them, so let's just stay with what we know works."

Sheila was firm in her decision. "We just hired this guy from one of the biggest agencies in New York, and I need to get him working on some projects. He'll be fine, I know change is hard, but your client will love his work, I promise." Bill had learned to not argue with Sheila when she spoke with her impatient, declarative tone—this always indicated there was no room for discussion. And if someone made the mistake of thinking they could or should offer an alternative viewpoint, she was quick to cut them off at the knees. Occasionally she was quick to show them the door.

"Sheila has spoken" was the phrase used throughout the agency to indicate there was no point in any further debate or discussion.

When Bill came back from the client meeting he went directly to Sheila's office and gave her the bad news. "They hated it, and if they don't get a new concept and campaign they like by this Friday, they're going to talk to other agencies about the project." Bill tried to minimize the I-told-you-so tone in his voice, and he expected Sheila to be at least a bit contrite and reassign the previous designer to make things right. Instead, she was annoyed at Bill, and put the blame on his shoulders.

"The design work is fine. I reviewed it all myself before we released it to the client. Clearly you didn't sell the concept. What you need to do is rethink your whole approach, go back and sell this to the client. If you can't do it, I will."

Sheila had spoken.

Bill knew the client well enough to be certain that if he went back and tried to persuade them that the original design work was in fact great for them, he would lose the project, and the $20,000 commission. He also knew that if Sheila showed up and tried to sell the client, he would lose the account permanently along with almost half of his annual income.

He had no idea what he was going to do. He left the office and walked a few blocks to the nearest Starbucks. Sitting in a corner nursing his coffee, Bill thought through all of his options, and none of them were good. Mostly he felt the urge to walk into Sheila's office and quit, then march down the street to another ad agency, but he had spent years building his client base, and starting over again didn't appeal to him at all. He rubbed his eyes, feeling a headache coming on.

"How's it going, Bill?"

He looked up, caught off guard, to see one of the other account managers, Sonya Thorpe, and he waved her away. "Not a good day, Sonya, probably best to just leave me alone." But Sonya sat down at his table with an expression of genuine concern.

"What's going on?

"There's no point in even talking about it," Bill replied. He really just wanted to be left alone, but Sonya had always been decent to him and he didn't want to be rude to her. She was one of the few people in the office who seemed genuinely kind and funny and interested in the success of others. She wasn't gossipy, wasn't competitive, wasn't jealous when she heard about another account manager's big win. She was great at her job, always friendly, happily married with two kids, and a decent human being. Right at this moment, Bill found himself hating her.

"I have to admit, you look pretty down in it, whatever it is. And I was just going to walk past and pretend I didn't see you," she said. "But I didn't."

"You should have."

"But I didn't," she repeated. "So what's going on?"

Sonya had always been the kind of person that people open up to, and sure enough Bill spilled out the whole story. He was hoping for some sympathy, or at least a little bit of righteous indignation toward Sheila who was clearly at fault for creating this whole situation. Instead Sonya listened carefully, nodded as he spoke, then smiled as she said, "You're screwed."

They walked back to the office together, and Sonya asked to see the designer's work that the client had criticized so harshly. Again, Bill was hoping for some validation, with Sonya acknowledging that the work was clearly inferior and unacceptable. Instead she said, "Well, maybe not the best I've ever seen, but there's potential here." Then she asked, "Do you mind if I talk to Sheila about this?"

Later that day Sonya met with Sheila, and Bill never found out exactly what was said. But the next morning he was called into a meeting with Sheila, the new graphic designer, and the designer who had worked on the client's previous agency projects. "We're going to put our heads together and make some adjustments," she said. "We're going to incorporate some of the new concepts but also pull in some of the old elements that we know the client is fond of." They worked throughout the morning until the design package felt like something Bill could confidently deliver to the client. By lunchtime Bill was actually feeling good about the whole process, though still confused about Sheila's turnaround. Then she dropped a bomb on him.

"I'd like to be there when you present this to the client," Sheila said, and Bill's heart immediately sank, imagining her reaction if the client offered any push-back at all. She noticed his pained expression and smiled. "All I want to do is to open with an apology. I'll take full responsibility for our misfire the first time, then I'll turn it over to you and shut up." She reached out to put a hand on Bill's shoulder and look him straight in the eye. "I promise I won't mess this up for you."

Weeks later Bill mentioned this turn of events to a colleague, who replied, "Yeah, when we need to get Sheila to do something, or to change her mind, we ask Sonya for help. We call her the boss whisperer."

Sonya didn't have any particular method or inside track regarding her boss Sheila. Instead, she simply had a way of communicating and talking through challenges that Sheila found to be productive, positive, and sometimes even enjoyable. Sheila was just as harsh and tough with Sonya as she was with anyone else. But instead of being intimidated or frustrated, Sonya was able to relax and smile and continue the dialogue. It helped that Sonya had great respect for her boss and the agency she had built almost single-handedly, and her calm confidence in the face of Sheila's "I have spoken" demeanor seemed to work wonders.

Sonya was charming and likable and exceptionally persuasive because Sheila liked her and enjoyed their conversations. Even their arguments were enjoyable. So Sonya had no specific persuasion techniques—she had a connection. That is probably the core definition of charm.

SHOW GENUINE INTEREST IN OTHERS

Even if you have a healthy ego, even if you are in fact the smartest person in the room, even if the life you live is vastly more interesting than the mundane existence of everyone else on the planet—you will still be much better off, from a career advancement standpoint, if you show more interest in others than in yourself. Nobody likes a showoff or a braggart who is only concerned about getting everyone to pay attention to him.

One of the most powerful ways to show respect for others is to show genuine interest in them. By asking questions about their thoughts and ideas, their life experiences, their opinions, you show them how much you truly respect them.

Sonya had a unique way of responding to "Sheila has spoken" moments when others tended to sit in stunned silence. Sonya would almost always ask follow-up questions like:

- "Can you walk me through your thought process? I'd like to learn from it."
- "I know you're basing this on your instincts and experience, can you share some of that with us?"

Just to be clear, Sonya was asking questions like these because she REALLY wanted to know the answers. But these questions also told Sheila how much Sonya respected her thoughts and per-spective, which of course helped to create a strong rapport between the two.

When you really want to let someone know that you are truly interested in what they have to say, always find a way to ask two or three follow-up questions that build upon what the person has just said. These questions actually pull the person more deeply into the conversation and let them know that you're truly listening.

Journalists use this technique often when they want an interview subject to open up more fully. They will ask questions that start like:

- Tell me more about how you . . .
- What was your reaction to that . . .
- How did you feel about that . . .

You get the idea. Sonya's use of follow-up questions helped drive many of their conversations deeper. Some people in the office were surprised at how much Sheila had opened up to Sonya, sharing stories of her past, the problems she had overcome in building the agency, even some of the tough things she had experienced in her childhood.

Another reason that Sheila had shared so many professional and personal details was that Sonya went first, talking about her own challenges and struggles. If you are willing (at an appropriate place and time) to share with others a little information that makes you vulnerable and human, they will be much more willing to share the same sort of information with you. Essentially you can "prime the pump" by sharing personal information (again, at an appropriate place and time) and then showing real interest (with follow-up questions) when the other person reciprocates.

IF YOU WANT SOMETHING, ASK DIRECTLY

We've said that one of the keys to charm and likability is showing genuine interest in others without wanting anything in return, and this is very true (or we wouldn't have said it). But of course there are going to be times when you do in fact want or need something.

And when charming people want or need something from others, they don't beat around the bush. Because they know that nothing is more frustrating or disrespectful than having someone try to "work" you to get something, without being upfront about what it is they want.

This doesn't necessarily mean that you should be harsh or abrupt or rude about it, of course not. But if you want something, let the other person know what you want. Directly. Respectfully. And if you can (genuinely) frame it in mutually beneficial terms that is even better. But don't try to stretch the win/win thing. Sometimes the truth is that we want something and it isn't win/win. We just want it or need it. And the most gracious and charming thing we can do is ask for it directly.

When Sonya approached Sheila to talk to her about Bill's situation, she didn't tip-toe. She started with "I'm worried about Bill, I have a proposal, and I'd like you to hear me out." She was direct, respectful, and straightforward. And Sheila initially said no, which Sonya fully expected. So she asked follow-up questions and gained a better understanding of Sheila's thought process.

"I was trying to help Bill get stronger," Sheila said.

"I understand that, but right or wrong, if we lose this client, Bill is going to blame you. And that's not going to be good for him, for you, or for the business," Sonya said to Sheila. "You've always taught me to put ego aside and do what's best for the business."

Sheila couldn't help but smile because . . . Sonya had spoken.

Sonya's ability to persuade Sheila was clearly based upon her personal charm and likability—her confident humility, respect, humor, and genuine interest in others. And you can become a "boss whisperer" yourself, although this will take an exceptional commitment of time and mental energy. To make a strong personal connection with a boss and develop the ability to charm/persuade them when necessary:

Study the Business: Your depth of knowledge regarding the business has to go much deeper than what is required just to do your job. You will need to become a continuous and never-ending student of the business. Understand every department, every function, the competitive market dynamics, how the business succeeds, and the threats to business growth/stability. Your colleagues in the business can help, but do not expect your boss to be the source of this information, you will only engage in discussion after you are able to ask well-informed questions (see below).

Understand the Boss Bubble: Because they have power over others in the workplace, every boss operates within a "bubble" that tends to diminish the accuracy and authenticity of the information which makes its way to them. Many people will try to make sure the boss doesn't hear "bad news" even if this is information the boss needs to make effective business decisions. Many people will celebrate the boss's ideas and actions even if they don't actually support them. They will laugh at the boss's jokes even if they aren't especially funny. Your goal isn't to judge the bubble but to study it for your particular organization. Make sure you understand how well insulated the boss is, or isn't.

Study the Boss: Observe carefully how the boss interacts with others, how the boss prefers to absorb information—some want verbal highlights, some want detailed data in written form, some want time to read in private, some want to discuss openly with groups. And some want a combination of these, or something else entirely. Study how your boss takes information in, and then study how he or she delivers information to others. Also observe to determine just how competent your boss really is, how well informed, how effective. Is there anyone else in the business who has a great relationship with the boss? What can you observe about their interactions with that person? Notice any pet peeves the boss may have. Again, your goal isn't to judge but to gain a deeper awareness.

Ask Smart Questions: Based on your study of the business and observations of the boss, you should be in a position to occasionally ask smart questions that subtly communicate to the boss that your depth of knowledge goes deeper than expected. For example, "I read your letter to the shareholders in our annual report and wondered what we're doing now to address some of the strategic threats you mentioned?" A question like this, asked at the right place and time, gives the boss a chance to talk about something he or she has probably been thinking a lot about, and also lets them know a lot about you. Another example would be: "I've noticed that our competitors are investing a lot of resources into new technologies. Is that something we are considering? Or do you have a different perspective?" When you frame the question this way, you aren't implying that the competitors are doing something better, just giving the boss a chance to talk about his or her thought process.

Create Unexpected Value: You have to do great work in your assigned area of responsibility, that much is a given. But you should try to find other areas in which you can create value for the business, or value specifically for the boss. If a leader mentions that she wishes that she could get more feedback from customers, you might find a way to connect with a few customers and get feedback for her. If a leader expresses frustration that during the monthly Q&A sessions with employees, no one asks the tough questions that people are really wondering about, next time you could ask such a question (carefully, not too tough). Every situation and career are unique, but you can always find ways to create unexpected value that will be noticed and appreciated by the boss.

Align Your Communication Style with That of the Boss: After you have spent time observing the boss's behavior, you should have a strong sense of his or her typical communication style. Some people speak very directly, even bluntly, making quick points and expecting quick responses in return. Others tend to ramble in a friendly give-and-take conversational style, and might actually be put off by someone who is too abrupt. Some use lots of data and others tell a lot of anecdotal stories. Some leaders are exceptionally polite and proper, with an excellent vocabulary and perfect diction. Some frequently spout off malapropisms and others swear like sailors. You don't have to copy the boss's communication style, but you should know it and align with it in a way that feels natural.

Diminish the Natural Tension: There is always going to be a natural tension between someone with power and the person over whom they have the power. And typically that tension makes *both* individuals a little uncomfortable. Yes, you are probably more uncomfortable with the natural tension than your boss might be, but just be aware that the discomfort on his or her part is there. And when you can find natural, appropriate ways to diminish the tension (it will never go away completely) you will find that the boss very much appreciates it. This may mean finding opportunities for humorous commentary during meetings. It may mean engaging with the boss during after-hours work events. This very much depends upon the boss's individual personality, but your objective is simply to find ways to help the boss become more comfortable with you.

Be Sensitive to Colleagues: As you develop a stronger working relationship with your boss it is not uncommon for other employees to take notice, and some will be put off, maybe even a bit jealous. It is important that you are sensitive to the perceptions of others and not create the impression that you somehow have special access to the boss or special privileges or special knowledge. Even if in fact you do have some of these things, you should work to minimize the problematic perception of other employees. Do not boast about your conversations with the boss, do not adopt an air of informality around the boss when others feel the pressure to remain formal. If a boss notices that others perceive you to be "favored" in any way, many bosses will immediately stop any conversations or activities that contributed to the perception, and your boss-whispering days are over.

Know When NOT to Engage: There are going to be issues and circumstances that you simply should not address with the boss, no matter how strong your working relationship may be. In other words, you always have to know your place. Business leaders often have to balance issues of confidentiality and legal compliance with the desire to be open and transparent. In addition, anything related to personnel tends to be sensitive, so if two other employees are having a conflict in the workplace, don't assume that it is your place to try to resolve it with the boss.

Help the Boss Win: Once you have a better understanding of your boss, you should be aware of his or her own career goals, and other things they want to accomplish in the workplace. Sometimes there may even be non-work-related goals that you can help with. If the boss mentions that he has always struggled with learning golf, and you know of a truly great golf instructor, you can certainly mention this. At work, if you know that the boss has specific goals, or just a general desire to look good to his or her own boss, anything you can do to help will certainly be appreciated.

All of these suggestions should be implemented with the charm and pleasant demeanor we have been discussing in this chapter. It should never feel—to you, to your boss, or to others—like you are "working" the boss. Any whiff of this, and the whole process will shut down quickly.

IF HERB CAN DO IT, YOU CAN TOO

So Herb agreed to meet me for lunch. And I fully expected it to be a short, somewhat uncomfortable experience similar to our previous lunch. But instead of being harsh and abrupt and overly opinionated, Herb was actually . . . nice. I might even venture to say that he was kind. And funny. Really.

"I've spent a lot of time thinking about my career. I have maybe ten more good years in me as far as work is concerned, and I want to spend those ten years as wisely as possible."

Herb said that he had spent most of his career just working as hard as he possibly could, pushing himself hard, and others harder. The CEO position at PlayerTrak was his ultimate dream and he had been determined to make it a success.

"Unfortunately I was so determined that my inner demons got

the best of me," he said. "And ironically, all of that drive and push to succeed, that's what did me in." Herb mentioned that he was soon going to be traveling to work on a consulting assignment for a casino in Macau, China. He had been studying the social etiquette of China and even trying to learn a bit of Mandarin.

"Herb Luttrell in Macau," I said. "That'll be quite a stretch for you."

"Yeah, sort of like a bull in a China shop," he said, grinning.

Herb . . . actually . . . made a joke. And later told me the China experience was life changing for him because he had to be polite and sensitive and respectful and a whole bunch of other things that didn't come naturally to him.

THINK NOW

Objectively assess your own level of charm and likability. Are you about as likable as everyone else? Are you very likable with some people and less so with others? Are you charming and likable enough to ACCELERATE your career growth?

- How do you really feel about people in general? If you tend to be judgmental toward others, what is this costing you in terms of your own likability?
- How comfortable and confident are you in terms of knowing your own flaws but not being embarrassed or debilitated by them? Do you have work to do in this area?
- How often do you poke fun at yourself in a good-natured way?

If you think that you would benefit from increasing your likability and charm at work, follow the action steps below.

- When you want something from people, are you able to ask directly while also leveraging your charm and warm personal connection with them?

ACT SOON

- Without making any obvious or abrupt changes in your behavior, begin to more frequently and naturally use people's names in your day-to-day conversations.
- Find natural opportunities to more frequently show respect to others at work.
- Find ways to show genuine interest in others by:

  — Expressing curiosity about their goals and interests.
  — Asking more questions.
  — Asking follow-up questions.

- Find ways to bring laughter and joy to others. If you are not a naturally funny or amusing person, you can still share YouTube videos of funny kittens. (That's a joke.) (But you could still do it.)
- How often do you poke fun at yourself?
- Do you ask thought-provoking questions and follow-up questions?
- If the interpersonal connection with your direct supervisor is difficult, or just sort of "flat," you may want to begin thinking about ways to warm up that relationship.

LONG-TERM THOUGHTS AND ACTION POINTS

It would be insulting to you if we attempted to condense this topic into a few oversimplified tips and bullet points. If you make a sincere effort to enhance your charm quotient and personal likability, in every area of your life, the questions and tips below will help to give you direction for further development. But the hard work and deep thinking is all up to you.

- Who is the most charming person in your life right now? Who are the most charming people you have interacted with in the past?

- Who do you know who has a natural interest in and respect for other people? How do you show respect to others?

- Who do you know who laughs easily, always seems to be in a good mood, and seems to often bring emotional "sunshine" to the lives of others?

- What sort of behavior can you learn and "model" from these people?

Postscript: Herb has gone back to Macau several times and continues to do independent consulting for casinos throughout the world. He is enjoying his work more than ever, and enjoying the PEOPLE he works with, which is a very new experience for him.

8

Buddha, Spock, Patton, and Sherlock

◆

Choices are the hinges of destiny.
—EDWIN MARKHAM

Throughout the course of your work life there will be a few key decision moments that will have a significant impact on your career trajectory, either upward or downward. Because these moments are relatively few and far between, most of us simply apply our normal and instinctive decision-making process, which generally serves us well for day-to-day problem solving. But often when it comes time to make big career decisions, you will be better served by a more thoughtful process, such as:

- What type of career path should I pursue?
- Which job offer should I accept?
- Do I take the offer or try to negotiate for something more?
- If things aren't working out, should I quit or try to make things better?

- Should I address difficult issues directly with my boss or a colleague?
- Should I keep my safe job or try something riskier with greater upside potential?

When I talk to people who have had long and successful careers, and ask them about the key decision points that made a difference for them, I'm struck by how often their decision was counterintuitive or went against the "rules" of typical business decision making.

"I have no regrets," he said. "Everything in life is a learning experience."

I was speaking with Halvor Bjorkson, the operations director for a regional printing company in the Midwest, and he had just recounted a series of difficult experiences with previous companies. Halvor ("Hal" to his friends) was exceptionally competent in all matters related to print production. He was a hardworking straight arrow, perhaps a little rigid, but that's often a good thing when you are depending on attention to detail in a commercial print production environment. One minor mistake and you've got thousands of useless brochures on a palette waiting to be trashed.

Hal told me the story of how his career was derailed for several years when he left a very large company to work for Grainger Printing Company, a smaller printing business. "It was a big step up in responsibility and income, plus they promised me company stock and a short track to a senior leadership position." In the larger company Hal would have had to wait a decade or longer to get to a similar leadership role, if it was ever going to happen. "So I decided it would be better to be a bigger fish in a smaller pond," he said. But the new work environment was not at all what he had expected. The smaller, family-run business at Grainger had a much different culture, and he was surprised at how many family members worked in various roles throughout the company. "Most were not especially good at their jobs," he said. But they were "protected" by their family ties and were rarely held accountable for their poor work.

One of Hal's direct reports was the nephew of the president and son of the marketing director (the president's brother) and he seemed bored by the job. When Hal tried to give him corrective feedback, he just rolled his eyes and walked away. Hal was unable to fire him, unable to coach him, unable to do anything other than let him continue to receive a paycheck. This was demotivating to everyone on Hal's team, but especially to Hal.

Once Hal realized how difficult and stifling the family-run business culture was at Grainger Printing, he decided to begin looking for another job. But he ended up working there for three years before he was able to find equivalent work with another commercial printer. Of course, when he was looking for a new employer he was careful to be sure that there was no family-run culture within the business. He had to take a small pay cut, but it was worth it to get out of his current situation. Unfortunately he stepped out of the frying pan and into a (very different) fire.

Once Hal began working at Bonner Print Solutions as a production director, he found that some projects were being delayed because materials (specialty inks and paper) were not yet available. Hal found that the business's finances were so tight that for large and specialty print jobs they were ordering paper and other materials only after initial payment (typically 50 percent of the order) had been received. This often meant that a job would actually be started a week later than Hal had planned for, and sometimes the delay was longer.

This made project and timeline planning very difficult. Printing presses would sit idle for a half day or longer, then suddenly would need to be run through the night to get a print job completed on time, which meant paying overtime to the production crew. And the business had not budgeted for overtime pay. So Hal was expected to find other ways to cut costs.

When Hal interviewed for the position at Bonner they had not in any way mentioned how tight the business's finances were. Of course he didn't ask, either, but it's unlikely they would have been upfront about it. He was in production, not sales, so there was little he could do to bring in more business, and after less than a year Hal realized that things were not getting any better. If anything, the financial pressure was getting worse. When one of his workers quit, Hal was asked to delay hiring a replacement for a few months, to save money. "How do you expect me to get the work done," he asked, before realizing they expected him to pick up the slack personally, for no additional pay.

The financial pressure was also preventing the company from acquiring new digital printing equipment, and this was at a time when most commercial printers were transitioning from traditional printing presses to high-speed digital printers. This lack of investment meant that Bonner Print Solutions was losing certain jobs that required the speed and flexibility of a digital press. Plus the new digital printers were putting downward pressure on pricing for everyone in the industry. So it was no surprise that Bonner's finances were tightening like a noose.

It took less than six months for Hal to realize that he needed to find a new job, but it was almost another year before he was able to find a position that was even close to his current responsibilities and pay. The job he eventually landed was in a remote part of the state, almost a two-hour drive away. But the pay was good and the company, Great Plains Media, was heavily invested in digital print production. In fact they were planning to completely phase out traditional offset press printing within two years, sooner if possible. While there was a lot of pain in the process of jumping from employer to employer, Hal was actually excited and felt he could have a real future at Great Plains. Plus, his wife and son were willing to consider moving to the much smaller town, once Hal was sure this was a long-term fit for him.

Hal had been working at Great Plains Media for about six months when I first met him. I was facilitating a leadership workshop focused on employee loyalty and engagement, and Hal was clearly struggling with some of the core concepts we were discussing. He was used to the blue-collar command-and-control culture of a traditional printing facility, where supervisors were lauded for micromanaging every aspect of the print production process. Production employees were mostly male, low-skilled, without college degrees, and eager to work hard to keep their jobs, which paid fairly well and were relatively easy compared to other blue-collar work.

The modern digital printing culture at Great Plains was very different. Employees were typically younger and college-educated with computer skills, including design as well as print production. There were almost as many women as men, and the business had to compete for the best employees because they were able to leverage their computer skills within many different industries in nearby cities, so the company needed to attract them to its smaller rural location. Hal was frustrated because, from his perspective, the employees were very well compensated but did not seem to be especially grateful. In fact they "whined and complained" (his words) about even the most minor inconveniences.

Even the common language was new and somewhat off-putting to him. His direct reports were "team members." They embraced "shared accountability" and "strategic whimsy." Huh? Sometimes he felt as if he had landed on a different planet.

I liked Hal and we stayed in contact after the workshop. A few months later we were having lunch and he mentioned that he was looking for a new job. He had just received his annual performance review, which included 360-degree feedback—this is where your direct reports, peers, and supervisors (often including your boss's boss) provide anonymous commentary. Hal was really stung by some of the feedback. His own boss, in reviewing the comments with him, was trying to coach Hal to be more open, inclusive, and flexible with his staff. Hal nodded and smiled, but all he could think about was the feeling of betrayal—that he had been stabbed in the back by these people and there was nothing he could do about it. This was definitely not the way things worked in the traditional blue-collar world, the world that Hal was used to. Frankly, it had been many years since anyone had ever given him such direct, critical feedback. It seemed wrong to him, on many levels. "If someone has a problem with me, they should just come to me directly," he said. "I don't see the 'strategic whimsy' in stabbing me in the back."

Hal just couldn't see himself fitting in long term, so he was once again beginning the search for a new employer. He wasn't particularly sour or angry. A little sad, perhaps, but ready to move on.

"I have no regrets," he said. "Everything in life is a learning experience."

Such a reasonable and nonblaming attitude is certainly a mature way of thinking. It also reflects Hal's stoic Scandinavian heritage. Never complain, just do the work. It's easy to admire this everything-happens-for-a-reason high-road mind-set. But this also presents a problem. Because by taking the high road, Hal was also avoiding any truly deep analysis of the decisions he had made.

Hal would have been so much better off if he had simply said, "I made some mistakes, and I need to learn more about how that happened so I don't repeat them again." Yes, all of life is a learning experience and, yes, we should not live a life of regret for past mistakes—but we also should not pretend that we haven't made mistakes.

Recognizing that you have in fact made career-limiting mistakes in the past, that certain decisions have had a negative impact on your professional progress, this is where you must begin in order to maximize your career potential moving forward and improve your ability to make positive career-impacting decisions.

Whether you are a college student contemplating your first full-time job, or a fifty-something professional looking toward the last decade of your career, there are some key decisions that will have dramatic career impact. You will help your career progress enormously if you think DEEPLY about decisions such as:

- Which college you attend and the focus of your education.
- Your extracurricular activities and projects during college.
- The first full-time job you accept after college.
- What to do if you hate your job, your boss, and/or your colleagues.
- What to do after having a child.
- Which job and project offers to accept, which to turn down.
- What to do if you are suddenly laid off or unemployed.
- Which ongoing professional development activities to pursue.
- Which people to align with at work, whom to socialize with, whom to avoid.
- Should you take credit for a failed project or shift the blame?

Sometimes the "right" answer to these questions is easy and straightforward. But the focus of this chapter is what to do when the right answer is elusive and uncertain. Or when you have a history of making suboptimal choices, even when the best decision seems obvious. And by getting better at answering these somewhat difficult but profound career questions, you will also get better at answering the mundane but important career questions as well, such as:

- Date a coworker, or not?
- Be honest with your boss, or not?
- Tattoo or no tattoo?
- Share the story of your weekend with coworkers, or not?

The purpose of looking back and fully acknowledging any decision-making mistakes you have made isn't to beat up on yourself, it is instead to ensure that you are able to fully and deeply analyze exactly what went wrong, and reduce the likelihood of repeating the thought process.

"I have no regrets," Hal said to me. "Everything in life is a learning experience."

I took a sip of coffee before responding, not wanting to annoy Hal, but certain that he needed a different perspective. "It's been almost eight years since you left the job with the large printing company," I said. "If you had stayed, where do you think your career would be right now?" I tried to keep it nonchalant and casual, but it apparently struck a nerve because Hal went silent for a moment.

"You sound like my wife," he said. Then he told me that one of his old direct reports was now a senior leader at the company. And others on his team had also experienced significant progress in their careers. Hal, on the other hand, was now making about the same income as he had eight years ago, plus he was planning to quit (again) and look for a new job (again), and his future career prospects weren't great.

"Well, when you—and my wife—put it that way," he growled with defensive sarcasm, "I guess I really screwed up."

It took a lengthy conversation for Hal to ease up on his defensiveness, and to his credit he eventually became comfortable acknowledging that, yes, he had made some poor decisions. I don't know if he really screwed up or he didn't. No one can firmly predict how life would have changed if different decisions had been made. But Hal and I agreed that there was, at the very least, something missing in his decision process. He might have been annoyed at me initially, but this is what it took for Hal to finally think DEEPLY about the decisions he had made. Why hadn't he been more discerning when he decided to look for a new employer?

"I was so ambitious years ago, I knew what I wanted and I wanted it now," he said. "I was so drawn to the possibilities, I don't think I even wanted to see the reality of the situation. I was impatient. And when things didn't go as planned, I wanted so badly to get away from my mistake, quickly, to get away from the frustrations, again I think it sort of blinded me to the reality of the situation," Hal said. And that was the moment when he began to gain real clarity. He recognized that he didn't see a lot of the negatives and difficult aspects of the potential future employers because he didn't WANT to see them. His impatience to move on was blinding him.

Sometimes when confronted with a difficult decision we allow ourselves to be blinded by our desire for money, recognition, power, love, sex, validation, new experiences, or something else we deeply desire (or a combination thereof). So the first step in making any tough-and-profound decision is to question your own mind-set. Question your deepest desires.

BORROW THE BUDDHA MIND-SET

I'm a plain vanilla Midwestern Lutheran boy, but I've learned a lot from the Buddhist teaching that when we free ourselves from desire, we will know serenity and freedom. I am not asking you to become Buddhist (or Lutheran), or even to permanently eliminate desire from your mind-set. I've tried, and it seems almost impossible, because there are still things in life that I really, really want. Many of these things contain chocolate.

But when faced with a tough-and-profound decision, first ask yourself, what it is that you most deeply desire? As you contemplate the decision, what are your main emotional drivers?

Are you being driven by a deep need for recognition or validation from others? Or the fear of embarrassment? Or the desire for money? A profound longing for love or acceptance? A wish that others would know your pain and feel sorry for you? A need to prove yourself right? Or to prove others wrong? Fear of failure? Fear of irrelevance?

You are the expert on you, and when you acknowledge your deepest desires related to a potential decision, this gives you the opportunity to set aside that desire, at least briefly. Ask yourself if there is anything you are not seeing because you are blinded by your desire.

When Hal and I talked about this, he again was quiet for a long thoughtful moment. "Yeah," he said. "I wanted out so badly, I didn't want to see the reality." He realized that in every situation when he was considering a potential new employer, there had been signs and indicators of the trouble to come, but he ignored them. Then I asked him if it was possible that his decision to leave Great Plains Media was also driven by some deep desire—perhaps the sting of embarrassment and the need to not be wrong. And was that blinding him to some degree?

Hal took a sip of coffee and after a long Scandinavian pause, he looked at me with a slight smile and said, "Damn you."

Sarah Langtham was coming to the end of her twelve weeks of maternity leave and really didn't want to go back to work. Finances would be incredibly tight if she and her husband had to live on his salary alone, and she worked in a technology job where even six months away meant that her technical knowledge and skills would be falling behind. But she really, really wanted to stay home with her baby.

"It's better for a child to be with its mother during the day. No one will care for my daughter the way her own mother will," she told herself. And she was right. So she and her husband made the decision to have her stay at home for at least the first year.

"It's better for the child," she told herself a year later, and many times after that. And she was right. Whenever she would feel pangs of regret or uncertainty regarding the career that was slowly pulling away from her, this was the mantra that made her feel better. It is also the phrase that stopped her from deeply contemplating the price she would eventually pay. After five years (and another child) she knew how out-of-date her technical knowledge had become, and the idea of interviewing for a new job, and possibly being embarrassed by her lack of knowledge, was something she didn't want to face. Plus, of course, it was better for the children if she stayed at home. And she was right.

No decent human being would ever ask a mother to stop thinking about what is best for her child, but when it came to making her career decisions, Sarah eventually realized that her deepest emotional desires had blinded her to the reality of the decisions she was making. After more than ten years, she felt trapped. There was simply no way (as far as she could see) to reenter the workforce at anything near her previous capacity.

"Of course I love my children. But I wish I had recognized how much I allowed myself to be blinded by that love," she says. "I should have found a way to make better decisions."

Her decision to stay home was not wrong. And if she had made a decision to go back to work, that also would not have been wrong. That's the nature of really tough career-impacting decisions. To be clear, this is not about setting aside your feelings. When you are contemplating an important career decision, only a fool would ask you to remain emotionless. Emotions are powerful forces within us and often serve to help us make better decisions, but it is critical that you at least recognize the deep desires and emotions that are in play. Ask yourself if you are potentially blinded by your deepest desires.

Ross Bernhal hated his boss with a passion. First of all the guy was a jerk, treating his direct reports like servants. Second, he really didn't know what he was doing. He didn't understand the business and didn't have the skills to be an effective leader. And while the boss expected everyone on the team to work long hours and come in on weekends when necessary, he was the first one out the door at five p.m. sharp every weekday and never, never would he be seen in the office on weekends. Not only was the guy incompetent and lazy, but Ross was pretty sure that he was unethical as well. There had been several decisions to award contracts to specific vendors whose bids were clearly not the lowest, and Ross thought his boss was probably taking a kickback under the table in return for approving these vendors. But there was no proof, just a gut instinct. But what Ross definitely knew was that his boss was incompetent.

"I have no idea how he managed to work his way up in this business," Ross said. "The guy orders people around, never does anything himself, and always makes sure he has a fall guy for every project, just in case something goes wrong."

Now, on the flip side, Ross liked his job, liked everyone else that he worked with, and the pay was really good. Ross struggled with what to do. One side of him said to just let it go, wait until the guy moved on. Or wait until a better job opportunity came along, then Ross could get out and not have to deal with him any longer. Take the high road, this side said. Be the bigger man, keep your head down, and just continue to do a good job.

But the other side was furious that such a lazy incompetent boob could be so successful and had the power over Ross and others in his work group. Ross talked to many of his colleagues, mostly he ranted, but no one was willing to rock the boat. One woman who had worked with the boss for years told Ross, "He wasn't always like this, maybe he's under a lot of stress." She advised Ross to just let it go, but there were a few others who encouraged him to take action. Of course, they weren't willing to take action themselves, and when Ross actually suggested that they file a group complaint, everyone backed away and went silent.

Ultimately Ross gave in to his deep emotional need for justice. He set up a meeting with the company HR ombudsman, who was supposed to be someone that an employee could reach out to anonymously to report concerns. When Ross met with the ombudsman he explained all of his concerns related to the ethics of some of the vendor decisions, plus he mentioned the harsh leadership style.

About three weeks later Ross was given a "promotion" into another department. The pay was the same, and he was happy to get out of his current situation. Then two months later Ross was abruptly laid off. The explanation from HR was that his position was being eliminated in a company restructuring. His old job was no longer available because it had already been filled by a new hire. Ross was absolutely certain this was all related to his coming forward with concerns about his old boss, but he had no way of proving it. He met again with the HR ombudsman, who told him there had been follow-up after his complaint, though his identity was kept anonymous, and the ultimate outcome could not be revealed because of employment privacy laws. Ross didn't believe a word of it. He even contacted a labor rights lawyer, but was told there was almost certainly no way to prove illegal discrimination.

So did Ross make the wrong decision in bringing forward his concerns to the HR ombudsman? Did he allow his emotional need for "justice" to blind him? Well, we don't really know because he didn't gather enough information before taking action. Ross had plenty of ranting talks with colleagues, but his intense emotional desire for "justice" caused him to take action without doing all of his homework in advance.

CHANNEL YOUR INNER SPOCK

When you think of the *Star Trek* character Spock, the first thing that comes to mind is probably his commitment to logical decisions devoid of emotion. If you think about this a bit more deeply, because of Spock's lack of emotion he based his decisions on information, and he would typically wait until he had all the information he needed in order to make a reasoned, fact-based decision. Most of us would not argue with the wisdom of fact-based decisions, and most of us have an "inner Spock" who tries to guide us. But we sometimes let our emotional desires convince us that we already have enough information, when in fact there are usually many opportunities to gather more information.

In Hal's case he had ample opportunity to learn more about each of his potential employers. He belonged to a local commercial printing trade association where he certainly could have leveraged his contacts to find out more about the specific printers he was considering. Some of Hal's colleagues had worked at these companies and they would have been great sources of information. "I didn't really think of that, because I didn't want people to know I was looking," he said when I mentioned this idea.

Obviously I wouldn't recommend saying, "Hey, I'm interviewing over at Great Plains Media, what do you think of them?" But a person could certainly ask, "I heard you used to work over at Great Plains, what's it like there? Do they do anything especially well that we could try over here?"

Hal could have also done more online research. There are numerous sites where people can post online "reviews" of their current or previous employers. Of course some of these online opinions are nothing more than sour grapes, but even taking that into account you can often glean valuable information.

Hal could also have asked much better questions during the actual job interviews. He asked all of the basic tactical questions about the job itself, the work process and requirements, etc. But he didn't dig deeper into the culture and what made each business a unique place to work. When he did bother to dig a little deeper it was only to make sure the new employer didn't have the same problems as the old employer.

He could also have asked to meet with a few of the employees. He could have connected with some of them through social media online and asked for their perspective on their employer. He could have asked to "job shadow" for a day or two to get a feel for the actual culture within the business. I'm not saying that he should have done all of these things—I'm saying that he could have done more than just sit at a couple of interviews and ask basic questions.

I noticed that as I mentioned these ideas to Hal, there was a certain cadence to our conversation. It went something like:

"Maybe you could have tried this idea . . ."

"Well, that sounds good but it wouldn't have worked because . . ."

"Hmm, what if you tried it this way . . ."

"Yeah, I suppose that could work, but . . ."

This pattern was repeated after each idea and suggestion for gathering more information about an employer before making a decision. I have found that when I'm having a conversation with someone like Hal, if I'm always the one trying to figure out how to make the ideas work, there usually isn't a successful outcome. Until the person who HAS the problem is fully engaged in OWNING the problem and solving it (not expecting someone else to do the hard thinking), generally speaking, the problem won't get solved.

"So you're planning to leave your current company," I said. "Are you sure that you have all the information you need to make that decision?"

Hal started to nod, then stopped himself. "Well, like, what do you mean?"

"I don't know, you tell me. What assumptions are you making? What actual information are you basing this decision on?"

When you find yourself at the point where you have a difficult decision related to your career, and you want to ensure that you have acquired all of the information you need to make a reasoned, intelligent decision, here are a few questions I have found to be helpful:

- What information am I certain of, and why am I so certain?
- Is there any possibility that my certainty is misplaced?
- What information is, in reality, just my (perhaps well-founded) perception?
- What information could I gather to confirm (or dispel) my perceptions?
- Where is this information most readily accessible?
- Who do I know who has dealt with similar decisions? What could I learn from them?

Ross Bernhal was absolutely certain that he had made the right decision to bring his concerns to the HR ombudsman. He was also absolutely certain that this had led to his orchestrated ouster from the company, and that there was nothing he could do about it now.

But it turns out there was a lot of information Ross didn't know, although he probably could have learned it if he had been willing to set aside his preconceived perceptions. Ross had complained to a few long-term employees, passionately expressing his frustration with the boss. When some of them tried to share a different perspective, he didn't want to hear it, interrupted with more of his commentary, and essentially shut them down.

So there were two things Ross never heard. First, no one was sure that the HR ombudsman truly kept things confidential. There had been rumors that occasionally the details shared with him went directly to the owner. No firm evidence, just rumors. Second, Ross never heard that those who had worked for the abrasive boss for many years had seen a marked change in his behavior and personality. Only a very few people knew that this was the result of a mild stroke he had suffered two years ago. It wasn't something people were comfortable talking about, but if Ross had been more patient and open, less ranting, someone surely would have shared this information with him.

What Ross also didn't know—but he could have—was that the owner of the company approved every invoice for every vendor. This was a policy implemented at the request of the boss when he came back to work after the stroke, because his memory was sometimes fuzzy and he didn't want to make a mistake. So it was the owner who was making the ultimate determination to work with a certain vendor whose project bid may not have been the lowest.

The entire issue of suspected vendor kickbacks was something Ross had created in his head. When he had shared his suspicions with the HR ombudsman, these were shared with the owner, along with all of Ross's other opinions about his boss. The owner was very protective of the boss, who was a long-time loyal employee. The owner of course had seen the significant behavior changes after the mild stroke, but he was loyal and determined to help him through it. Ross's complaints struck the owner as petty and paranoid, and at that point the owner made a determination that Ross should probably move on.

The point of sharing all of these details with you is to highlight how easy it is to be absolutely certain your opinions are fact-based, and yet be totally wrong.

Author's note: I heard this story directly from the HR ombuds-man, who definitely should not have been sharing it with me. He was close to retirement, had known the owner most of his work-ing life, and there seemed to be an implicit understanding that he would have a few final comfortable years at the company, as long as he served as the owner's "ears." I'm not saying it's right, I'm just saying it happens.

Sarah Langtham, the reluctant stay-at-home mom, had of course done her homework. She read dozens of books and hundreds of online articles about the career impact of staying at home to raise a child. There was (and still is) no shortage of opinion on this topic, and plenty of facts to support either position:

Staying at home to raise a child is ultimately better for that child's emotional and intellectual development. No one will care for your child the way you do. And mothers who try to "have it all" end up being unhappy at work, which makes them even less effective at home.	Having the confidence and assurance of a robust career, being able to have a professional life beyond child rearing, is best for a woman's mental, emotional, and financial health. Which ultimately translates into her being a better mother for her child.

Sarah struggled with her decision, had endless conversations with her husband and anyone else who would offer an opinion, or at least a willing ear. Some suggested that she try a "hybrid" approach where she was essentially a stay-at-home mom but also had a professional life. She could leverage her computer expertise to be an at-home telephone tech support person, but this wasn't really the career path she wanted. Her company actually offered her a part-time position, in customer service, but they wanted her to work in the office (she didn't try to negotiate this requirement) and coordinating with her husband's work schedule would be very difficult. Someone suggested that she start a tech blog for women, but she didn't see how that would make money, and she wasn't a great writer.

Everyone she spoke with had opinions and ideas, but nothing seemed truly workable. So Sarah never actually decided to be a permanent stay-at-home mom, but over time it just happened. She truly felt that there were no viable options, and with each passing year the barriers to career reentry (at her previous level) became higher and higher. After ten years out of the workforce, she had given up completely.

"When I look at where things ended up, I know I should have stayed active in my career somehow," she says now. "We paid a high price financially, but more important, I get depressed when I think about the potential I wasted." Sarah is sure that there could have been a way to achieve both of her goals, but she never figured it out.

PUT ON PATTON'S BOOTS

General George S. Patton, remembered for his fierce determination and ability to lead soldiers, is considered by many to be one of the greatest military figures in history. His military strategy and tactics often surprised the enemy. His speeches often inspired his soldiers. But what is often overlooked are the behind-the-scenes battles that took place as Patton worked to prepare his army for war. There were political battles at home, with many politicians opposed to America's entry into the war. There were funding battles, which sometimes meant that Patton's army lacked the necessary equipment and support. There were battles with other generals, who felt that Patton was an egomaniac and were unwilling to lend support to his battle plans.

In virtually every major battle fought in World War II, Patton was tasked with developing a strategy, then executing it to win. Which is exactly what he did. However, he was never able to develop a "perfect" strategy because of all the limitations. Patton's army had many new and poorly trained soldiers, inadequate equipment, uncertain information about the enemy's positions, unpredictable weather, and scarce medical supplies.

When asked how he developed a strategy with inadequate resources, Patton said, "A good solution applied with vigor now is better than a perfect solution applied ten minutes later."

In other words, he never let the lack of a perfect solution get in the way of taking action. Many decades later Secretary of Defense

Donald Rumsfeld stated, "You go to war with the army you have, not the army you want to have." He took a lot of heat for that statement with some choosing to interpret it as a lack of commitment to adequately fund, support, and protect the troops. But Rumsfeld's actual point was similar to Patton's—you can't let the lack of a "perfect" solution get in the way of taking action.

And when you are confronted with career decisions, there may be times when you are faced with a whole range of imperfect options. What you should not do is avoid the decision altogether. Or put too much time and effort into trying to craft a perfect outcome.

Often a "good enough" solution executed with vigor now is better than a perfect solution executed later, or never.

And unfortunately Sarah Langtham allowed herself to get stuck in an "imperfect decision loop" meaning that she kept talking and thinking and considering, rotating from one imperfect idea to the next, never putting on her boots and stepping into battle.

General Patton probably would have said, "Goddamn it, Langtham! Get your whiney ass in gear and do the fuckin' tech blog, do the fuckin' in-home phone tech support, and see what the fuck happens! At least you'll be executing SOME sort of goddamn strategy! Learn from what works, and what turns to shit. Make adjustments and move on. But, goddamn it, do NOT just sit there in your own whiny-ass shit whimpering because you're not sure. Who the fuck is sure about ANYTHING in this goddamn world? Now, put on your fuckin' boots and get moving!"

Yes, Patton was also known for his colorful language.

So to summarize what we've covered up to this point regarding how to make the most effective career-enhancing decisions:

- Be aware of your deepest emotional desires and needs related to the issue and make sure they are not blinding your decision process. Borrow the Buddha mind-set.

- Make sure that you have acquired all of the information you need (no assumptions or interpretations) to make a well-reasoned decision. Channel your inner Spock.
- Do not let the lack of a "perfect" solution get in the way. Create the best plan possible with the information and resources available, then take action. Put on Patton's boots.

But application of these three principles will not always guarantee a successful outcome. You can set aside your deepest emotions to ensure clarity of thought, gather a ton of fact-based information, and develop a solid plan for action—and still fail. Just ask Joseph Horton.

Joseph Horton was in his early forties, working as the VP of product development for a manufacturing company whose target market was teenagers and parents of teens. They had recently been acquired by a private equity firm through a leveraged buyout. The CEO (who made a huge amount of money from the buyout) was planning to retire soon, and Joseph was determined to be the next CEO, but he had competition. The VP of marketing was also positioning himself as a possible successor to the CEO.

The private equity firm thought highly of both men, but made it clear they were looking for an "innovative thought leader" to take the company forward. They wanted a leader who "wasn't afraid to make mistakes" and was willing to stretch the organization to "think outside the box."

In that spirit the VP of marketing had negotiated an agreement with Disney to manufacture and market a special line of the company's products within all Disney theme parks. Joseph had scoffed at the idea when he first heard the proposal because Disney was demanding a huge royalty on every item sold, which meant the profit margin was less than half of what they were accustomed to. And Joseph also thought the volume projections were inflated.

But the private equity company loved the idea. They gushed about "cobranding synergies" and it seemed that everybody loved Disney. And as the man who had spearheaded the entire effort, it looked like that VP of marketing's star was rising rapidly.

Joseph Horton needed a big win. Something bold. Outlandish. He hired a consulting firm from New York to do some quick research on the current teen mind-set—trends, interests, values, what was hot, etc.—and propose specific marketing or product options.

The consulting firm presented Joe with a very detailed analysis that indicated the Disney brand wasn't particularly hot with teenagers anymore. He was secretly thrilled to hear this, but was even more pleased with their additional research. They offered detailed data showing how much influence the hip-hop culture was having on teens throughout the country. It was no longer just an urban trend but in fact even in middle America suburbia teens were embracing hip-hop music, fashion, and terminology. The hip-hop trend was almost the opposite of Disney in terms of teen values and lifestyle.

The consulting firm wasn't just presenting their opinion, everything was backed up by thorough research. They proposed development of a specific line of products to be designed by several leading hip-hop stars such as Jay-Z, Beyoncé, and Russell Simmons. While the large royalty fees of these stars would reduce the profit margin, Joseph was very excited about the whole initiative. The consulting firm's sales projections were based upon actual sales of other products introduced into this market, so Joseph was definitely channeling Spock and felt confident that he was on solid ground. It was exactly what he had been looking for—new, different, innovative . . . and definitely un-Disney. The consulting firm was able to advance the project quickly by providing quick access to artists and designers in the hip-hop world.

When Joseph presented his proposal to the private equity firm, the VP of product development was in the room and clearly not enthusiastic about it. "I'm not sure this is our target demographic," he sniffed.

"I'm trying to expand our target demographic," Joe responded. "With some out-of-the-box thinking."

The private equity firm decided to move forward with both initiatives. Clearly they would be targeting different demographics, but maybe this was a way to capture a much larger piece of the overall teen market. For the next six months both VPs were locked in an unspoken battle for dominance, each determined to outdo the other. Disney vs hip-hop.

One of Joe's advantages was that with the help of the consulting firm and all of their contacts in the hip-hop world, he was able to execute and go to market quickly. He put on Patton's boots and marched.

Ultimately both initiatives failed miserably.

But Joe's hip-hop project failed first, which caused his career prospects at the company to spiral downward. On the other hand, the VP of marketing had lots of high-profile events with Disney executives, invited key leaders of the private equity firm to participate in several meetings at Disney headquarters, and was appointed to the CEO position while the Disney project was still in long-term development. It took two years before they were ready to launch, and the actual sales results were abysmal. But by then it was too late for Joe. And the new CEO was easily able to deflect blame to some of his underlings.

SEE THROUGH SHERLOCK'S EYES

You see, but you do not observe. The distinction is clear.

—Sherlock Holmes, *A Scandal in Bohemia*

So what went wrong? It was only years later that Joseph began to understand what had really happened. It turned out that the New

York consulting firm had contractual relationships with each of the hip-hop artists they had recommended to Joseph. In some cases they co-owned branding companies with those artists. What was supposed to be an objective, fact-based consulting research project was actually nothing more than a slick sales presentation. They didn't do any original research for Joseph, they simply recycled the same data they used when pitching to every other prospective client, with the goal of getting hip-hop branding and endorsement deals. That was their real objective.

They made money on the initial consulting project. They made a percentage of the upfront royalty payments. They recommended a separate manufacturer for some of the specialty products—Joseph's company could have done it but it would have delayed the rollout six months—and received a commission from that manufacturer (with whom they had a "special" relationship).

None of this came to light until years later, when Joseph was having a conversation (job interview) with the CEO of another manufacturing company, and found out that they had gone through virtually the same process, with the same consulting firm.

The lesson? When it comes to making significant career-impacting decisions, sometimes you have to be a detective. Not everyone is always honest with you. Not everyone has your best interest in mind.

Companies will often avoid telling you the whole, unvarnished truth about their organization if they think it might dissuade you from wanting to work there.

Individuals will selectively omit information that does not serve their cause. Some people will just outright lie to you in order to achieve their objectives.

So, to be a good career decision maker you should ask yourself: What are people NOT telling me? What motivations might others have to give me less than accurate information? What could go wrong? What is the worst possible downside?

amn you," Hal said, but at least he was smiling a little. The more he thought about his current career situation, the more he realized that what was really driving him away from Great Plains Media was embarrassment. He was so used to being the most competent guy in the room when it came to traditional print production, this new environment sometimes made him feel . . . inadequate.

Hal had a tentative job offer from a traditional printer, and it seemed to be a perfect fit for him. "Seemed" is the operative word. Hal agreed that he needed to be more of a Sherlock and gather additional information about the company before making a decision. He also agreed that he needed to gather more information at his current job—he was assuming that they were disappointed in him and wouldn't mind if he moved on. But that was all assumption, and he really needed to have some genuine conversations with a few people to determine what they thought about his future there.

Then I asked him to put on Patton's boots and assume that whichever path he took, nothing was going to be perfect and he would have to deal with uncomfortable issues no matter what. If that was the case, that every path was going to present challenges and discomfort and disappointment, then where did he want the path to eventually lead him? To a traditional printer, or to the new world of digital print production? A "new world" decision wouldn't necessarily mean that he should stay at Great Plains, but it would help him decide whether or not to accept the other job offer.

Fast forward two years—and Hal is still at Great Plains Media, has been through some serious coaching and leadership development work, is enjoying his job like never before, and finds that he actually likes working with so many "young pups," as he calls them.

THINK NOW

Have you made any major career decisions that did not work out as planned? If so, think about the information in this chapter and ask yourself if you could have been more thoughtful in your decision-making process. Which specific part of the process we've outlined would have been most helpful for you:

- Buddha
- Spock
- Patton
- Sherlock

In the future, recognize when a career-impacting decision is so potentially significant that you should take the time to review this chapter again and then think through your options.

ACT SOON

While this approach is designed for big decisions, you can begin to apply some of the thinking to your smaller day-to-day decisions, which will better prepare you for the time when a big decision is at hand.

....

**You can learn more at
www.workplacepoker.com/decision-making/.**

....

LONG-TERM THOUGHTS AND ACTION POINTS

Whenever you are faced with a significant career-impacting decision, take the time to think more deeply and come to the conclusion that is most likely to accelerate your career trajectory.

• Be aware of your deepest emotional desires and needs related to the issue and make sure they are not blinding your decision process. Borrow the Buddha mind-set.

• Make sure that you have acquired all of the information you need (no assumptions or interpretations) to make a well-reasoned decision. Channel your inner Spock.

• Do not let the lack of a "perfect" solution get in the way. Create the best plan possible with the information and resources available, then take action. Put on Patton's boots.

• As others get involved in your decision making, listen and observe carefully. Do not just accept information at face value. See though Sherlock's eyes.

9

Like a Rubber Cat

♦

I returned, and saw under the sun, that the race is not to the swift, nor the battle to the strong, neither yet bread to the wise, nor yet riches to men of understanding, nor yet favor to men of skill: but time and chance happeneth to them all.

—ECCLESIASTES 9:11

Shit happens.

—NOT ECCLESIASTES

There will come a time in your career (if it hasn't already) when you will be hit by a sudden job loss, or a big project failure, or learn that a trusted colleague is stabbing you in the back, or some other really awful thing will happen. And even if you've already had more than your share of awful things in your career, you need to be ready for more. Because hardworking people get fired. Good companies go out of business. Well-deserved bonuses get canceled, coworkers get mean and nasty, and yet . . . your career goes on. What doesn't kill you makes you stronger. Unless it kills you.

Whenever I have the opportunity for thoughtful conversation with an exceptionally successful person, I ask them about the tough times in their career. The worst moments, and how they recovered. When the person I'm talking to can't think of any truly major career difficulties, I generally slip some ketamine into their drink and end the discussion quickly. Because I'm bored and a little annoyed.

Seriously, people who have had major troubles in their career are so much more interesting than those who have experienced nothing but a smooth upward arc of success. And as it turns out, the vast majority of uber-successful folks I've talked to have had very interesting lives filled with plenty of adversity.

"I'm like a rubber cat," an executive at a Fortune 500 company once told me. He was describing a series of business failings and errors that should have ended his career. "I've had at least nine lives, but I always bounce back, and land on my feet."

Of course it's easy to tell someone to bounce back—but when the really bad stuff happens, most of us struggle to figure out what to do. Sometimes we are so dumbfounded that we can't think clearly. I met a group of twenty people who had just been laid off by their company. Most were on the mature end of their careers (meaning they were old) and more than a little stunned by the sudden job loss. The company had paid for what is euphemistically known as "transition coaching," which is essentially helping people write résumés and look for new jobs. I was part of the team helping this group, and at our first meeting I noticed that of the twenty people, about half just sat through the meeting in dazed silence. This was a week after their layoff had been announced.

The ones who were more vocal spent most of their energy bitching about the company and the unfairness of the whole situation. Several talked about suing the company and one woman started to cry. One person—just one—was totally focused on rewriting a résumé, updating a LinkedIn profile, finding out about networking events, learning more about the job search process, and finding out where to go to polish up on computer skills. One person. And while many of these people (but not all of them) eventually found jobs, who do you think got hired first, and who actually managed to step up into a better paying job rather than having to settle for something less? Exactly—that one person. The one who transitioned from stunned surprise to massive action—QUICKLY.

When the really bad things happen in your career, managing your mental and emotional state is probably the most critical task. And, yes, I know this is much easier said than done. When career adversity strikes, many of us are initially stunned and inert. We aren't sure what to do, feel confused and uncertain, and often spend a fair amount of time in denial, contemplation, desperate bargaining, and, finally, sometimes panicked action. Most people wait too long to jump into action and the action they do take isn't enough. Then when something they try doesn't work they tend to get stuck again in a stunned pause, overthinking and inert again.

SLAP YOURSELF AND START RUNNING

Researchers have found that even during natural disaster situations, most people react with a delayed, lethargic response ("no need to panic here folks . . .") and these people actually have a greater tendency to perish. The survivors tend to be those who take quick, targeted, and massive action.

Cassie Eddington woke up at 5:30 a.m. and smelled something strange. She was an eighty-five-year-old widow living alone, and within moments she recognized the smell of chlorine in the air. "I looked out my kitchen window and saw a cloud of white gas," she said. Cassie's small home was isolated and nestled at the bottom of a valley, so she knew that whatever the source of the white cloud, it was drifting down and settling near her home. "The smell was getting worse pretty fast, and I knew I had to get out of there." So

Cassie quickly poured cold water over a towel and held it to her nose as she scooped up her cat and car keys, intending to drive to higher ground.

"When I opened the door to go outside, the chlorine hit me in the face. My eyes were burning and I almost turned back, but thank God I didn't," she says. Cassie knew the shortest route to the highest ground nearby, and after a few minutes she was clear of the chlorine. Her cat was annoyed and meowing loudly, its eyes watery and stinging from the chlorine, but they were both safe.

Within less than an hour a rescue team arrived, responding to an overturned railway car containing liquid chlorine less than half a mile away. Luckily the spill occurred in a relatively isolated area and the poisonous vapors were contained in the valley. After two days in the hospital Cassie made a full recovery. But unfortunately several of her neighbors died that night. A retired husband and wife were found huddled in the far corner of their basement. They had apparently tried to seal their basement off with wet towels under the door. Another woman was found in her basement, and a man was found in his bathroom with his dog, the cold shower water still running. All had attempted to seal themselves off from the poisonous gas with wet towels under doors and around windows. And all had perished.

Cassie's response to the crisis—taking quick decisive action— was uncommon, but it is what saved her life. Those who died unfortunately responded the way many people do when disaster strikes— hesitate, retreat, huddle.

And this tendency to delay active response to a disaster is very relevant to individuals who have suddenly lost their jobs or experienced other career adversity. Often they will "freeze" for days, weeks, sometimes months. But those who survive and prosper tend to be the ones who take action quickly.

So the first question to ask yourself when a career disaster strikes should be: What can I do? A subtle but important point is to not start with what SHOULD you do—begin first with all the possibilities of what you CAN possibly do.

You should clearly and very consciously think through all of the possible actions available to you. Is there anything you can do to change, alter, or impact the event? In those situations where there are a variety of possible actions, quickly assess your alternatives, take massive action, with a positive attitude and a specific goal in mind. If that action doesn't work, learn from it and try another action. And if that doesn't work, learn some more and try another.

As long as you know that you can impact the negative event in a positive way, stay action-oriented. And your actions should be:

- Quick
- Targeted
- Massive

WHEN THE STORM BUILDS SLOWLY

Sometimes the adversity jumps up and screams at us, and sometimes it just creeps up slowly behind, subtly sucking the oxygen out of the air around us. We don't see it coming until it feels hard to breathe and we are almost ready to pass out.

Brian Cisneros is a great example of someone for whom adversity snuck up slowly, eventually overwhelming him. Brian was a salesperson for an office supply company in Charleston, South Carolina. This was his first full-time job out of college, and although Brian had no formal training in selling strategies or techniques, he was doing pretty well. He was a naturally outgoing guy and viewed his job essentially as maintaining good relationships with all of his accounts. This was pretty easy for him, so what would be the point of any sales training, he thought. "To be honest, even the term 'sales training' was kind of gross to me," Brian said.

Newly married, he and his wife wanted to live near the beach, where housing is definitely on the expensive side. They bought a small house within walking distance of Folly Beach and both were still paying off college bills, so money was pretty tight, but they were happy.

They started a small home-based business selling nutritional and weight-loss supplements, hoping to make a little extra money to cover some of their housing expense. Since Brian was a "natural salesman" this seemed like a good option for them. They invested a few thousand dollars for inventory, brochures, and other marketing materials, but most of their inventory just sat on a shelf in their laundry room.

At one point Brian lost a couple of big office equipment accounts to a competitor, which really set them back financially. So they had to be even more careful about money. Brian knew that his car needed some repair work, but he kept putting it off, until eventually, on his way to a sales presentation, it stalled out on the freeway.

The cost for towing and car repair was far more than it would have cost for proper maintenance. The mechanic mentioned that he should probably replace his tires because they were worn pretty thin, but Brian decided to wait at least until the next paycheck. Of course the next payday came and went without replacing the tires. And then a tire went flat in the parking lot of another prospect. Brian continued to have trouble starting his car in the morning—so he was late to more than a few sales presentations.

But it wasn't just the car. "I felt like I just couldn't catch a break," Brian says. Over time other troubles started to pile up. He had checks that bounced, so he had to spend time dealing with that issue. He forgot to pay a few bills, so he was getting harassing phone calls from creditors. He was working hard trying to make up for the lost accounts, so he had stopped taking the time to exercise, and he was eating in his car more, so of course he was gaining weight.

"I think it was about two years where things just seemed to

get a little worse, week after week," he says. "But it felt like a life-time." Over the course of those two years Brian gained almost forty pounds, felt a lot of pressure from his manager to win back his two big accounts, and rarely spent time at the beach.

Brian came home at the end of a long workday and his wife announced that she was pregnant. She was probably hoping for a reaction of joy and excitement, but all she got was stunned silence. "With everything else that was going on, this just sort of pushed me over the edge," he said. "There was no way we could afford this." For the next two days, Brian left for work earlier and stayed at the office longer, not because he was doing more work, but because he was avoiding home—and avoiding any talk about the pregnancy. His reaction was the common natural disaster response: denial, stunned contemplation, avoidance of reality. ("This can't be happening.")

Eventually Brian and his wife had a huge blowout argument, she threatened to have an abortion and to leave him. Then just days later, when he thought his life couldn't get any worse, his manager told him he was being put "on probation" and if he didn't get his sales volume up in the next ninety days, he would lose his job.

Later that day after being put on probation, Brian sat at the beach, afraid to go home, not sure how to tell his wife that he might be out of a job. "My head was spinning, trying to figure out what to do," he said. As Brian sat there his mind ticked through all the things he could possibly do, and none of his ideas seemed particularly good. He wasn't sure if he should really dig in and try to improve his sales, or if he should start looking for a new job. He had already been trying to sell more, so it wasn't like he could truly work harder at it.

His manager suggested a sales training workshop, but that seemed like more of a long-term solution and Brian needed results now. It was going to be hard interviewing for a new sales position when he couldn't point to stellar performance at his previous employer. Plus he should lose some weight before going to job interviews. He could try harder to sell some of the nutritional supplements gathering dust in their laundry room. Or maybe they should move away from the beach area to save money. He could sell his car, which was still giving him fits, and they could try to get by with only one vehicle.

Eventually he had to go home and tell his wife. She was of course surprised and scared, but he was grateful that she at least wasn't angry at him. The panic they were both feeling was finally spurring them to focused action. They knew something had to change, so they sat down and listed all of the things they could possibly do. I won't share with you their entire list because it filled several pages, but a few of the possible actions included:

- Sell the beach house, move to an apartment (neither of them wanted to do this).
- Polish up his résumé and start actively looking for a new job.
- Tell Brian's manager about the pregnancy, maybe he'll be sympathetic and this will buy a little more time (Brian hated this idea).
- Attend a sales training course (ugh, he hated this one too).
- Sell Brian's car and try to get by with one vehicle.
- Put more time into selling the nutritional supplements.
- Start eating better (both of them) and exercising again (Brian).

As they started trying to decide which actions to take, Brian was clearly avoiding two of them: selling the house and sales training. Selling the house felt like admitting defeat. And attending sales training felt like admitting that he wasn't good at his job. But as they scanned the pages, his wife looked at him with dead seriousness and said, "We have to do it all."

And that is exactly what they did. Massive action.

In fact, the reason I met Brian was that he attended a sales training workshop I was facilitating. It wasn't easy for him because he had kind of a chip on his shoulder, didn't really think there was much for him to learn. He was naturally great at talking, not so good at asking questions and listening. He wasn't very organized or naturally strategic in his thought process, so he had to work hard to develop a more systematic approach to his sales activity. But to his credit he stuck with it, and applied the new skills immediately upon returning to work.

They sold their house, which removed a lot of the short-term financial burden, and they actually spent some of the proceeds to buy a newer car for Brian, because the repair bills on his old one were killing them financially. He also started taking much better care of his health, eating better and exercising every morning.

The point of sharing Brian's story with you is that through massive action, he and his wife were finally able to turn the tide of their financial situation. Which turned the tide of their marriage. And that turned the tide of Brian's professional life. Yes, his manager gave him a little more breathing room, but within five months Brian had accepted a new sales job that paid more and would give him a more regular schedule.

"The only thing I regret," Brian told me recently, "was that I waited so long. I could have easily taken those same actions a year or two earlier."

PANIC CAN BE YOUR FRIEND

If you find yourself in a situation where there is no single dramatic negative career event, just a slow steady trend in the wrong direction, you might want to try inducing some positive panic. Focus on the worst-case scenario, how bad it could possibly be, and immerse yourself in all of the potential negative outcomes. To be clear, I'm only recommending you do this if you need to panic yourself into action. If you are instead fully ready to move forward, no need to slap yourself.

When you are determined to be action-oriented, it's usually best to try and come up with a list of as many possible actions as you can think of. Then choose those that are most likely to get you the outcome you want, but keep the others in reserve. This works well because it reinforces that you are in control of the situation—you have options, many options—and you can make a rational and objective decision about which actions to take, and if need be, you immediately have other backup actions available to you.

"If we had just sold our home and done nothing else," Brian said to me, "it would have felt like an act of desperation." But because they were taking massive action and making many other changes, selling their house felt more like part of a plan, a process for moving forward.

Of course not everything you try is going to work out. If one action doesn't get the desired result, try another one as soon as possible. Learn from your mistakes but avoid being overly contemplative. If you spend too much time and energy analyzing why something didn't work, you're going to lose your action momentum.

YOU CAN'T FIX CRAZY

Heather McAdams was a marketing manager for an advertising agency with offices in Los Angeles, New York, Atlanta, and Minneapolis. She worked in Minneapolis, one of four managers reporting to the marketing director, who worked out of the New York office. The agency had grown rapidly, primarily because of the creative reputation of one of the partners, Raul Toma, who was flamboyant, amazingly talented, and annoyingly arrogant.

Raul traveled each week from office to office (LA on Tuesdays, Atlanta on Wednesdays, etc.) bestowing his rarified talent upon the creative staff in each location. The company chartered a jet for his frequent travels, and his constant travel companions were two large black pit bulls, Rocco and Rufus. There was simply no way to not notice Raul Toma wherever he went, with his long black ponytail, Maori tattoos, and matching black pit bulls. He was tall, but the rumor was that he wore lifts in his black boots to make himself even taller.

Heather had worked at the agency for a little over six months and had sat in on many meetings where Raul conducted reviews of the creative work on every current project. Raul's pit bulls always sat in a corner of the meeting room on a mat placed there for them. A staff person in each office was assigned to ensure that they had a large bowl of fresh water (filtered, not tap) and organic grain-free dog treats. But no one was to feed them the treats except for Raul.

During the creative review meetings Raul was brutal with his criticism—"This is shit!" was said so often that it seemed to be his catchphrase. An intern thought it would be funny to come to work one day with a "This is shit!" T-shirt. He was gone the next day.

Almost everyone had figured out how to survive these meetings. Shut up, take notes, agree with Raul, and never, ever disagree with one of his ideas. Heather had apparently not gotten that memo.

She sat in a creative review meeting one week watching as Raul shot down a lot of pretty good concepts, then presented an idea of his own which of course he thought was "unique and compelling" (his words). Heather thought the idea was pretty similar to one that had been presented to Raul weeks ago, and his response back then had been . . . you guessed it . . . "This is shit!" There was certainly no harm in Heather having a different opinion. But she didn't stop there.

"This seems a lot like the concept we proposed to you three weeks ago," Heather said. "And you thought it was shit then. So what has changed?" Her tone of voice was sincere, not snarky. Professional and courteous, not critical. But that didn't really matter.

No one said a word. Only a few dared to look at Raul directly. But almost everyone was thinking "Oh . . . my . . . God." Except for Heather, who waited for an answer with a sincere expression of professional curiosity.

Raul smiled at Heather. "Perhaps you're right," he said, and then simply moved on to review the next creative project without another word about her question.

After the meeting adjourned everyone scattered back to their offices and cubicles to continue another long workday. There were a fair number of emails and text messages sent back and forth commenting about Heather's question and Raul's response. Almost all of these messages were sent from personal phones and tablets to personal recipient accounts. Because the business was paranoid about losing creative intellectual property, everyone understood that all company computers and mobile devices were heavily monitored.

Heather was oblivious to most of the online chatter because she had her head deep into a big project on a tight deadline. Plus she kept her personal mobile phone in her purse most of the time so that she wouldn't be distracted by nonbusiness emails and calls during the workday.

At about six p.m. that day the office was quiet, most people having gone home or down to the faux-Irish pub on the first level of their building. But Heather stuck with it at least another thirty minutes before finally shutting her laptop down and heading for home. As she walked out of her office and turned a corner to a very long hallway that spanned almost the full length of the building, she saw Raul and his two "boys" at the other end. She hesitated because there was no way she wanted to reach the elevators at the same time. But they had clearly seen each other, so she couldn't just turn back. She decided to walk slowly and if they reached the elevators together she was going to pretend that she forgot something in her office. He wouldn't believe her of course, but she didn't care.

What happened next Heather can recount almost like a slow-motion movie. "It took a moment for my mind to understand what was happening, but his dogs were rushing toward me from the other end of the hallway," she says. "I stood frozen at first, not believing it. And by the time I knew it was real, it was too late."

The two black pit bulls rushed at her, growling, and they were on her so fast that she barely had time to run before they jumped up on her back and pushed her to the ground. She screamed, but there was no one in the office to hear her except Raul.

Flat on the floor with her face pressed to the carpet, her purse and belongings scattered, both dogs kept their front paws pushed into her back, keeping her pressed to the floor. They didn't bark, and didn't bite. As long as she stayed still, they apparently just intended to keep her pinned to the ground.

"Rocco! Rufus! Back!" Raul called to them as he walked down the hall toward her. He didn't run, he walked. He wasn't rebuking them, he was simply giving them an order, and they backed away.

"So sorry," he said without an ounce of sorry in his voice. Raul reached down to help Heather up and she let him, before realizing what was happening and jerking away. "Sometimes they have a mind of their own." He then grabbed their leashes and walked with his boys toward the elevator without another word, without looking back.

Heather was shaking as she gathered up her things and unsteadily pulled herself up. She wasn't physically hurt, but as she heard the elevator door close behind Raul as he headed down with his dogs, she began crying. "I can't remember ever being so frightened as during those few seconds when they were rushing at me," she says. And of course with no witnesses, and no physical damage, there was little or nothing she could do about it. She knew how things worked at the agency, even if she made some sort of formal complaint to HR, nothing would happen, but she might pay a price, so she did nothing.

In individuals, insanity is rare; but in groups, parties, nations and epochs, it is the rule.

—FRIEDRICH NIETZSCHE

Heather told a few people about the incident, personal friends, not work colleagues. And within a few days she thought that she was pretty much over it. But the following week when Raul was back in the office and they had another creative review meeting, she froze when she saw his dogs come into the room and take their place on the mat. Raul made direct eye contact with her, saw the look of panic, and smiled.

"There was no way I could work there, but I couldn't afford to just quit," Heather said. "And I hated the idea of leaving because it felt like he was winning, getting exactly what he wanted." Heather eventually found another job, lower paying and with less career potential, but she was happy to be out of there.

Even years later, injustice of the whole situation still frustrates Heather. "I have to be careful about telling the story because I can easily get worked up again," she says. "I feel as if my career took a hit and I still haven't fully recovered."

Any honest discussion of workplace adversity has to acknowledge that sometimes the really crappy experiences are just that—really crappy. There's no deeper life lesson. There's no "inner journey" to make you a better person. There's nothing you can do except call it what it is. A piece of life crap that landed on you.

So what do you do when you can't do anything?

"The one thing I always have control of," Tom Ciccione told me, "is my mind. Life can fuck with my job, my bank account, my stuff—but nothing fucks with my mind, except me." You may not be surprised to hear that Tom is a successful boxing promoter. He was a fighter himself for a few years, and still has a slight bend in his nose to show for it. "When I follow my nose, I tend to go in circles," he laughs.

Tom has had people steal from him. "Millions," he says.

Tom has had people lie to him. "Because they don't have the guts to tell the truth when it's hard," he says.

Tom has had cancer—three times. "Fuck cancer," he says.

Tom is a somewhat extreme example of a person who has decided to choose his emotional reactions to people and events, rather than merely reflect the natural reaction to difficult situations.

Most people are "emotional echoes." Their feelings simply echo what has happened to them in life. When someone is mean or rude to them, they get angry or hurt. When someone makes fun of them, they feel embarrassed (and hurt and angry). When they suddenly lose their job, they feel sad and embarrassed and fearful.

SING AN EMOTIONAL ARIA

A bad thing happens, and the emotional echo feels—bad. Well, that makes sense, doesn't it? Only an idiot would feel good about bad things happening, right?

In my experience, the most successful career professionals have a different perspective. When something happens that they absolutely cannot control, when there simply is no "massive" action possible, or even a single minor action that will make the slightest difference, these people still know they can control two things: their perspective, and their emotional reaction to the event.

These people ask "what emotional response will serve me best?" And then they adjust their perspective to achieve that response. These people are emotionally arias, not echos. They choose the emotional "song" they will be singing in reaction to the event. I know that sounds kind of highbrow. In Tom's case, his "emotional aria" in response to cancer was "Fuck cancer."

When you choose to respond with your own emotional aria, this means acknowledging that you, personally, have the power, freedom, and ability to choose your emotional response to whatever happens to you. You see that your circumstances don't control how you feel. In fact, the exact opposite is true: you are in total control of your emotional reaction to every circumstance—and you ALWAYS have the choice to use what happens to you, even the most awful negative things, as building blocks to create the results you want.

How do you change your perspective in order to change your emotional response? Sometimes by changing the questions you ask yourself. Instead of "Why me?" you might ask "How can I grow from this?" Instead of "Why does God let this happen?" you might ask "What does God want me to learn from this?" Instead of "How can they be so cruel?" you might ask "How can I help others who have experienced the same pain?"

Sometimes thinking about how someone you admire might react differently to a situation can help you adjust your own emotional response. I have to admit that occasionally when I feel like a particular person or situation is beating me down emotionally, I think of Tom "Fuck cancer" Ciccione and imagine how he might react. Then I imagine how someone like the Dalai Lama might react to the situation. Typically the Buddhist reacts very differently from the boxing promoter. And then I'll think about someone I admire from my career and ask myself how that person might respond to the situation.

The beauty of this simple technique is that it tells my brain there are in fact many different and reasonable ways to react, and this helps me adjust my own emotional response.

Sometimes it helps to compare and contrast your situation with others who have experienced much greater difficulty. I remember one evening I was complaining to my wife about someone at work who had taken credit for a big project when I had done most of the work. She was quite understanding, and then mentioned a story she had read earlier that day about a woman in Brazil who had to go to the local garbage pit each day and fight off wild dogs to get scraps of food for her children. "But I know you have it hard too," my wife said. I'm guessing she was being sarcastic. But it certainly did change my emotional perspective.

Of course none of these techniques are magical. It is really hard to develop the ability to consistently respond to bad situations with productive emotions. And I have found that the best way to develop this ability is to start with small baby steps in your ordinary day-to-day activities. Start with the way you react to the work colleague who sometimes annoys you, or the boss who is sometimes harsh or abrasive, or someone else in your life with annoying qualities.

You already know your natural emotional echo response, so ask yourself how you might respond differently to this person. Is there anyone you respect who might respond differently to these situations? Just to be clear, I'm not asking you to pretend that the person in question isn't annoying or abrasive or frustrating or whatever. You can fully acknowledge a person's annoying qualities and yet still choose a productive emotional response to those qualities.

One of the quotes I recount to myself at these times comes from Wendy Mass, an author of young-adult novels and children's books: "Always be kind. Everyone you meet is fighting a battle you know nothing about." This quote reminds me that whatever I am experiencing with a particular human being, there is so much more going on within them that I will never know about.

And as you develop your ability to consciously choose your emotional responses to those who sometimes annoy you, this will better prepare you for the big difficulties that eventually impact almost every career.

THE BIGGEST BATTLE MAY BE IN YOUR HEAD

Justine Stuart had been in sales and marketing for more than fifteen years, and her greatest strength was making powerful presentations to large groups. She had been successful in a direct client sales position, then was promoted into the marketing department where she became the go-to person any time they had a large group presentation. Ultimately her company chose Justine to deliver all of their major industry trade show presentations and her formal job title was changed to "Chief Evangelist" for the company and its products.

Justine was a great example of someone whose rapid career rise was based on true innate talent. No one could work a large group presentation like Justine. She had a deep mastery of technical product details but also knew how to communicate complex information in a clear, simple way. She was fit and attractive, which of course helped. But she also had a great sense of humor, could make any audience laugh and enjoy the show while she sold them on the unique benefits of her products. Justine loved everything about her job and the people she worked with, and her future truly looked bright and limitless.

But a skiing accident left her paralyzed below the waist.

Justine was an inherently optimistic person and determined to make a full recovery. Even when her doctors indicated there was no hope for regaining use of her lower limbs, she insisted on occupational therapy to try to gain some use of her legs. But this was not a matter of will or determination or attitude. She eventually accepted that she would be in a wheelchair for the rest of her life.

Her long recovery was emotionally and physically draining, but Justine was eventually welcomed back to the company. Everyone was incredibly supportive and they made it clear that there was no reason she should not continue to be the Chief Evangelist. Everything she used to do while standing, she could still do in a wheelchair.

Justine appreciated the support and kindness, but she also hated it. "I could see the kind pity in their eyes," she said. "And I was repelled by it." She couldn't stand the thought of seeing that same pity coming from a large group of people as she was conducting a presentation in her wheelchair. She eventually took a leave of absence, then quit.

Colleagues who tried to stay in contact with her were ignored as Justine found it more comfortable to deal with people who had never known her before she was wheelchair bound. "The people who had only known me in a wheelchair, for some reason it was more comfortable being with them," she said. "Because I never saw that sad pity in their eyes."

Justine eventually took a job as an at-home telesales person for a technical systems company. The pay wasn't great, but she did enjoy having conversations with people who had no idea of her physical limitations. "I even sort of liked it when they were rude to me," she said. "Because their rudeness was so real, and so . . . normal."

Justine's situation was of course extreme, with her career trajectory crumbling because of a freakish accident. But her story is helpful because her emotional echo was natural and normal after her life-changing accident. She was repelled by the look of pity from her colleagues and she removed herself from an environment that was uncomfortable. Many of us would have reacted the same way.

"But over time I came to realize that the reason I so hated the look of pity in the eyes of my colleagues," she says, "is that I was feeling pity for myself, but I didn't want to admit it." I doubt that anyone would ever say that Justine didn't deserve to feel at least a little pity for herself. But the important question isn't whether or not the emotion is reasonable, but whether or not the emotion is serving her well. And in Justine's case, she was definitely not being well served by her emotional echo.

Justine had actually come to enjoy her telephone sales job, but it was obvious that she was capable of much more. She had created a comfortable world for herself and was hesitant to step out of it. "But there came a time when I was able to have a little more empathy for how people were reacting to me," she says now. "I realized that they were uncomfortable, and uncertain what to do or say, and I should have been more sensitive to their discomfort." As Justine gained a level of emotional acceptance and peace with her new life in a wheelchair, she began to think about the possibility of returning to her old job. "I realized the only thing standing between me and a much more productive career was my own emotional response."

The big emotional shift for Justine occurred when she began thinking more about helping others be comfortable around her, rather than focusing on wishing that others would make her feel more comfortable. "That shift made all the difference," she says. And today she is once again the Chief Evangelist for her company, conducting large group presentations at trade shows across the country.

SOMETIMES WE CREATE OUR OWN TROUBLES

Joe Temora is a good example of self-inflicted adversity. He was a pure Teflon Rhino salesperson who pounded the phones to get appointments and closed hard with every prospective customer. He had his own business, with an exclusive license to sell a patented in-home water purification system in Arizona. The manufacturer was based in China, and Joe had free rein to market their product in any manner he wanted. He focused most of his sales efforts on retired couples living in Phoenix and Scottsdale. "I focused on retired couples for the same reason that Jesse James robbed banks," he says. "That's where the money is."

Joe had also found that it was easier to get in-home appointments with retired couples, and for him they were relatively easy sales. His aggressive style—along with a lot of stories about the life-extending benefits of purified water as well as the (unverified) list of potential carcinogens in the local tap water—made it a relatively easy sale for him. "I couldn't sell ice to Eskimos, but I sure could sell expensive water to old people," he said with a chuckle.

Joe got a phone call one day from a retired couple who wanted a sales presentation, saying they had been referred to him by a previous customer. This should have made him suspicious because in the five years he had been doing this he had never received a customer referral. His only contacts from previous customers were typically complaints about high-pressure sales tactics and requests for a refund. But Rhino Joe charged forward and gave the retired couple his standard sales pitch. When they resisted making a quick decision he pulled out all of his best stories and even made up a few new ones on the fly. Eventually they relented and made the purchase, so Joe had another notch on his belt and another nice commission.

And then one evening, about a week later, Joe began to get calls from friends who had just seen him on the television news. It turned out the retired couple had been working with a local news investigative reporter and there were hidden cameras throughout their house. They had recorded every moment of their interactions with Joe.

Joe's stories (lies) were laid bare for the whole world to see. At least the whole world covered by local Phoenix and Scottsdale television. And the reporter also had an analysis of Joe's actual purification system completed, determining that the system was no more effective than one purchased at the local Walmart for less than a tenth of the cost. Ultimately the state attorney general investigated and sued Joe's company, and Joe personally, for consumer fraud, and within six months he was totally out of business. No money. Bad reputation. Unemployable in Phoenix/Scottsdale. He barely avoided jail time.

The morning after Joe Temora's debut on the local television news, he stayed home the entire day and ignored all of the phone calls coming in on both his mobile and home phone. He was scared, ashamed, stunned. Being outed on local television as a fast-talking con man is probably never a good thing, but for Joe it was the lowest point in his life. Especially since he had grown up in Phoenix and most of his family lived in the area. So by the end of the day everyone would know. Everyone. "I could have easily ended it all that morning," Joe says now.

There was a knock on the door early that afternoon, and he tried to ignore it. But the knock persisted, and whoever it was clearly wasn't going away. When he looked through the peephole he saw every adult man's worst nightmare when he's been caught doing something really, really wrong. The police? No, it was his mother.

Joe's father had passed away a few years ago, but Rita Temora was still going strong and had always been a force to be reckoned with in the family. "Is it true?" she asked him. Joe nodded. "Then stop feeling sorry for yourself, because you deserve this."

Joe didn't disagree, but those words coming from his own mother had a special sting. And Rita wasn't finished. "Now the only thing to think about is how are you going to make up for it," she said, "and how are you going to move ahead?" She refused to let her son sit in his apartment, stunned and isolated from the rest of the world. Rita really didn't know what to do, but her instinct told her not to let her shell-shocked son sit alone and stew on the horrible situation he had created.

And as horrible as it was that day, over the next few months it got worse. Eventually Joe was left without a home and just a few hundred bucks to his name. He had to move in with his mother, which actually turned out to be the best thing because Rita Temora was all about action. Joe saw no point in looking for a job because there was no way anyone would hire him. He would have moved out of state, but he couldn't afford to. Rita didn't judge him—but she pushed him. "She pushed me every day," he says. "Look for a job, any job. Send out résumés. Make calls. Follow up with every past customer who wanted a refund and promise to make restitution, eventually." Joe kept a list of every unhappy customer and the amount of the refund due to them. At the high point the amount was over $200,000.

Rita's pushing paid off. Joe eventually got a job as an orderly at a nursing home in Phoenix, on the night and weekend shift. It was tough, grueling work and the pay was awful. But it was a job. "And somehow, it felt right that I should be emptying bedpans and cleaning up old people's shit," he says. About six months later he was hired by a home health care products company to sell equipment in their Phoenix store. He kept the orderly job as well, so he was working days and nights, and most weekends. And still making a lot less than he used to.

After a year at the nursing home, Joe had saved a few thousand dollars and was planning to make a down payment on a used car. When he mentioned this to his mother, she didn't have to say a thing—he knew what he had to do. "Almost a full year of savings, just to give a refund to one customer. It was painful," he says. "But it was right."

Today, about five years after the initial television news report, Joe is no longer a nursing home orderly. But he does volunteer regularly at an assisted living facility near his home. Rita has passed away. "But she was able to see me come full circle, so I'm grateful for that," he says. He is still in sales, doing relatively well financially, and has paid off about half of his debts to past customers so far.

When I asked Joe what lessons he has taken away from the experience, he says, "First, of course, there's the whole 'don't screw people over' lesson, I definitely learned that one. And second, my mom was right, don't run away from your troubles, face into them. When your panic freezes you, take action, almost any action, just to get yourself unstuck."

THE ADVANTAGE OF EARLY ADVERSITY

There was an interesting research study conducted a few years ago, focused on the top 2 percent of income earners. Thirty-two percent of these individuals had started out life with some distinct advantage, either family money, business connections, or an elite education, sometimes all three. Fifty-two percent had started out life with some distinct disadvantage, such as no formal education, an abusive home environment, physical disability, health issues, violence, abandonment, extreme poverty, or some combination thereof. Only 16 percent of the top income earners came from what we might call "normal" backgrounds without significant advantage or disadvantage.

Hmm . . . so what's the lesson here? Well, first, of course, it's better to have the early advantages in life. Family money is good. Family connections, good. Elite education, ditto.

However, it seems that in terms of ultimate success, the worst possible upbringing is the average, normal, middle-class childhood with no unique advantages, but also no profound problems. Here's my theory. If you grow up with loving parents, a large supportive family, in relatively comfortable surroundings, and a stable community, with enough money for the things you need and some of the "extra nice" things you want, if you are treated well at school and have good friends, if you get relatively good grades and are happy with yourself—then there is very little internal need to push yourself beyond your comfortable existence.

Don't get me wrong; this is perfectly fine, and probably great for most people. They grow up without that deep internal need to be something more, to do something more, to overcome—they don't have that thing you have inside of you. And I know YOU have it, because why else would you be reading this book?

So in many ways, early adversity in one's life is a bonus. It's great training for what you may experience later in life. If you've learned early on that you can eventually overcome hardship, I believe it becomes part of your deepest mental wiring, and those circuits are available to you for the rest of your life.

THINK NOW

- What has been your typical pattern of thought/action when you have faced adversity in the past?

- Has this pattern served you well, or would you be better off by adjusting your approach?
- How specifically would you adjust your thoughts and actions when faced with adversity in the future?

ACT SOON

For the next few weeks try this. Focus on the mundane annoyances you may experience during a typical week at work. And practice your "emotional aria" in those relatively minor situations:

- When someone continually interrupts you.
- When someone is harsh or abrasive with you.
- When someone abruptly dismisses your opinion.
- When someone tells a lie and you know it.
- When someone takes credit for work they didn't do.
- When someone shifts the blame for their own mistake to others.

In any of these situations you know what the natural "emotional echo" would be. Typically a combination of frustration, anger, hurt, embarrassment, and judgment. So try instead to choose your own "emotional aria," a response that might perhaps be more empathetic, more understanding, less judgmental. Over time this will help you build new "emotional muscles" to better prepare you for extreme adversity when it eventually comes (and it will).

You can learn more at
www.workplacepoker.com/adversity/.

LONG-TERM THOUGHTS AND ACTION POINTS

- When you are confronted with a difficult career challenge, first ask yourself if there is anything you can actually do to impact the specific event.

- If you can in fact take action to impact the specific event, then take QUICK and MASSIVE action. Learn from any mistakes or missteps, adjust, then take more action.

- If you cannot take action to impact the actual event, remember that you always have control over your emotional response to the event. Don't just be an emotional echo, choose your own emotional aria.

- You can build emotional resilience every day by reacting to day-to-day annoyances and frustrations in a productive way. Every day you can choose to:

  - React to frustration with kindness and patience.
  - React to harsh judgment with empathy and curiosity.
  - React to disappointment with a more positive perspective.

CONCLUSION

♣

Hadia Badrai graduated from Kabul University in Afghanistan with a degree in computer engineering. Her parents and younger brother were killed by the Taliban in retaliation for her father's cooperation with the US armed forces. Hadia immigrated to the United States, sponsored by a family in Greenville, South Carolina.

She is a devout Muslim living in a community that does not universally embrace her presence. Her English was not strong at first, but she has become a quick study. And her first job was in customer service for a local flower shop. As a university graduate she was perhaps a bit overqualified but she appreciated the opportunity. And within six months she was working in customer support for a local technology company in Greenville. Hadia is a truly talented computer programmer and eventually she had a chance to use those talents within her company. Within four years she was actually leading a small team of developers and helped the company launch a new online video chat system that today is a major profit center for them.

Hadia worked very hard, was clearly talented and ambitious, and eventually achieved the career ambition she had always hoped for.

End of story.

See what I did there?

As much as we have focused on all of the things that can hold your career back, on the limits of talent, hard work, and ambition in a hypercompetitive workplace, it's good to be reminded that sometimes the good guys (and gals) win.

And that's my deepest hope for you. That you take from this book the ideas and strategies that will serve you, add to these your own talent and hard work, and achieve the positive, productive life you desire.

Over the years as I've met and learned from the people you've read about in this book, I saw my own career trajectory rise as my ability to read people and navigate workplace politics increased. But the biggest change occurred when I began to fully embrace this as a natural part of career success rather than as an "extra" set of skills I had to learn. And I know that fully embracing these ideas only came after I had truly mastered them.

So I would encourage you to focus not just on learning, but truly mastering these skills and strategies so that you can begin to fully embrace them as quickly as possible.

If you are curious about some of the stories featured in this book and where those individuals ultimately ended up in their careers, visit my blog at www.workplacepoker.com, where I keep my readers up to date on new ideas and practical approaches to success in the workplace. I'd also love to hear YOUR stories, which you can share at this site. And occasionally I have an "update" interview with some of the folks featured in this book.

But I have to tell you about Tony from San Diego right now. Because he started all of this, and when I began writing the book I was naturally curious to find out how he was doing, in life and in his career. I hadn't spoken to him in almost twenty years so it took some time just to find him. And then I wasn't sure if I wanted to know the truth. Because if it turned out that Tony was now a homeless man living in a cave under the railroad tracks in Lonely Gulch, North Dakota, my whole premise would be called into question.

Well, Tony is doing quite nicely, thank you. You hopefully remember that Tony landed a great new job while the rest of us were struggling to get interviews. At that job, Tony met a wonderful girl and today they're married with three amazing kids. Years later Tony's father-in-law encouraged him to invest in a small coffee company based in Seattle that was about to go public.

Lucky bastard.

ACKNOWLEDGMENTS

♣

First I have to thank all of those who shared their stories with me. While your identities were changed to protect relationships with bosses and coworkers, I'm grateful that you were willing to share your experiences with the rest of the world and let us all learn from them.

My wife, Paula, and son, Quinn, were daily sounding boards as this book transitioned from ethereal concept to final manuscript. Thanks to both of you for your ideas and unvarnished opinions. We can finally pull down all of the Post-it notes from our dining room wall.

Eric Nelson and Susan Rabiner of the Rabiner Literary Agency were much more than just agents for this project. They helped to refine the initial concept and proposal, and I have no doubt that this book would not exist without them.

Eric Meyers, Hollis Heimbouch, and Colleen Lawrie at Harper-Collins all poured tremendous time and mental energy into this book. They coaxed me along with mostly gentle nudges and occasional sharp elbows when needed.

Larry Julian, bestselling author of *God Is My CEO*, has been on this journey with me from the beginning. Our wives sometimes worried what two guys could possibly talk about for hours and hours on Saturday mornings. Now they'll know. Most of it.

My father, Franklin D. Rust, passed away before publication. He and my mother, Darlene Rust, deserve credit for nurturing the soul of a young writer and letting him wander the world to find his own way. My brother, David Rust, deserves a public apology for being tied to trees more often than was necessary when we were young, plus he helped me understand a whole new universe of workers in a way that truly helped to expand the scope of this book.

ABOUT THE AUTHOR

♣

Dan Rust writes and speaks about career acceleration, workplace culture, and related issues. He is the founder of Frontline Learning (frontlinelearning.com), an international corporate training company.

Twitter: @danrust
LinkedIn: linkedin.com/in/danrust
Email: dr@danrust.com